Dedication

I dedicate this work to my fellow global traveller and partner in life –
Susan Murphy, and to my two daughters Margaret and Ann who have
always given me support and encouragement.

Acknowledgements

I wish to acknowledge the extensive assistance received with this book. Its inspiration came from the pioneers in this field – Chuck Gee, Clare Gunn, and Edward Inskeep. The encouragement has come from my Mt Buller Resort Management students; the assistance in putting it together has come from Glennis Derrick and Sally North. The academic content and practical details have come from countless individuals involved in resort research and businesses. Of these Wendy Magee (Australia), Rick and Cathy Stolle (Canada), Alison Gill (Canada), Patrick Long (USA), Kit Jenkins (UK), Miriam Jansen-Verbeke (Belgium) and Luna Bajracharya (Singapore) deserve special mention and thanks. But, as always, it is the author who is responsible for any misinterpretations, errors and omissions.

Contents

List of tables

List of figures

Part A

History and features of resorts

1

Constants and changes in resort development

Introduction

Many people consider resorts represent the best of vacation experiences because the term is associated with luxury products and with destinations which cater specifically for the tourist. When tourists see the prefix 'resort' attached to a hotel the implication is they can expect superior facilities and service at that hotel. Likewise, when one visits a resort destination, it has been designed primarily for tourist needs rather than for general service and industrial purposes. It is the difference between Blackpool and London, and between Miami Beach and Miami. While the latter examples may receive more visitors in general, it is the former locations which have been designed to meet the needs of tourists and have been designated as resort destinations in marketing and the literature. Dictionary definitions reflect this strong association between resorts and vacation travel with reference to places frequently visited, especially for vacations, rest or relaxation and cures.

Resorts have been a feature of travel and tourism for a long time. Their origins can be traced back to Roman times when the concept spread throughout Europe in the wake of their conquering legions. From the simple origins of public baths and restorative mineral springs their typical structure became 'an atrium surrounded by recreational and sporting amenities, restaurants, rooms, and shops' (Mill, 2001: 4). In short, this structure forms the basic model of a modern resort. For example, a resort is often designed to emphasize a core activity, be it a beach, a golf course or a heritage site, and to support that with key accommodation, restaurants and retail opportunities.

Since these early days of resort development its popularity has waxed and waned; but it has survived the changing times by adjusting to suit new tastes and conditions, to become a new force in today's relatively stable and prosperous times. Early on the original health purpose of resorts was supplemented and eventually overtaken by social and political motivations, as exemplified by the resurrection of the hot springs at Bath, England which became an important part of the English royal court circuit in the seventeenth century. This pattern was followed in the 'New World' by the railways, using hot spring resorts in the wilderness national parks to draw the wealthy and privileged westward, as in the case of Canadian Pacific's (now Fairmont Hotels) Banff Springs Hotel in Alberta, Canada.

Today, similar grand and enticing resort concepts are being developed by corporate entities to appeal to the wealthy populations of industrial societies and to develop the hinterlands of industrial-urban regions in Europe, North America and Asia. Clifford (2003) has noted the corporate development of ski resorts in North America, which has been partly a response to demographic changes and partly an attempt to create new products, such as the ski villages and associated second homes in the mountain regions. He notes that one of the three big corporations in the vanguard of such changes is already looking to the future, with Intrawest turning its attention to warm-weather destinations and golf resorts for the aging baby-boomers (Clifford, 2003: 222). This type of strategic planning is occurring in the Gulf States, where several major luxury integrated resort complexes have been built or are under construction to assist them in diversifying their economies.

An example of this trend is the US$2.9 billion Emirates Palace in Abu Dhabi, where:

> Although it has fewer than 400 rooms, the hotel features 128 kitchens and pantries, 1002 custom-made Swarovski crystal chandeliers . . . a layout so sprawling staff will soon be equipped with golf carts to navigate the corridors, 'some of them are over a kilometre long' . . . room prices range from a modest US$608 a night to US$12,608 (subject to a 20 per cent service charge).
>
> (Pohl, 2005: 12)

It is not only the wealthy who now enjoy the benefits of resorts, for the growth of industry and commerce has brought such delights within the reach of the masses. They have either followed the past elite to their secluded 'hide-away' resort retreats as exemplified by the development of Brighton around the Prince of Wales' Brighton Pavilion; or they have stimulated the building of their own style of mass resort, as in the case of seaside resorts like Australia's Gold Coast or the gambling resorts like Las Vegas, and even combining the two interests in Atlantic City.

The spreading of the resort market to the masses can be seen in the historical development of Waikiki on the island of Oahu in Hawaii. Prior to the 1960s Waikiki was a small beach oriented destination, with a few major luxury hotels catering primarily to wealthy American tourists. These tourists had travelled to the island over several days via passenger liner and chose to linger in this tropical paradise for several weeks or months. Its relative inaccessibility with its slow and expensive transport link made this resort an upscale and elite destination until the advent of the commercial jet airliner. Then Waikiki became available to anyone who could afford an airline ticket, could handle a few hours flying time, and who wanted a short annual vacation.

Although there has been a steady evolution of the resort concept there have been constants within the changes over the past centuries. These constants often represent continuations of the original model developed by the Romans, and it is these constants that have helped to maintain the resort as a particularly sustainable form of tourism product and activity.

Academic interest

Despite this track record of successful adjustment over the centuries the study of this particular phenomenon has generated only a modest level of interest among tourism academics – even in this era of supposed attention to sustainability! A major reason is the ubiquity of resorts, which has helped camouflage their individual characteristics within the domain of tourism and hospitality studies. Resorts occur over a wide range of locations and in many functional forms, so their study has often been subsumed under other topics and approaches. In the process this approach has minimized or overlooked resorts' particular needs and market differentiation, because these have been incorporated into larger-scale enquiries and more general discussion. While there is a natural broad interface between the issues found in resort domains and those examined in other areas of tourism research, some feel that resorts deserve to be studied in their own right – because they are an identifiable subset of the tourism market with their own needs and issues.

Included amongst those who feel resorts should be examined on their own merits are Inskeep, Gee and Mill, each of whom makes a case for paying special attention to resorts due to some distinctive differentiating factors. If we examine their thoughts in chronological order we find some characteristics that can be identified as specific resort characteristics.

Inskeep (1991) states particularly well-designed resorts can become attractions in themselves and he devotes a chapter to 'planning tourist resorts' under the umbrella of community tourism. Within this framework he emphasizes two factors:

- *Resorts are a business*: They need to start their planning with a market analysis and demand assessment, which should then be matched with a product assessment of how well the proposed area can match expected market demand.
- *Community relations*: Need to be considered carefully if there is a resident population living on or near the resort site, because of positive and negative impacts from such a development.

Gee (1996: 14–21) considers resorts differ from other sorts of tourism destination in that they:

- cater primarily to vacation and pleasure markets;
- the average length of stay is longer, so hotel rooms need to be larger and better equipped;
- because most resorts are isolated they must be self-contained;
- the recreational bias of resorts makes them highly seasonal;
- resort management must be 'visible management', that is everyone 'must be infused with the idea of total hospitality, warm relationships, and unstinting round-the-clock service to guests'.

Mill (2001: xv) considers resorts have a combination of elements that make them distinctive. These are:

- the recreation attractions that draw guests to the resort;
- activities to occupy the guests during their stay.

Within these descriptors of resorts and their management needs certain *commonalities* can be identified. Resorts are distinctive in that they:

- *Are established as tourism businesses*: When they are planned and financed it is with the specific intent of creating an attraction that will draw visitors.
- *Convert visitors into guests*: To make a profit and long-term success of the business most resorts must convince enough visitors to become overnight guests. The exceptions are those resorts focussing on a local day-trip market.
- *Attempt to hold their guests on-site*: By providing a critical mass of activities – in addition to the accommodation there must be sufficient attractions and activities to keep the guests occupied during the day and night.
- *Attract guests and hold them with superior quality facilities*: To keep the guests on-site these attractions and activities need to be of the highest quality.
- *Cosset guests with superior service*: To complement the quality facilities and to obtain the most from the experience for the guest and the resort, the resort needs quality staff who can deliver superior service.

Such descriptions of the resort structure and management approach are considered sufficient by the quoted references and this author to distinguish resort management from other forms of tourism management. It involves a pre-planned business approach that emphasizes value. It does not mean every resort needs to be an up-market affair, what it does mean is that every resort from budget to luxury must offer a guaranteed special experience that provides value for the price paid and will convert guests into repeat customers and goodwill ambassadors.

Resort management analysis

If one is going to study a phenomenon such as resorts, with the goal of providing useful management information to the business at hand and its host community in general, one appropriate analytical approach would be to use classical scientific enquiry. This involves three stages. First, the *description and classification* of a research topic – in this case the resort.

Second, attempts to explain what is happening and why, within the resorts themselves and in terms of their external relations with the host community. Finally, to combine the first two stages into an ability to *predict future outcomes and behaviour*. This for many is the ultimate goal of science, and provides the direction that resort communities and individual business operators within them are seeking. At this point in resort management analysis most would claim we are at the explanation stage, attempting to understand the internal and external forces that are moulding current resort patterns.

This book will use the scientific approach to identify business issues and management strategies that can help to create healthy and attractive resorts. To maintain resort sustainability in economic, social and environmental terms will require more work in all three stages, since society and the tourism industry is continually evolving. As we shall see in the last chapter even the concept of sustainability needs to be re-examined if current ecological balances come under threat from global warming.

Descriptions and definitions

To start with the first stage involves a discussion of and decision on terms and definitions. As is common in leisure industry research and many areas of social science we find that resorts have several definitions. A review of the following academic descriptions and definitions, again in chronological order, illustrate the variety of features and functions of the resort business, but hidden within them are some fundamental consistencies:

Pearce (1987: 167): 'A spectrum of resorts exists, ranging from those with a wholly tourist function to those where a significant amount of tourist activity occurs alongside a variety of other urban functions'.

Krippendorf (1987: 70–71): 'Self-sufficient holiday complexes, designed and run on the basis of careful motivation studies as enclaves for holiday makers'.

Ayala (1991: 571): 'There is a growing number of self-contained, international resort hotels, master planned with an ambitious goal of captivating the guests and giving them no reason to leave the hotel'.

Gee (1996: 22): 'The resort concept is accomplished through the provision of quality accommodations, food and beverages, entertainment, recreational facilities, health amenities, pleasant and restful surroundings, and most important, an extremely high level of service delivered in a friendly and personalised manner'.

Huffadine (1999: 1): 'Traditionally, resorts have been places to make social contacts, attend social occasions, and improve health and fitness'.

Prideaux (2000: 227): 'Put simply, the resort market is the location where goods and services are produced and sold. The market can be viewed from a number of perspectives such as the demand-side, supply-side and at the point where equilibrium occurs'.

Ernst and Young (2003: 4): A resort is 'tourist accommodation catering primarily to leisure travelers, providing a range of recreational facilities and differentiated by experiential qualities in the context of a particular regional destination'.

Within these varied descriptions of resorts several consistencies emerge that help to distinguish resorts from other forms of tourism. *First*, there is confirmation of the business focus of resorts in the vast majority of the definitions. *Second*, the business focus is one that emphasizes capturing and holding guests. *Third*, an important part of that business process is to satisfy guest expectations with outstanding facilities and service. *Fourth*, these facilities and services are designed to enhance the visitors' experience with the resort's prime attribute or activity. *Fifth*, the scale of resorts can vary from an individual establishment to an urban destination, and this will impact the level of control business operators can apply to the resort's development.

With the business emphasis of this book and the desire to develop management strategies that can benefit both the resort business and surrounding host destination the above descriptions and definitions of a resort can be reduced to the following key components, to provide the following definition of resort management:

> *A resort is a planned vacation business that is designed to attract, hold and satisfy its guests so they become repeat visitors and/or goodwill ambassadors. To achieve these objectives requires a management strategy that can operate at a variety of scales and with a selection of target markets, but its constant must be the creation of a valued experience.*

Explanation

To achieve the above description and definition of a resort, management will need to examine the social science, environmental and business literature that has attempted to explain what is happening to resorts. There

9

are several key management considerations that have been discussed in this literature or have arisen from practical experience, these include:

- *Capture through differentiation*: If a resort is to capture rather than simply attract it must have something significant to draw the visitor and then turn them into a guest, by engaging them in an experiential association that leads to some form of revenue generating activity. Given the wide range of tourist interests and intense competition in today's global tourism market this magnetic attraction needs to be outstanding, and has led to a strong emphasis on Porter's (1980) 'differentiation' and 'segmentation' focus in his competitive analysis strategy. This has resulted in resorts emphasizing their core features, be it snow or beach, health and wellness centres, gambling, sport or a gastronomy emphasis.
- *Attempt to be self-contained*: By providing a sufficient critical mass of activities, attractions and accommodation to keep guests engaged for the whole extent of their stay and their expenditures within the corporate business. This is one of the big lessons that Walt Disney learned from his original foray into theme parks. His initial Disneyland theme park in California was just an attraction at first, until Disney recognized that much of his visitor expenditure was being captured by local hotels and restaurants; so he added and connected the Disney Hotel to his Anaheim theme park to tap into that lucrative aspect of the market (Bryman, 1995). The effect of this lesson can be seen in Walt Disney's subsequent development plans for the Walt Disney World Resort in Florida. Now the theme parks within this resort complex are viewed as the principal attraction to draw guests, who would now be accommodated in Disney or leased hotels on-site, and their extra interests accommodated through a variety of sport or other activities also available within the huge Walt Disney World grounds. If a guest insists on visiting the outside world during their stay the resort attempts to arrange such forays through its own booking and transport facilities. After all the guest came to stay with them, so they should receive some benefit from these local excursions.
- *Deliver fabulous facilities and super service*: To hold the guest within the resort requires quality in addition to a critical mass of activities. The core attractions are expected to include the latest technical advances in their field, and to be staffed by experts – at times by some outstanding 'professionals – instructors'. The hotel rooms should be bigger and better equipped than those in downtown hotels because the guests are expected to spend more time in them compared with the business traveller, who often dominates the city accommodation market. The

service should be spectacular, since staff have the opportunity to get to know guests and how to cater to all their needs – even to the point of offering advice regarding local activities and sights, and increasingly about local gastronomic delights.

■ *Determine the appropriate target market scales*: Different target markets will lead to different scales and complexities of operation (Prideaux, 2000). Resorts dependent primarily on a *local market* will need to emphasize local recreational day-use activities, with convenient access to local urban areas. There is still room for these types of resorts, even in the ultra-competitive global market conditions of today. Clifford (2003: 216–240) describes in his book on the North American ski industry the potential for small ski hills to compete with the mega-corporations by emphasizing community control, the spirit of skiing and more affordability. Resorts serving a *regional market* will need to supply more substantial and possibly more challenging recreational activities that will encourage short stays and therefore require the provision of accommodation and entertainment options. Resorts serving *national or international markets* will need to supply a larger critical mass of attractions and activities, that are not only of the highest quality but are competitive on a global basis. Such has been the development of the Whistler – Blackcomb international ski resort in Canada, the Port Douglas international resorts and attraction of the Great Barrier Reef in Australia, and Las Vegas in the USA. As in all hierarchies there are far more local and regional resorts than in the last category, but it is the national/international resorts that have received the most extensive promotion and have captured global attention.

■ *Range of resort operation scales*: It is apparent that resort management can and should operate at a variety of scales. At the *micro-scale* of a single facility, a 'resort hotel' needs to encompass internal activities that will hold its guests all day and in combination with quality rooms, gastronomic opportunities and entertainment provide no reason to leave the establishment. A traditional example of this would be the Hotel Badehof resort hotel in Tokyo, where an elaborate series of pools and spa facilities involving waters from a local hot spring provide a relaxing respite from the pressures of working and living in such a bustling metropolis (www.badehof-q.co.jp). At the *meso-scale* of an integrated resort complex, where several hotels and ancillary functions support the prime function and differentiator of the resort, the component parts should work together to hold and satisfy the guests within the complex. An example of this would be Daydream Island Resort on one of the Whitsunday Islands off the east coast of

Australia (www.daydreamisland.com). At the *macro-scale* of a resort destination, such as Las Vegas, all the above considerations are in play, but within the broader context of a multi-purpose community with multiple planning and development goals (www.visitlasvegas.com). In this situation the resort facilities and business are still important to the local community, as outlined in Pearce's definition, but they are part of a larger economic base and wider community aspirations. So more collaborative strategic planning is called for, to unite the various community stakeholder groups behind a consensus development strategy.

■ *Varying Levels of Control*: As the scale of resort development increases from a single facility to an urban destination the business operators have to share their degree of control. This is reflected in the environmental scanning process (Bourgeois, 1980; Daft et al., 1992) and the planning collaboration (Murphy and Murphy, 2004). Environmental scanning reveals the level of control is highest, but not absolute, within the confines of individual business units; and weakens as the scale of influence increases to a destination or national level. When resort operators need to consider the business ramifications of operating with others in the destination or national market it often leads to collaboration and partnerships as individual businesses attempt to sell the destination first and their particular business second in order to prosper.

Forecasting and prediction

All resort operations will need to consider their future returns on investment (ROI) if they are ever to recoup the extensive capital investments that are involved in establishing the distinctive resort features outlined above. They will need to predict future trends in consumer preferences and spending patterns. Such considerations of present and future development situations will involve both their internal business environment, the external physical and social environment of their host community, and global trends. For those resort destinations with a strong community base there will need to be a more collaborative approach regarding strategic management, including the use of participatory models and consultative processes (Bramwell and Lane, 2000)

Many resorts in the past have been swept up in the dream of creating something special without the constraints of careful analysis and forecasting. A Tourism Task Force report (Ernst and Young, 2003: 4) on Australia's resort situation stated 'Despite the growth of domestic and international tourism in the last two decades, resorts in Australia have performed poorly from a profitability and investment perspective'. Such experiences are common around the world, and need to be addressed if resorts are to continue to provide their unique contribution to tourism's array of options.

For example, the rapid expansion of North American ski resorts over the past few decades has been questioned in terms of its sustainability. Clifford (2003) forecasts the demise of current corporate ski resorts because they have attached their growth philosophy and operational designs to a single demographic cohort – the post-World War II baby-boomers. This group and those serving their interests have benefited from the most sustained period of economic expansion in recent times and from significant inherited wealth that has enabled them to fulfil recreational fantasies and to buy expensive second homes in their selected resort destinations.

The emphasis of this book is to use a scientific analysis approach to guide resort management to a continued sustainable development future in very challenging competitive circumstances. To achieve this objective a paradigm or framework is offered to guide the process from analysis and theory to practical management considerations, as outlined in Table 1.1. This uses the business emphasis of resort management to first describe the key features of resort management, followed by the various types of explanation that currently support those key features and finally by predicting possible future outcomes.

Resort management framework

Table 1.1 presents a framework by which resorts of all sizes and emphases can examine their management requirements. The columns start with a *description and definition* of the term resort management. Given the business emphasis of this book the earlier definition of resort management on p. 9 will be adopted. At all scales and standards it will involve the need to attract, hold and satisfy guests by creating a valued experience.

This is followed by the need for *explanation* of a resort's current development using a variety of sources and approaches. One key to understanding resort development patterns is their exposure to external forces as well as internal and local conditions, which is portrayed in the structure of this book. Part B examines external challenges while Part C investigates internal challenges and strategies. The external forces shape the market opportunities for resorts and, while beyond the direct control of resort management, need to be monitored and understood for resorts to make the best of the situation. Internal challenges and strategies are ways in

Table 1.1   Analytical framework for resort management with a seniors market example

Description and definition	Explanation (external and internal challenges)	Prediction (risk management)
Attract	■ Competitive market ■ Differentiate ■ Branding	■ Health and wellness ■ Light exercise and recreation ■ Second or retirement homes.
Hold	■ Attractive setting ■ Critical mass of activities ■ Supportive staff	■ Independent to dependency ■ Flexible delivery ■ Security
Satisfy	■ Skilled staff ■ Service profit chain ■ Value creation	■ Caring service ■ Rest home component ■ Hospital links

which resort management can respond to external forces and develop specific strategies to take advantage of opportunities in the external environment. Just as Billy Butlin did with his original resort camp product, which was designed to meet the anticipated holiday needs of rising numbers of British workers who were receiving paid annual leave for the first time.

The resort sector's future involves a *prediction* of what future guests will want and what the environment and society will permit. This becomes the realm of forecasting, extrapolating present patterns into the future, combined with a mix of conjecture regarding what directions the future will take. Since all business involves risk and risk increases with the unknown, this matrix and book introduces risk management as an ideal way to approach the future, as shown in Part D.

Risk is viewed in three ways. The normal business risk, that the interpretation of market analyses and associated feasibility studies is correct. The litigation risk, that the product development and duty of care are sufficient in this era of increased liability. We are now in a social environment where many individuals fail to accept any personal responsibility for their actions and seek redress for their pain and suffering by suing others. The third form of risk is that the world is becoming a different place in which to conduct business. This involves increased knowledge of crisis management, which shows up not just in the courts but through increased evidence of global warming and climate change. If the recent Inter-governmental Panel on Climate Change reports are correct, humans are 'very likely' to blame and should set about repairing this situation. It will mean that resort management needs to add this new worry to its existing problems of natural hazards such as earthquakes and cyclones, and play its part in reducing carbon emissions.

A good way to demonstrate the applicability of such an analytical framework in resort situations is to examine a specific question. This is illustrated by examining the framework's relevance to a common challenge and opportunity for many resorts now and in the near future – the emerging seniors market.

Resort management analysis: seniors market

Accepting the proposition that demography represents our destiny to a large degree, the example in Table 1.1 focuses on one factor that is expected to influence resort futures and is susceptible to management influence, namely the growing significance of our seniors market. The electronic newsletter *Travel Impact Newswire* reports on 'The Impact of Demographic Change' in one of its issues. One story relates to a Mastercard Insights Report on Japan's older women – the 'silver aristocrats'. Japan is at the forefront of aging societies and its older women have become 'a powerful and important segment, expected to command some US$313 billion of spending power by 2013' (Travel Impact Newswire, 2005: 6). It goes on to say:

> A whole new industry has come into existence catering for their special needs (including health spas, continuing education centers, and amateur associations dedicated to the pursuit of a wide variety of hobbies and interests). Demand for consumer goods and products tend to have a low threshold, whereas demand for services could expand virtually indefinitely as long as consumers are provided with new and satisfying experiences. The growth of demand for services will be limited only by businesses' ability to innovate.

Resorts are well placed to become a part of such business practice and innovation.

To *attract* guests in the today's highly *competitive market* all resorts need to stand out by *differentiating* themselves from their competitors.

Many are attempting to do this by applying competitive advantage principles and through *branding* to increase their top of mind awareness amongst consumers. We can already see movement in these directions for the seniors market.

There is a strong expectation that *health and wellness* will be a major feature of the senior's market, and that such interest will not be confined to the traditional hot springs resorts. For example, the Daydream Island resort in Australia's Whitsunday islands has resurrected itself around a wellness theme in order to differentiate itself from nearby competitors. In addition to the health facilities seniors will be tempted by the *light exercise and recreation* opportunities provided by many resorts, particularly the golf and swimming pool facilities, and by the healthy menu creations emerging from the various kitchens. Some guests will be so pleased with their pampered body servicing they will be tempted to repeat their visit or even to relocate to the resort. More resorts are accommodating such thoughts with the building of *second or retirement homes*, which in many cases provide them with the sort of cash flow they need to maintain or enhance the facilities they provide.

To *hold* seniors, resorts need to provide *attractive settings* because they have the time to observe and comment. In some cases the natural environment will be an integral part of the resort's product, in others it will function as a backdrop; but in all cases it must be healthy and attractive in appearance. The resorts will need to provide a sufficient '*critical mass*' *of activities*. Critical in the sense of quantity, that there are enough different things to do to hold seniors with their various interests and physical abilities. Critical in the sense of quality, that the facilities and activities on offer are all top quality because the seniors are experienced and critical consumers. There is an increased emphasis in many resorts on learning new skills and more about the resort area's heritage and culture. To help the setting and facilities function to their full potential there needs to be a trained and motivated *support staff*, who will help the seniors derive the most from their experience.

To hold the senior guests in the future may well require resorts to become combination leisure and retirement centres, because it is anticipated that the retirement years for many will extend to 20 years or more, and during that period their physical and mental faculties can be expected to slowly deteriorate. Under those circumstances the guest will pass from a state of *active independence* to one of *dependency* on others, and may well need to move to different forms of housing and activity within the resort. This will require greater *flexibility* on the part of resort facilities and the presence of increased *security*, which will need to include internal unit monitoring as well as the usual external controls.

To *satisfy* the seniors market will require quality service, one that builds on super service, to include watchfulness and companionship in later years. Staff will need to be *skilled* in both the technical and personal components of their positions. Heskett et al. (1997: 11) state:

> *service profit chain* thinking maintains that there are direct and strong relationships between profit; growth; customer loyalty; customer satisfaction; the *value* of goods and services delivered to customers; and employee capability, satisfaction, loyalty and productivity.

Future seniors can expect to spend longer in retirement than preceding generations, and some resorts are developing *quasi-rest home areas* within their grounds. They will offer the full range of resort facilities for healthy independent retired couples who can mingle with other and younger guests, plus more specialized facilities and smaller units to those who become widowed or who encounter poor health. These specialized units will be located in quieter areas, often attached to a central socializing area, and have features such as safety bars in the bathroom, emergency call buttons and 24 hour nursing assistance on call. Such resort facilities are starting to appear along the Sunshine Coast of Queensland, Australia's prime retirement state, and in parts of Asia such as Thailand. In addition these types of resort are establishing *links with local hospitals* for their elderly guests who may need attention at short notice.

Like all demographically driven scenarios the seniors market future for resorts outlined in Table 1.1 is already underway. Several of the case studies in this book will illustrate various features of the table's predictions. However, it should be appreciated that this is only one of several market segment opportunities that resorts will face in the future, so several alternative or complementary futures should be studied and managed using the classic scientific enquiry method and proffered matrix analysis.

Summary and book structure

This chapter has shown that resort management is a distinctive part of general tourism management, with its defining feature being the creation of a business model designed to attract, hold and satisfy its guests. The very use of the term 'guest' over that of consumer or visitor implies that resorts are something special, something that goes out of its way to please its customers. Focus on the quality of technical facilities and personal service ensures an emphasis on value, but as in all cases it must be directed at appropriate and appreciative market segments. To provide the type of special experience that would attract guests to a resort requires a considerable and long-term investment, so a major challenge facing resorts revolves around the concept of sustainability – the need to develop a profitable conjunction of economic, social and environmental dimensions over an extended period.

The remainder of the book illustrates how the business of resort management can be examined using the type of analysis outlined above with regard to the future seniors market. Part B demonstrates the importance of using management theories and techniques to monitor and respond to the external forces which can have such a strong influence on the future success of resorts. Part C then focuses on internal aspects of the resort operation, where management decisions have a more direct impact on meeting the needs of guests and other stakeholders. Both of these parts attempt to explain what is happening to current resort business using selected theories and literature examples, but the goal of scientific analysis is to predict what will happen in the future and the best way to prepare for it. This author is no clairvoyant but being a positivist he believes in a stochastic approach to the future, where our options are ruled by probabilities. Hence, Part D looks into the future through the medium of risk management. It acknowledges that all business involves an element of risk, that some of that risk has already been recognized and quantified in terms of financial and liability matters; but other factors like global warming and climate change may be changing the ground rules for everyone and could represent the biggest challenge to a continuing sustainable long-term resort sector.

At the end of each chapter some case studies are offered based on the author's visit and interview or literature accounts. The purpose of these cases is to offer illustrations of how specific resorts around the world are tackling some of the issues raised in the associated chapters. Some of the resorts are large and internationally recognized benchmark operations, others are less well known primarily because they are smaller operations, but in their own way they have developed some thoughtful and successful responses to the challenges of operating a modern resort. At the very end of each chapter several questions have been put forward to stimulate further thought. Some may have a fairly obvious answer, but others are questions that continue to tease the resort sector and this author, because there is no apparent simple answer; and if you can come up with one you are on your way to making your mark in this field.

Case studies

Spa, Belgium

The town of Spa, nestled on the edge of the Ardennes region of Wallonia, Belgium is the origin of the current term 'spa', which signifies a health resort associated with a mineral water spring. The town of Spa's various mineral springs were appreciated and developed by the Romans, but its rise to prominence did not come about until the eighteenth century and lasted through to World War I, when it became Kaiser William's general head-quarters for the western front. Over that extensive time period we can see its evolution was determined by a combination of natural endowment and political forces, but since then this resort community has had to re-invent itself in the face of growing competition and increased consumer options.

Despite Spa's early start with the Romans, and the arrival of celebrity guests at certain periods, like Peter the Great of Russia and his successful convalescence, the town did not emerge as a major resort destination until the eighteenth century when certain external political factors came into play. These involved the Prince-Bishop of Liege, who built on the principal-ity's reputation for neutrality and safety by encouraging the building of Europe's first casinos – the Redoute (café where people play) and the Waux-Hall. In return the Prince-Bishop received a handsome share of the profits for the casinos' exclusive privilege of organizing public balls, festiv-ities and gambling games. With this development the mineral springs were now combined with entertainment, which made it an attractive package for the wealthy and influential of Europe. Over this boom period it is esti-mated Spa drew 600 to 1200 people a year, plus their retinues, leading the town to receive the title 'Café de l'Europe' (Figure 1.1).

Over this boom period many significant buildings were constructed and customs were created. Major buildings were erected over individual springs; substantial private homes were built to accommodate the aristoc-racy and nobility; public facilities were built to encourage gatherings and to provide green space for healthy exercise. Combined with this construc-tion was the growth of peripheral activities, such as the souvenir business. Some of the early mementoes were small and attractively decorated wooden boxes, made by local craftsmen from the wood of the nearby Ardennes forests. One particular local box was in the form of a tube and was designed to hold 'billet-doux' (love-letters) which fanned the roman-tic assignations that blossomed under such social circumstances.

After World War I, which decimated much of Belgium and brought an end to the traditional high society era, Spa had to re-invent itself in order

Figure 1.1   The early resort destination of Spa, Belgium.

to survive. An important element in this was a form of 'commodification' and 'democratization', in that the town started to export its mineral waters to the masses. In 1921 the Spa Monopole Company was created to bottle and export the local mineral waters and this has become a major business in the town. In the same year the Spa-Francorchamps racetrack was built for the fast developing innovation of the twentieth century — the car, and this track now hosts Belgium's annual Formula-1 race.

Since World War II, which fortunately spared the town, the appeal of spa therapy has widened to include more immersion, swimming and health treatments. In this regard, Spa replaced its old nineteenth century 'Thermes de Spa' with a modern and enlarged facility in 1997, set on top of a hill overlooking the town centre, to which it is linked by a funicular railway. The thermal centre and railway connection are a €14 million investment, and a French spa company 'Eurothermes' manages the operation. Spa and its new thermal centre are promoted as the 'pearl of the Ardennes', with its emphasis on water fitting nicely with the region's general cooperative advertising campaign of 'Ardennes Bleues' (Mawet, 2005).

Over time Spa's tourism market has changed, from the aristocracy to select mass markets. The town now focuses on the family and business markets, but there is also an important retirement market that helps to provide a year-round business. The family market is essentially a pleasure market, enjoying the thermal baths, the heritage, the spas and restaurants, the water activities, golf and of course the casino. The business market is both a seminar-conference market, which uses the modest conference facilities around the town, and an incentive travel market, providing small holiday packages as business rewards. Both of these markets tap the nearby areas of Germany and the Netherlands, in addition to Belgium and France, thanks to the good local freeway system.

Within this case one sees the constants and changes that can occur with a successful and sustainable resort destination. The principal constant is the appeal of the mineral waters, whose restorative powers have been appreciated over the centuries. Along with this physical attraction has developed an associated social pattern of behaviour. People cannot drink the water or stay in the waters all day, so it was imperative to develop a supplementary activity. Early socializing became transformed into formal entertainment and gambling, which is now supplemented by a wide range of recreational activities and special festivals.

Both of these consistencies have evolved over time, so that within them we can detect change. The major change has been a broadening of choice and a move to the mass market. In terms of health, instead of private or restricted springs Spa now has public facilities and instead of simple drinking or immersion there is a wide range of health and beauty procedures. In terms of socialization, there has been a build-up of supplementary recreation and support activities, a greater variety of accommodation, and more peripheral services. Most notable among these is the regional context in which Spa is now promoted. It is no longer sufficient to sell Spa alone, it needs to be sold as part of a distinctive regional package, one that can be enjoyed to the full by those who have their own cars or come on a tour. The regional package is seen as a way to encourage more visits and longer stays.

It is reassuring to return to one of the origins of resort development, to find it still recognizable as a resort destination and still earning a good livelihood from this same, but much changed, sector of the tourism industry. Naturally, it has experienced peaks and troughs as society's needs have changed, tourists' expectations have grown and it has been caught up in some major calamities which we call 'world wars'. Along the way it has had to re-invent itself; either by renovating and upgrading its period buildings to meet new standards and expectations, or by broadening its appeal with the addition of events like the Belgium Grand Prix Formula-1 race and combining with the region to present a combined attraction to more mobile tourists. But it has survived and evolved into a beautiful heritage centre in a scenic region. It now offers a tranquil oasis of health therapy within the frantic post-industrial age of Western Europe.

Waikiki, Hawaii, USA

The long-term evolution of a resort destination can provide several twists and turns, but there is always that combination of constancy and change, even if it is located in a very different part of the world from Spa and linked to another century. Such is the case of Hawaii's resort area of Waikiki, on the island of Oahu. This tropical paradise is a child of the twentieth century, which has grown and prospered due to the technological advances of that century, but it has been endangered also by the growing conformity of our global economy.

The isolation and relative expensiveness of Hawaii which would normally deter significant growth and development has not stopped it evolving into one of the world's major resort destinations, because it is the 'Aloha' state and is special to many people. Waikiki receives an average of 72 000 visitors a day, which represents 44 per cent of the state's total visitors (State of Hawaii, 2003). About 43 per cent of Waikiki's visitors are international, but this statistical definition fails to take into account the US mainland visitors who to a large extent are sufficiently foreign and distant travellers to qualify as 'international visitors' to this part of their country. In 2002 Waikiki had an accommodation inventory of 31 717 units, most of them being full-service hotel rooms. 'Directly and indirectly, the small one-square-mile area of Waikiki can be associated with supporting about 11% of all civilian jobs in the state and 12% of state and local tax revenues' (State of Hawaii, 2003: 7).

When Waikiki started out as an international beach resort in the 1920s Honolulu was a popular destination for ocean liners plying the Pacific Ocean. These ships, small by today's standards, brought wealthy and influential visitors who looked forward to a long stay visit after a crossing of several days. Many were drawn to the Waikiki area, now a suburb of Honolulu, because of its attractive beach, the surf, its views of Diamond Head and its two luxury hotels – the Moana Surfrider and the Royal Hawaiian. The elegant style of this early resort environment can be seen in old photographs and posters and in today's Sheraton Moana Surfrider and Royal Hawaiian hotels which have been restored to their original glory (Figure 1.2).

The arrival of jet airliner travel changed everything and that can be seen most clearly in the spread of tourism throughout Oahu and the style of hotel that emerged in Waikiki after 1965 (McDonald, 1999). In addition to the island's natural attractions of the beach and surf, the cultural and heritage attractions around Oahu became more developed, such as the Polynesian Cultural Center on the north shore and the Battleship Arizona memorial in Pearl Harbour, which has recently been joined by the Battleship Missouri to symbolically mark the beginning and end of World War II for the USA. Entertainment started to focus on pop culture and was associated more with Hollywood's version of Hawaiian culture, as exemplified by the Elvis Presley films and some Hawaii-based television shows. As its popularity grew and customers changed new accommodation had to be built and international chains started to build fine resort hotels alongside Waikiki's sweeping beach, while nearby a local hotel company 'Outrigger' developed less expensive accommodation with more of an Hawaiian style and feel.

In the process of this development Waikiki followed Butler's (1980, 2006) Tourist Area Life Cycle curve, shifting from his 'exploration' stage to 'stagnation' or beyond according to some local observers. By the 1990s, some 25 plus years after the start of Waikiki's mass tourism,

Figure 1.2 Early resort hotels of Waikiki, Hawaii.

the resort destination was beginning to loose visitors and some considered it was starting to tip into the 'decline' phase of the Butler model. One such person is the past mayor of Honolulu, Jeremy Harris, who claims 'By the end of the '80s, tourism was already hurting. Waikiki the economic engine of the state was looking tired and run down' (Harris, 2004: 86). However, a study of resident attitudes by Sheldon and Abenoja (2001: 442) suggests 'residents have made the affirmative choice to live in Waikiki and (still) hold favorable attitudes towards tourism'. They conclude that a critical step to revitalizing Waikiki and any mature destination is to identify the local culture and sense of place and include the residents in such a process. This is exactly what has been happening in Waikiki.

In 1998 the state's Economic Revitalization Task Force recommended the establishment of a Joint Waikiki Task Force to focus attention on this area and to help restore its competitiveness in an increasingly competitive global market which was offering more and more tropical paradise destinations. The Joint Waikiki Task Force was created and viewed as a platform to enhance public and private investment and initiatives. The Waikiki Improvement Association is a public–private sector partnership, designed to 'keep Waikiki on the top of the S curve wave' according to its president Rick Egged (2005).

The Association started out by asking its members from the travel industry, supporting businesses, the community and public sector three key questions:

1. What would differentiate Waikiki from the growing number of similar destinations around the world?
2. Why did they think Waikiki is no longer an automatic 'top of mind' consideration by world travellers?
3. How are they going to ensure that whatever plans they made were going to be brought to life?

The answers to these important questions would have an impact on Waikiki's future as a sustainable long-term destination, one that could continue to draw visitors thousands of kilometres to its shores in the face of increasing travel costs, terrorism and growing competition.

The group's answer to the first question was that Hawaii has a distinctive culture and history in addition to the attractive environment and climate of a tropical paradise. The history of the Polynesian people's arrival, their early struggles, their encounters with the Cook expeditions and later the American business barons, and more recently Hawaii's significant role in World War II and subsequent Asian conflicts has left a unique historic-cultural presence on these islands, and particularly on the central island of Oahu. One clear sign of this is the multi-racial composition of modern Hawaii's population, which is now a blend of American, Asian, Pacific and European people who now exceed the indigenous Polynesian population, where there has been much intermarriage leading to the delightful self-description of Hawaii as a 'chop suey' community. What fosters such an inclusive feel to these different groups who have migrated to the island is the Polynesians spirit of 'Aloha', a single word that symbolizes welcome and love. It is hard to describe the warmth of a Hawaiian welcome, especially from those of Polynesian descent, but in a service environment it transcends the standard greetings and service levels of most destinations. With this history and spirit the Waikiki Improvement Association felt it had a distinctive and unique base on which to build its future tourism.

Their answer to the second question was to raise the awareness of this cultural and historic sense of place in the minds of potential travellers. It was felt that local customs and history had become subsumed by the power of global business practices and the selectivity of the global media, both of which tended to favour standardization over local diversity. To restore the balance it was considered that the tourism product of Waikiki should stress the cultural and social features of Hawaii, rather than the standard American lifestyle that could be experienced back on the mainland and increasingly elsewhere around the globe. There are now cultural markers and regular heritage tours throughout Waikiki.

The answer to the third question was to start with a small and simple physical problem, before tackling the larger and more fundamental issues. By tackling something specific which upset a lot of people, locals and tourists, it was hoped that the positive and visible outcome would symbolize a new era of sustainable tourism planning and development had arrived. One of the obvious areas to start was to clean up the waterfront areas of Waikiki and to make it a more attractive area for walking. Now the sidewalks /footpaths have been enlarged and landscaped to provide a more appealing walking space and environment.

To achieve the above goals the Waikiki Improvement Association needed both internal consensus and outside support. It has managed to achieve this task and in the process released a local community energy that has started to transform the appearance and prospects for Waikiki. The efforts of the Association have led to considerable investment and renewal in Waikiki. In its 2002 Report the Association reported, 'the private sector has invested more than US$325 million in renovations and developments' (Waikiki Improvement Association, 2002: 8) which is only a part of the investment snowball that has been generated. According to Mayor Jeremy Harris' book on *The Renaissance of Honolulu*, of which Waikiki is a most important suburb, 'the public investment of US$70 million has triggered over US$1 billion of planned private sector re-development' (Harris, 2004: 117).

Thus, we can see Waikiki has faced the demon of a decline stage in the S curve and produced strategies that can help it regain its position at the top of the Tourism Area Life Cycle (TALC). It has achieved this by reaffirming its core values and distinctive product and by tapping the collaborative forces of the tourism industry and local residents to produce a community destination brand.

Questions

1 A scientific method of enquiry has been offered as one way to examine the development and future of resort management. What are the weaknesses of such an approach and can you suggest alternative ways of analysing resorts and resort management?

2 Resorts have been identified as a Roman legacy. Examine this link in more detail and discuss other ways the ancient Roman Empire may have influenced current travel and tourism.

3 Critically assess the resort definitions identified in this text and elsewhere, then create and justify your own comprehensive definition of the term 'resort'.

4 The author offers three distinctive features of resort management – attract, hold and satisfy. How much do these differ from regular tourism management strategies and how would you apply them in a resort of your choice?

5 Resorts can operate at a variety of levels. How would you categorize the resort of Whistler, Canada (or any other resort of your choice) and how would this categorization influence your subsequent strategic planning?

References

Ayala, H. (1991). Resort cycle revisited: the retirement connection. *Annals of Tourism Research*, **18(4)**, 568–587.

Bourgeois, L.J. (1980). Strategy and the environment: a conceptual integration. *Academy of Management Review*, **5**, 25–39.

Bramwell, B. and Lane, B. (eds) (2000). *Tourism Collaboration and Partnerships: Politics, Practice and Sustainability*. Clevedon: Channel View Publications.

Bryman, A. (1995). *Disney and His Worlds*. London and New York: Routledge.

Butler, R.W. (1980). The concept of a tourist area cycle of evolution: implications for management of resources. *The Canadian Geographer*, **24(1)**, 5–12.

Butler, R.W. (ed.) (2006). *The Tourism Area Life Cycle*, Vols 1 and 2 Clevedon: Channel View Publications.

Clifford, H. (2003). *Downhill Slide: Why the Corporate Ski Industry Is Bad for Skiing, Ski Towns and the Environment*. San Francisco: Sierra Club Books.

Daft, R.L., Fitzgerald, P.A. and Rock, M.E. (1992). *Management*. Toronto: Dryden.

Egged, R. (2005). President, Waikiki Improvement Association, Honolulu, Hawaii, Interview, August 23.

Ernst and Young (2003). *Resorting to Profitability*. Sydney: Tourism Task Force (TTF) Australia.

Gee, C. (1996). *Resort Development and Management*, 2nd edn. East Lansing, Michigan: Educational Institute of the American Hotel and Motel Association.

Harris, J. (2004). *The Renaissance of Honolulu: The Sustainable Rebirth of an American City*. Hawaii: City and Council of Honolulu.

Heskett, J.L., Sasser Jr., W.E. and Schlesinger, L.A. (1997). *The Service Profit Chain: How Leading Companies Link Profit and Growth to Loyalty, Satisfaction, and Value*. New York: Free Press.

Huffadine, M. (1999). *Resort Design: Planning, Architecture and Interiors*. New York: McGraw-Hill.

Inskeep, E. (1991). *Tourism Planning: An Integrated and Sustainable Development Approach*. New York: Van Nostrand Reinhold.

Krippendorf, J. (1987). *The Holiday Makers*. London: Heinemann.

Mawet, J.P. (2005). Director, Aqualis, Spa, Belgium, Interview, September 27.

McDonald, M. (1999). Who owns Waikiki? In *Hawaii: New Geographies* (D.W. Woodcock, ed.), pp. 179–219. Department of Geography, University of Hawaii-Manoa, Hawaii, USA.

Mill, R.C. (2001). *Resorts: Management and Operation*. New York: John Wiley and Sons.

Murphy, P.E. and Murphy, A.E. (2004). *Strategic Management for Tourism Communities: Bridging the Gaps*. Clevedon: Channel View Publications.

Pearce, D. (1987). *Tourism Today: A Geographical Analysis*. Harlow: Longman.

Pohl, O. (2005). Lazing in the lap of luxury at $A16375 a night. *The Age*, (Melbourne paper) 12.

Porter, M.E. (1980). *Competitive Strategy*. New York: Free Press.

Prideaux, B. (2000). The resort development spectrum – a new approach to modeling resort development. *Tourism Management*, **21**, 225–240.

Sheldon, P.J. and Abenoja, T. (2001). Resident attitudes in a mature destination: the case of Waikiki. *Tourism Management*, **22(5)**, 435–443.

State of Hawaii (2003). *The Economic Contribution of Waikiki*. Honolulu, Hawaii: Department of Business, Economic Development and Tourism.

Travel Impact Newswire (2005). The impact of demographic change. *Travel Impact Newswire*, 68th edn. 2 November, 6–8.

Waikiki Improvement Association (2002). *Vision: Waikiki A Place of Aloha*. Annual Report 2002. Honolulu, Hawaii.

2

Management definitions and theory applicable to resorts

Introduction

This chapter discusses some of the major management definitions and theories that are particularly relevant to resort management. As the book title states the emphasis will be on business definitions and theories, but since resorts involve environmental and social matters the text will stray into biological science and social science regimes, where it is considered those disciplines can help direct resorts to a sustainable development outcome.

This book will view resorts as businesses, which are attempting to be comprehensive long-term sustainable operations. This will involve achieving the following objectives:

1. *Making a profit*.
   This is the economic rationale of most businesses. Without it all other objectives will fail in the long run.

2. *Developing an attractive and competitive product.*
   To attract customers in an increasingly competitive environment the resort must offer a core attraction that is desirable and located in an attractive setting.
3. *Developing an attentive and skilled workforce.*
   Resorts need to offer high-quality service to build on objective 2, and that requires skilful management and staff.
4. *Becoming a sustainable operation.*
   Given the long-term nature of resort development and the symbiosis between its business success with the health of surrounding environments and communities, sustainable development becomes a fundamental principle for resort businesses.

To see how these objectives can be assisted by academic research we turn to the academic literature and some of the theories and techniques it has produced. Those offered in this book are not intended to be an exhaustive list, but should be viewed as indicators of how this literature can facilitate future resort management.

Management objectives

In general terms 'management' is all about marshalling one's resources, including time, to achieve a goal. We regularly undertake management on a personal and unconscious level to achieve life's major goals like higher education, a career and a home. We set a target and prioritize our time and efforts to achieve those goals we have set ourselves. This is similar to industry's interpretation of management in that business tries to operate in an *effective* and *efficient* manner to realize its goals.

Business management

The discipline of business management has developed a scientific management approach which identifies general principles of behaviour and outcomes for the management process. Within the overall management approach one specific sub-field that has particular relevance to resorts is the area of strategic management.

The strategic management process involves three steps:

1. *Strategy formation*: where decisions made by the *leaders* of resort businesses and local community determine the resort's vision, objectives and *planning* policies.

2. *Strategy implementation*: where a new strategy is installed or existing strategies are modified by *organizing* resources and personnel to achieve the planning objectives.
3. *Evaluation and control*: are the activities needed to monitor the plan's progress and to *control* the planning process by making any necessary course corrections over time.

(Based on Stahl and Grigsby, 1992: 5–6.)

Among the above steps are the four classic functions of management, which have been italicized above and are discussed in more detail below.

Leadership is required to initiate ideas and motivate others in order to bring these ideas to fruition. It is notable that many resorts are linked to the inspiration and drive of one or two people. These are the leaders who see the opportunity to innovate and fill a service or product gap. To be successful they need to be risk takers, with the ability to communicate their ideas and enthusiasm to a range of stakeholders. Often resort development involves development periods of five years or more, so we should also add stamina and commitment to the list of resort leadership characteristics.

Planning is the crucial first phase in that it communicates the leader's ideas via a tangible and negotiable format. This will involve public display of the resort's vision and its role within the local community. The vision, once accepted, can be converted into tangible objectives by proceeding through the planning process. This step will inevitably involve many stakeholder groups as the planning process moves through the legislative system of permits and bylaws for the resort to become an authorized entity.

Organizing becomes the next major task. The modern resort is a complex business at any level, that can be equated with the operation of a small town, so the leaders will need to create capable management teams and supportive staff to bring their plans to life. Much like Porter's (1985) 'value chain' resorts have the following general divisions and responsibilities:

Administration:	H.R. – Marketing – Finance – Environment and Social Responsibility
Functions:	Grounds – Attractions – Accommodation – F&B – Retail

These divisions need to be given resources, direction and coordination in order to achieve the planning objectives of the resort.

In terms of administration the resort will need to handle various major management tasks. Of crucial importance is the need to hire the right type of workers, ones who can deliver the promised quality product and service.

Marketing is an important challenge because of the growing competition for the guests' time and money, particularly when attempting to draw them over long distances with many intervening global opportunities. Finance is a consistent issue with asset rich and cash poor operations, and many resorts fall into that category. It becomes a major balancing act to acquire sufficient revenues to meet on-going costs, while upgrading or expanding the resort's product appeal. The final administration task of corporate environmental and social responsibility is one that has grown with the increasing awareness of tourism's negative environmental and social impacts, along with a demand for greater public accountability.

The functional divisions largely relate to the structure of resorts. Their physical setting must be attractive, so a great deal of investment goes into the infrastructure and appearance of the grounds and buildings. The primary core attraction must be of high quality and up-to-date in terms of the latest technology, if it is to compete in the global market. Secondary attractions will need to complement the core attraction(s) to help present a broader market appeal and convince guests to stay longer. For example, in many ski resorts there are a substantial number of guests who do not ski or snow board and are looking for other ways to occupy their time while their spouse, partner or colleague enjoys the slopes. Suitable accommodation and restaurant operations for the target market segments need to be in place to meet their needs and give them a variety of choice over their stay. The retail selection should support the primary attractions and activities and needs to help complete the guests' experience and to keep their dollars on-site.

Control of the development will be needed to ensure the plan stays on track or is altered where necessary to accommodate misjudgements and changing market conditions. An essential aspect of this process will be the monitoring of performance. This aspect will be easier to judge in terms of economic and financial matters, but becomes more challenging with respect to changing environmental and social conditions. In terms of resorts the monitoring and adjustment of performance revolves mainly around the guest, their levels of satisfaction with the experience and gap analysis of the disparity, if any, between established expectations and actual delivery (Parasuraman et al., 1985). Less has been done regarding the issues of environmental stress and community relationships, but that is starting to change (Hudson, 2006).

Service management

The basic resort product is the selling of experiences. Although this may involve many tangible products, the final output is an intangible and highly personal guest experience. This means regular business management and procedures to develop quality and reliable products must be augmented by service management principles and procedures to draw the best out of a resort's physical assets. Selling a resort experience involves a staff member combining quality products and service with a guest's expectations and mood, so the guest becomes a significant player and partner in the experiential resort product. This situation leads resort management clearly into the field of service management.

Normann (1991) one of the early proponents of service management, identifies significant differences between service delivery and the manufacturing process, but in a resort situation both facets will be needed. Good service in a resort requires an appropriate setting and quality tangible products which staff can work with to create the best possible individual experience for a guest. Simply managing workers does not result in great service they need to be nurtured, prepared and trusted to perform, plus they need to be rotated because the 'constant pressure of 'being on stage' and serving many customers in a short time frequently leads to fatigue and discouragement'(Berry, 1995: 7).

Value and revenue management

The guest's perceived value of any resort experience represents 'the consumer's overall assessment of the utility of a product based on perceptions of what is received and what is given' (Zeithaml, 1988: 14).What is received is a package of benefits from the experience that will be compared to expected returns from alternative leisure competitors; what is given is the time and money spent on the experience, plus the forsaken opportunity costs associated with alternative options. Within their perceived value assessments consumers are expected to consider three different value concepts, these being:

1. *Functional value*: the perceived utility derived from the product's capacity for functional, utilitarian or physical performance.
2. *Emotional value*: the capacity to arouse personal feelings in relation to the product experience, such as excitement and fulfillment.
3. *Social value*: the enhancement of social self-esteem, because the product has social status.

Turning these guest perceived value interests into actual experiences becomes the task of yield and revenue management. 'Yield management is the practice of maximizing profits from the sale of perishable assets, such as hotel rooms, by controlling price and inventory and improving service' according to Lieberman (1993: 35). Over time this concept has also been referred to as revenue management, and in a retrospective of revenue management Kimes (2003) notes revenue management needs to operate differently depending on two key dimensions – *product price* and *experience duration*. Where a business is predictable in terms of duration and relatively fixed in terms of price, such as a function space within a resort, it is the price factor that can be adjusted most effectively. So resorts present their seasonal range of prices. Where a business has a relatively fixed price for an experience over which it has little duration control, like a meal or round of golf, it can apply both duration controls and pricing management. In restaurants those diners making an early reservation could expect a discount or limited menu but must vacate the table prior to the later popular eating time.

One way to link value and revenue has been proposed by Thomke and von Hippel (2002). They recommend an advance on the customization techniques used by companies like Dell Computers, which provides a range of options to the customer who can then order a computer suited to their personal needs rather than choosing from a range of standard models. Thomke and von Hippel recommend five steps for turning customers into innovators and thereby enhancing personal and company value. While they focus on manufacturing we can see their relevance to resorts below:

1. *Develop a user-friendly tool kit for customers.*
   This involves designing an experience in conjunction with guests, be it a commonplace experience like a meal or something innovative like a new activity.
2. *Increase the flexibility of your production processes.*
   The operational aspects of the resort should be made as flexible as possible to cater for different guest tastes as well as different seasons.
3. *Carefully select the first customers to use the tool kit.*
   The best prospective customers are those guests for whom the resort was designed, and exploring with those guests ways to heighten their experience enjoyment.
4. *Evolve your tool kit continually and rapidly to satisfy your leading-edge customers.*
   Guest reactions to the proffered resort experiences should be monitored and adjustments made according to their observations and evolving technology and consumer preferences.
5. *Adapt your business practices accordingly.*
   'Outsourcing product development to customers will require you to revamp your business models to profit from the shift … Tool kits will

fundamentally change your relationship with customers (Thomke and von Hippel, 2002: 79).

Although such ideas may be revolutionary for the manufacturing sector, they should be relatively commonplace for service industries like the resort sector; for resorts sell personal experiences that naturally involve the guest as part of the overall product design and operation.

Applicable theories and frameworks

There are some theories and techniques from business and other disciplines that have particular relevance to the type of resort management discussed in this book. The following examples have been selected on the basis of the author's experience, but are not intended to be an all-inclusive summary. Rather, it is hoped that by suggesting direct links between some academic theories and resort management the reader will start to search for their own potential links when they read or hear about some theory or technique in the future. The presentation of these theories and techniques focusses on those that assist with the demand and supply dimensions of the resort business.

Demand side: Family/Household Life Cycle theory

The Family Life Cycle theory reflects the changing socio-economic circumstances that can be expected within a household over the life of its founders.

> Embedded within the larger sociopolitical culture, the individual life cycle takes shape as it moves and evolves within the matrix of the family life cycle. The family lifecycle is the natural context within which to frame individual identity and development and to account for the effects of the social system
>
> (Carter and McGoldrick, 2005: 1)

It was first mooted in the days of more stable nuclear family units, but its demographic principles can still be applied to the greater variety of household types that exist today.

The traditional family life cycle goes through various stages and has been used to analyse various vacation decision-making situations (Consenza and Davis, 1981). *Stage 1* is the formation of the household with marriage or some other form of commitment. At this stage the couple is labelled by the marketers as 'Double Income, No Kids' (DINKS) with few major commitments and often a desire to travel to exotic destinations, particularly in reference to the honeymoon. For some resorts and resort destinations the honeymoon market is a major market niche and needs to be planned accordingly in terms of privacy plus entertainment. *Stage 2* is the start of a family, and when the children are young and the house mortgage is large resorts are likely to be less of a priority. But holidays and short breaks are still important, so local or regional resorts offering a break to routine at reasonable prices are still a valid option, especially if they offer childcare or other options. *Stage 3* is child(ren) launching, when the mortgage is more manageable or gone and the children are older and starting to go their own way. This gives parents an opportunity to expand their horizons once again and to consider more prestigious and international resort locations. *Stage 4* is the early stages of retirement and is the second prime time for travel by those who have the time and money to spend on themselves and their wishes. For these people the lure of international travel involving first class resorts and cruises has become a major business opportunity. Finally, in *Stage 5* comes the loss of a spouse or partner and growing physical limitations for the survivor, which either means less travelling or none at all.

It should be acknowledged that this theory like all theories in social science and business is a simplified generalization. There have been many significant changes to the family and household structure since the rise of the nuclear family, such as the well-publicized growing divorce rates, single parent families and single adults going through life without a partner. While these social trends undoubtedly modify the life cycle for a growing number, many households still perform in the manner outlined by the Family Life Cycle theory. Furthermore, certain social changes like single adults and same sex couples appear to place even more emphasis on travel and entertainment than the traditional nuclear family, so resorts that choose to focus on those niche markets will also have the opportunity to succeed.

Demand side: lifestyle segmentation

Increasing prosperity and tourism options has given tourists greater latitude of vacation choices. There is greater opportunity for many to experience the personal fulfillment of Maslow's 'self-determination', rather than be restricted to standard vacations of the mass market variety. This has led tourism research to place more emphasis on the psychographic nature of vacation choices, the personal values, attitudes and lifestyles that can direct one's vacation choices. Under these circumstances the tourism market is not a homogeneous mass of buyers, but has split into a myriad of specialized markets where individuals follow their own vacation needs and desires.

Matzler et al. (2004) have applied a lifestyle segmentation analysis to Alpine skiing in Europe. They identified seven lifestyle segments amongst the skiers, along with five vacation style objectives, but were unable to detect a direct and definite relationship between the two. However, they did find a strong relationship between lifestyles and guest satisfaction and the intent to revisit. So like the life cycle theory there seem to be several intervening variables that at times confirm and at others confound the anticipated simple predicted relationships.

Supply side: Product Life Cycle/Tourism Area Life Cycle theory

The Product Life Cycle (PLC) Theory proposes that most products progress through various stages of development (Gordon et al., 1990). If they are successful products they will increase in production but will eventually decline to a modest output as they saturate the market, needing only replacement products for those which breakdown or for the new household markets being created – such is the case of the vacuum cleaner. Many will not last as long as the vacuum cleaner because they become superseded by new innovations and products, such as happened with the typewriter and VCRs. The first stage is the *introduction* of a new product, either a complete resort or a new attraction within it, bringing it to the attention of the public and in particular the intended target markets. The second stage is the *trial* of the new product, which is usually undertaken by the more adventurous and inquisitive members of society, called opinion leaders. It is upon their recommendation that others really notice the new product and begin to try it out. The third stage is the *adoption* phase and represents whether a product will be successful or not, because it is only at this stage that sufficient business volume will be generated to cover initial development costs. The fourth stage is a *saturation* of the market, meaning that in some cases one sale or experience is enough for most people (movie or bungee jump) or in other cases one purchase satisfies for many years (house, university degree). Stage five represents a *decline* in production, as the market now depends on replacement (repeat visits) or the arrival of new consumers via new household groups (new international markets).

The link between PLC and resort development in general is presented within Butler's well-known Tourism Area Life Cycle (TALC) theory.

In his seminal work on this topic Butler (1980: 6) states 'The pattern (his S curve) which is put forward here is based on the product cycle concept'. In a recent two-volume review of the TALC theory (Butler, 2006) several authors have noted its link with the PLC concept and relevance to resort development. In the scientific analysis spirit of this book Manente and Pechlaner's paper shows the TALC can become an early warning system, presenting criteria that can predict the onset of the decline stage; Berry's paper analyses the development of Cairns in Australia demonstrating 80 per cent of the original TALC indicators were positively related to Cairn's development experience and as such could have been used to predict events. However, Wheeler reminds us in the same TALC review that we should not expect TALC to be the sole predictor of resort fortunes. Resorts are people places and people businesses, so more than business economics and marketing will determine their future. It is the resort guest who will determine the future of a resort. Some may choose to age with the resort others may try to hold onto the original purpose and style of the resort, it will be up to resort management to determine which guest style they wish to encourage.

Supply side: competitive advantage

To help resorts stay on top of the PLC wave requires the maintenance of their competitive advantage, and in this regard the works of Michael Porter can be most helpful. Porter's (1985) seminal work on *Competitive Advantage* offers several theories and techniques that can assist resort management. The relevance of Porter's ideas to resorts is outlined below, but resorts are not simply mechanical products, they are experiential service products that have a strong regional character with respect to the environment and sense of place. Consequently, one must balance the productivity emphasis of Porter's industrial-business approach with a more balanced consideration of how well regional resources are deployed (Ritchie and Crouch, 2003), how competitive or complementary is the regional destination (Michael, 2007) and how well local social capital is being engaged.

The five competitive forces faced by all industries are:

1. *The entry of new competitors* – in a free market system of global tourism one can guarantee new entrants, especially where they see an existing successful business.
2. *The threat of substitutes* – in association with the first force is the development of substitutes and intervening opportunities between an existing business and its principal markets.

3. *The bargaining power of buyers* – individual purchaser's will have greater bargaining power when there are more choices (see force #1) and tour wholesalers have the major buying power because of their sales volume.
4. *The bargaining power of suppliers* – individual suppliers will have more power the closer they are to a monopoly situation.
5. *The rivalry between existing competitors* – the more intense the rivalry the more cutthroat will be the pricing.

Porter (1985: 4) states 'the collective strength of these five competitive forces determines the ability of firms in an industry to earn, on average, rates of return on investment in excess of the cost of capital'. He states further that strategic management policies can influence the five forces in a positive way.

To counter the possible entry of new competitors or development of substitute products, existing businesses can utilize strategies that make it difficult and/or expensive to copy them. This means they need to build their business on something that is unique, something that can be protected through copyright, or something that is difficult to duplicate. In the latter category this involves developing a product and service that is hard to match. The ability to influence the bargaining power of buyers and suppliers is largely out of the control of individual businesses in a free market situation, but buyers can still be influenced by making a business an attractive and satisfying experience. In tourism there has always been intense rivalry and competition for business; but there is also the growing recognition that a destination's businesses should work together to bring customers to their common location before they fight to draw customers into their particular businesses. In fact Porter's (1998) more recent work on 'clusters' emphasizes what there is to be gained through industry–government–education collaboration that utilizes local social capital.

Value is the fundamental reason consumers have for purchasing any product or service, so that value must be apparent to them and ingrained into the structure of the entire business. 'To diagnose competitive advantage, it is necessary to define a firm's value chain for competing in a particular industry' (Porter, 1985: 45). This *value chain* divides each business into its component parts, and analyses what each function contributes to the overall value of the product or experience.

The primary activities as laid out by Porter refer to manufacturing firms, but they can be adapted to a service business like resorts. Instead of bringing in raw materials a resort will need to draw in guests. To do this it needs adequate accessibility, like a nearby international airport or simply a good quality road; and an entrance that signals those guests should leave behind their daily woes and be ready for an exhilarating or restful retreat from their regular routine. Likewise, instead of shipping out finished products a resort should be sending home satisfied guests, who will either return for more or recommend the experience to others. The big difference will be with service, which is no longer viewed as an 'after-sales' activity, but as the core to the whole process. Resorts will need to ensure there is quality service to match the considerable investment in the land, plant and products of the resort.

To pull together the presence of the five competitive forces and the importance of judging each function's contribution to the value chain requires a generic strategy that emphasizes how to maximize a business' competitiveness. In this regard Porter offers his *competitive advantage theory*, which focusses on the need for cost leadership, differentiation and market segmentation.

'*Cost leadership* is perhaps the clearest of the three generic strategies. In it, a firm sets out to become *the* low-cost producer in its industry' according to Porter (1985: 12). To achieve this state a business must:

1. Conduct a meaningful cost analysis within each functional division and not across the entire firm (Porter, 1985: 64).
2. Develop a strategy to deliver lower 'relative' costs (Porter, 1985: 118)

Consequently businesses, including resorts, need to focus on the relative contribution of each functional division to the overall revenue structure; and to analyse their costs in relative terms, that is the relationship between actual costs and generated revenues.

Where businesses are selling experiences the ideal staff requires skills in the areas of technical knowledge, customer relations and sales. This triple capability is generally not available for minimum wage. Rather than thinking in terms of the nominal wage levels resorts should be thinking of real wages – the comparison between what is paid per hour compared with the earnings that hour produces within each functional area. For example, an employee who is adequately prepared to perform his/her functions within the total resort experience product should be able to not only serve the guests properly, but judge their mood and interests and 'up-sell' them onto other resort products and experiences.

A *differentiation* strategy encourages a firm to seek uniqueness along some dimension of its product that is valued by consumers. Differentiation can be based on the product, the delivery system, the marketing approach or a range of functions. The logic of a differentiation strategy is to stand out in a crowded marketplace. Resorts often select to focus on one primary core attraction or activity that can help them stand out from the competition.

Although differentiation can be obtained in several ways a common strategy in tourism is to emphasize a destination's 'sense of place'. This is the geographic setting and local history which make each area unique in the sense of possessing its own character. Such distinctiveness is now under threat from the standardization of globalization, which to some makes it even more important for tourism and resorts to nurture local character, like building designs and traditional costume. Resorts that emphasize their 'sense of place' can range over a variety of forms, from African safari park resorts profiling their wild animals and native customs to the Versace resorts selling a particular lifestyle and associated products.

The third aspect of Porter's Competitive Advantage theory is to *focus*. This aspect brings cost leadership and differentiation together, by focussing them on particular target markets. For example, if a resort chooses to offer the highest quality product and service possible this would cost a great deal, so it would only succeed if there was a wealthy market segment that wanted such luxury. If, on the other hand, a resort wishes to appeal to a larger market segment such as the middle income range, it is better advised to set its sights on more modest but still quality levels of product and service.

All resorts are advised to focus on the particular market segments they can best appeal to and satisfy. In terms of cost leadership if a resort is focussing on a budget market it should emphasize standardization, with limited core options and simple service. If it is aiming for the luxury market there should be many options and choices, along with personalized service. The selected differentiation should send a clear message to potential customers concerning what activities, facilities and service levels to expect. Local resorts will need to emphasize their core function and convenient road access, while national/international resorts will need to stress their airport access along with the variety of accommodation and entertainment options that support their core attractions.

Operational frameworks

To help identify and implement various theories requires the use of operational procedures. Three have been selected as being most helpful in terms of the previously discussed theories. Again this is not intended to be an exhaustive list, but simply to direct the reader to some of the more widely applied techniques in the strategic management of resorts.

Environmental scanning

Environmental scanning is the term applied to the process of examining the internal and external environments of a resort's demand opportunities, before making a major business decision. It commonly involves three levels of investigation and operation as shown in Figure 2.1 (Daft et al., 1992; Vesper, 1996)

- The *internal environment* involves operations within the organization, the resort business and site, and represents the scale at which management has the maximum control over its affairs. It can and should assess its ability to meet new demand trends and market circumstances by applying techniques such as SWOT analysis.
- The *task environment* is the immediately surrounding host community from which a resort would draw its local supplies and labour. Within

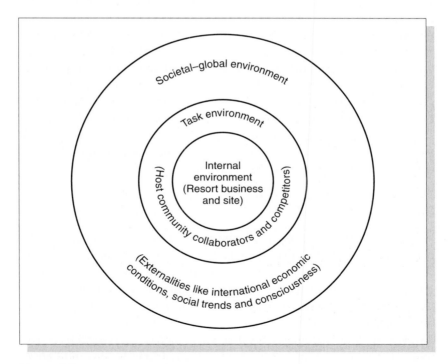

Figure 2.1　Environmental scanning structure.

that environment exists both collaborators and competitors, who would need to be considered if the resort was to develop an attractive destination package. To achieve the ideal unity of purpose and marketing would require inter-organizational collaboration between the internal and task environments.

■ The *societal/global environment* is the outer layer representing the external impacts of national policies and major global market and societal trends. Large scale impacts from this environment for resorts involve market trends like the move to shorter vacations and environmental awareness; and operational issues like the global price of oil (impacts transportation and operational costs), government legislation (working week definition and shift work regulations) and terrorism (publicity and insurance rates).

Resorts are influenced by all the above environments. Some they can control or strongly influence, others they can only watch and react to events. Interaction with the internal and task environments involves collaboration with staff and local partners, to develop strategic management plans that are regularly updated as feedback and global changes are taken into account. Contingency plans and risk management strategies are becoming a more regular feature of resort management, as successful resorts tend to have a long lifespan and society is changing more rapidly than ever. Even in terms of the societal/global environment resorts can be proactive to some degree by researching trends, by spreading their risk and forming associations and lobby groups to state their point of view on the national or larger scale. In Australia the *Tourism and Transport Forum* has been formed to monitor trends and to bring tourism's point of view to the attention of government, in the hope that this industry's contribution to the economy will be appreciated.

Stakeholder analysis

Associated with environmental scanning is analysis that focusses on the players within the three environments, the stakeholders. Stakeholder analysis essentially involves three steps – identify the relevant stakeholder groups, establish their needs and priorities, integrate their wishes into the business strategy wherever feasible and profitable. Hopefully, with this information and approach a resort business will be in a better position to develop win-win strategies; ones that will combine resort objectives with other stakeholder objectives in the three environments, to bring about profitable and sustainable partnerships.

The term 'stakeholder' in business represents 'those groups or individuals who are directly or indirectly affected by an organisation's pursuit of its goals' (Stoner et al., 1995: 63). Those *directly affected* are the internal stakeholders, such as owner operators, employees and customers; plus external stakeholders in the task environment like off-site employees, suppliers, shareholders and special interest groups. Those *indirectly affected* include community members not directly employed by or dependent on the business, plus people and communities further removed from the business site who might still be impacted by certain environmental, social or economic decisions.

Research in business and tourism has revealed the make-up of the direct and indirect stakeholders will vary from situation to situation; that some stakeholder groups, especially in the indirect category, will be hard to identify; and there is no guarantee of internal consistency within each group (Murphy and Murphy, 2004). Identifying both direct and indirect stakeholder interests at an early stage will assist a resort in developing a vision that works for the business and local community. A resort business does not have to fear being swamped by stakeholder involvement because experience has shown it is the opinion leaders of each group (officially – or self-appointed) who will step forward to discuss and negotiate with the business. This makes the process more manageable and permits the use of established planning and consultation techniques to set negotiations on a solid footing.

Murphy and Murphy (2004) in their chapter on 'Working Together' emphasize that conflicting strategies are not uncommon in a business setting and nor should they necessarily be avoided, because conflicting ideas have some positive components. What is needed are ways to harness the positive features of conflict, such as:

1. creating better ideas;
2. identifying and resolving long-standing issues;
3. clarifying individual views;
4. raising interest and creativity;
5. exploring new approaches and;
6. developing win-win situations.

'Emerging ways to deal with conflict, such as mediation and facilitation, offer great promise for addressing community tourism issues. Tourism proposals that include meaningful (stakeholder) participation from the start, are in a better position to build a climate of trust and cooperation' (Murphy and Murphy, 2004: 369–370).

45

Triple bottom line auditing

Stakeholders certainly need to be considered and consulted in the growing application of *Triple Bottom Line Auditing*, for this audit system brings together both the demand and supply components of business management. 'Today we think in terms of a 'triple bottom line', focussing on economic prosperity, environmental quality, and the element that business has preferred to overlook – social justice' (Elkington, 1999: 70). To pursue a sustainable development strategy Elkington suggests business combine its traditional economic accounting with assessments of its environmental and social impacts. This would be a good starting place for resort management that intends to work with the natural environment and local people to provide value and satisfaction for its customers and other stakeholders, which will lead to a profitable business for all concerned. The key tools for this approach would be sustainability accounting, auditing and reporting.

Sustainability accounting procedures need to extend beyond traditional accounting methods and move into 'full cost pricing', where 'all the costs associated with a product or service should be internalized, and, as a result, reflected in its price' (Elkington, 1999: 93). Where no market pricing currently exists, such as with a dependence on a 'free' public good like a national park or heritage site, 'shadow pricing' should be used to complete the picture of any proposed development or change. Shadow pricing occurs mainly with environmental and social impacts, where indices and other crude measures are being created and entered into the accounting and audit processes. The reporting of such audits needs to extend beyond internal business readership to a wider community of interest, reflecting the transparency that is in demand in many areas of business and government.

For tourism and resorts a move to triple bottom line audits would be a logical step with respect to long-term sustainability and a more successful integration of tourism into the local economies and aspirations of host communities. In a review of the relevance of triple bottom line audits to tourism Dwyer (2005) has noted many potential benefits to this approach. These include:

1. *Efficiencies and cost savings.*
   - Reduced operating costs through the detection of wasteful activities, such as recycling and reusing wastes.
   - Potentially lower compliance costs if organizations are proactive in terms of environmental and social legislation.

- Attracting and retaining competent staff by demonstrating an organization is focussed on values and its long-term existence.
- Improved access to capital from potentially more financial institutions and individuals if the organization can demonstrate its environmental and social credentials.

2. *Improved marketing positioning.*
   - Assists branding focus and message.
   - Creates value through enhanced reputation.
   - More positive customer response and more repeat business.

3. *Better stakeholder relationships.*
   - Encourages the consideration of both direct and indirect stakeholders.
   - Provides a competitive advantage in addressing stakeholder issues.
   - Encourages transparent reporting and good public relations.

4. *Improved strategic decision-making.*
   - Forces organization to be clearer about its goals and objectives.
   - Improves quality of information for decision-makers.
   - Systematizes and institutionalizes best practice and use of benchmarking.
   - Improves management of risk through stakeholder engagement and enhanced performance monitoring.
   - Supports the development of communication tools.
   - Promotes integrated decision-making within businesses and other organizations.

In conclusion Dwyer (2005: 91) says 'TBL is not about compartmentalizing activities/projects into the "three bottom lines", but rather is about integrating core principles that reflect a commitment to a sustainable organisation and society'. It is this goal that will now be examined.

Sustainable development

Sustainable development involves everything that triple bottom line auditing attempts to consider and more, the more being a commitment to creating a stable long-serving system that will meet the needs of future generations as well as this one, in a more equitable manner. The most popular description of the concept is that provided in the seminal Bruntland Commission Report entitled *Our Common Future*, which defines it as 'development that meets the needs of the present without compromising the ability of future generations to meet their own needs' (World Commission on Environment and Development, 1987: 43). A graphic presentation of the goals for sustainable development in tourism and their link with

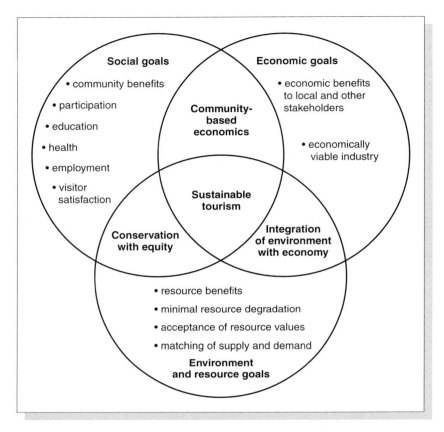

Figure 2.2 A model of sustainable tourism values and principles.
(Source: Hall, Jenkins, and Kearsley, 1997 cited in Murphy and Price, 2005: 175)

triple bottom line objectives is shown in Figure 2.2. This shows how the economic, environmental and social goals of triple bottom line auditing can be drawn together by developing economic objectives in harmony with the environment and social/community goals; and that the environment and its resources should be developed in an equitable manner so as to benefit the many rather than the few. Murphy and Price (2005) describe the complexity of this concept and describe the challenges in its implementation, especially for the small business operations that dominate the tourism industry. They agree with Pigram's (1990: 3) assessment that:

> Sustainable tourism has the potential to become a tangible expression of sustainable development. Yet it runs the risk of remaining irrelevant and inert as a feasible policy option for the real world of tourism

development, without the development of effective means of translating the idea into action.

Operationalizing the sustainable development concept is not just a tourism problem, as society becomes more aware of the globe's fragile state more pressure is being place on all businesses to function in a more sustainable manner, and one approach to resolving this problem has been offered by Iansiti and Levien (2004).

In discussing the long-term health of businesses Iansiti and Levien (2004: 76) find it useful to make biological analogies 'because the companies, products and technologies of a business network are, like the species in a biological ecosystem, increasingly intertwined in mutually dependent relationships outside of which they have little meaning'. If we take their 'business network' to be the resort, with the 'companies' representing individual businesses or departments within the resort, and their 'products and technologies' contributing to the overall guest experience, then we can see some close parallels between the steps Iansiti and Levien recommend for business in general and what can be achieved in the resort domain.

Iansiti and Levien (2004: 72–73) maintain there are three critical measures for a healthy business and healthy ecosystem. These are:

- *Productivity*: A healthy ecosystem is able to convert non-biological inputs, such as sunlight and mineral nutrients into living outputs (populations of organisms). The business equivalent is a network's ability to transform technology and other raw materials into lower costs and new products. One way to measure this productivity is to note the return on invested capital (ROI), and as noted in Chapter 6 some resorts around the world are not performing too well on this measure.
- *Robustness*: To provide durable benefits an ecosystem must prevail in the face of environmental changes, just as businesses must be capable of surviving disruptions to their system, such as unforeseen technological change. The simplest way to measure robustness is to look at survival rates, and on a global basis resorts have done well in this regard by adjusting to some major socio-economic changes over time.
- *Niche creation*: Healthy ecosystems exhibit variety and the ability to support a diversity of species. Businesses that are diverse are also in a better position to absorb external shocks. The best measure of diversity is the creation of valuable new functions or niches, which may at times involve the dropping of old niches. For resorts this means changing with the times as noted in this chapter's two cases.

The best way to implement the three above objectives is to become a keystone organization that improves the overall health of their local ecosystem by providing a stable and predictable set of common assets that other organizations also can use to build their own offerings. Iansiti and Levien (2004: 74) suggest:

> Broadly speaking, an effective keystone strategy has two parts. The first is to *create value* within the ecosystem. Unless a keystone finds a way of doing this efficiently, it will fail to attract or retain members. The second part, is to *share the value* with other participants in the ecosystem. The keystone that fails to do this will find itself perhaps temporarily enriched but ultimately abandoned.

In terms of a resort complex the keystone organization is likely to be the principal business and core attraction, which must create value for itself and the other secondary attractions and support businesses around it. If it fails to share the resort's overall market the other businesses will fail and/or move away, leaving the core business with a less diverse and attractive product.

Iansiti and Levien consider an ecosystem-based perspective has some important lessons for business, which again have direct parallels to the resort situation. They emphasize the importance of interdependency among businesses and the loss of direct control, which has been mentioned in terms of integrated resort complexes and resort destinations. Related to this is the process of integration, which is now seen as an important form of innovation through combining the technical and social capital of members to create new competitive advantage, as suggested by Porter's Cluster theory (Porter, 1998). 'Finally, a firm that takes an action without understanding the impact on its many neighbouring business domains, or on the ecosystem as a whole, is ignoring the reality of the networked environment in which it operates' (Iansiti and Levien, 2004: 78) and will fail to realize the long-term benefits of sustainable development.

Summary

This chapter has shown how past research and conceptualization has developed a cadre of techniques and theories that can be useful for resort management with the goal of sustainable development. The ones covered in this chapter represent some of the major business viewpoints within the literature, but it is not a complete sample and the reader is encouraged to delve into this interesting literature to find the answers or guidelines to their own specific management questions.

Very few of the cited works have been written specifically for resort destinations, the exception being Butler's TALC theory, which indicates the broad nature of the resort business domain and the need to consider multiple dimensions in adopting a sustainable development approach. Two of the highlighted management concepts are examined in the case studies at the end of the chapter. They reveal both the relevance and helpfulness of the respective technique and theory, but they also demonstrate one cannot expect to apply such concepts with textbook precision in the real world.

The remainder of the book will now disaggregate the generalities of these broad management concepts and apply them to specific issues and responsibilities within the resort domain. This starts with an examination of external challenges in Part B followed by an examination of internal challenges and management strategies in Part C. The book concludes with a look into the future, with reference to risk management in all its forms.

Case studies
Environmental scanning and Butlins Holiday Resorts, UK

An important component of environmental scanning is to look beyond the immediate conditions and issues associated with the daily operation of a business and examine the external forces and opportunities building up within the external societal/global environment. It is these external forces which will often direct future development and their implications must be understood and channelled to the benefit of the business. Butlins Holiday Resorts made excellent use of its founder's appraisal of societal trends in the 1930s. Billy Butlin's observations and influence on those trends placed his young resort business in a favourable position when World War II came to an end in 1945.

Butlins Holiday Resorts were founded in the UK by the late Sir Billy Butlin and are now part of the *Bourne Leisure Group*. The first resort was opened in 1936 at Skegness, Lincolnshire where it could serve the growing industrial cities of the English Midlands, the second in 1938 was opened in Clacton, Essex which could serve the London population. Although the resorts are now described as offering economical holidays (Nationmaster.com, 2005) they were planned as quality resorts for the growing mass market. Butlin described his Skegness prototype as a 'Luxury Holiday Camp' with:

> ... plans to accommodate 1000 people in 600 chalets with electricity and running water, dining and recreation halls, a theatre, a gymnasium, a rhododendron-bordered swimming pool with cascades at either end and a boating lake. In the landscaped grounds there were to be tennis courts, bowling and putting greens and cricket pitches.
>
> (Butlin with Dacre, 2002: 105)

His use of the term 'camp' to describe such a contemporary up-scale vacation business was due to his fond memories of summer camp experiences in Canada, when he was a young man working for the Eaton's department store. He wished to recreate that atmosphere for the working people of Britain.

Three external forces influenced the development and success of Butlin's vision for holiday camps in Britain. He notes 'I have come to believe that what people call 'luck' depends mainly on doing the right thing at the right time and this certainly proved to be the case with my holiday camps' (Butlin with Dacre, 2002: 118). He attributes his success in part to:

■ The development of *motoring* and particularly charabanc (bus) trips to the coast during the 1930s, that drew more people away from local metropolitan industrial conditions to a desire for sea views and bracing breezes; what we now refer to as the sea, surf and sand market. This change in accessibility has been placed here because Butlin acknowledged it as an external factor that gave his new concept of a coastal resort a real boost. It meant that those people crammed in the major and, by today's standards, polluted cities could now take a short break to the seaside and partake in its healthy attributes of fresh air, exercise and fun.
■ The introduction of *legislation* guaranteeing a week's paid vacation for all industrial workers by Parliament in 1938. This meant that with the stroke of a pen Butlin's potential market experienced a manifold increase. 'By 1946, some eight million workers would be able, and seemingly determined, to take a holiday by the seaside. Butlin camps were tailor-made to take advantage of that demand' (Butlin with Dacre, 2002: 118). Indeed, as a positive external factor for Butlin's camp business he did all he could to encourage the legislation, by lobbying Members of Parliament concerning its merits and contribution to national morale and productivity.

But like all opportunities this one had to be seized, and Butlin did just that with his new marketing theme. 'When this long-overdue reform took place I came out with the slogan "Holidays with pay: Holidays with play: A week's holiday for a week's wage"'(Butlin with Dacre, 2002: 119).

■ Butlin would not have been able to take full advantage of the above 'strokes of fortune' had it not been for another external factor – *war*, and his ability to be *optimistic about the future and to plan accordingly.*
In 1939 Britain went to war, and became one of the major combatants in World War II. War and tourism do not mix, but thankfully wars do end and those who look to the future can still benefit from such terrible external forces.
As Britain mobilized it needed to find and prepare camps for its rapidly expanding military forces. Butlin's two ready-made camps were requisitioned, namely his Skegness and Clacton resorts, and another that was under construction in Filey was converted to army specifications. Butlin's experience and workforce could provide military camps at a lower cost per head than the government so he was soon asked to build other military camps around the countryside. He agreed to assist the war effort, but

'I made one important stipulation though: I should be given the opportunity of buying the camp back at the end of the war for three-fifths (60%) of the cost. This was agreed. On the surface it seemed a good deal for Butlin's, but it was, in fact, quite a gamble: for I had no idea what condition the camp would be in at war's end'.

(Butlin with Dacre, 2002: 130)

What this quote does not state is that at the time of the agreement there was no guarantee that Britain and its allies would win the war. It also understates the fact that it was also a win-win situation for the government to have a potential buyer for a used military camp, one that did not need to be demolished and returned to its original use. The gamble was principally for Butlin, but with victory came the addition of several low-priced holiday camps for the exploding post-war demand for a seaside vacation in Britain.

These three external factors were used by Billy Butlin to advance his business. He not only observed the trends but actively supported two of them by lobbying and negotiating with the government of the time. But even more important was his conviction that a better future would emerge from the dark days of the war, when working people could enjoy the benefits of a week's holiday on the coast.

Tourism area life cycle and the Gold Coast, Australia

In order to plan for the future of an existing resort and resort destination it is imperative to know the resort's location on Butler's TALC theory. The relative location on that cycle helps to guide the resort's future strategic planning. If the resort is in the early stages of development it should be examining various growth options, if it is at the stagnation stage it should be looking for ways to kick start new products and attempting to rejuvenate its appeal. But how does a destination determine its place on the TALC curve? This is a question that the late Professor Bill Faulkner and his *Sustainable Tourism* Cooperative Research Centre team attempted to answer on behalf of the Gold Coast resort destination in Queensland, Australia.

The Gold Coast Australia, located to the south of Brisbane, offers a 40 kilometre stretch of holiday resorts and surfing beaches, along with several small and distinctive community centres to form the largest resort destination in Australia (Figure 2.3). Its modern origins can be traced back to 1933, when the community of Surfers Paradise was so named and the tourism emphasis of this coastal area began. Over the years various entrepreneurs and investors built up a range of leisure activities including theme parks and special events to supplement the natural attractions of the region, which include hinterland rain forests and national parks in addition to its better known surf beaches. By 2000 the Gold Coast City Council was responsible for the seventh largest city in Australia and one of the fastest growing populations in the country.

At the beginning of the new millennium some local people were beginning to question where Gold Coast tourism was leading and how it could be integrated with the growing residential population of young families and retirees. When Faulkner started to apply Butler's indicator of evolutionary change – visitor numbers to the Gold Coast at the beginning of the millennium, he noted that growth rates were slowing down, particularly for the international market; as noted in the later compendium of his works (Faulkner, 2003). Like others, Faulkner did not consider visitor numbers alone could provide a sufficiently detailed explanation of destination evolution and market change to help future planning. Firstly, there is always an element of estimation with such numbers, especially domestic visitors; and secondly their usage implies all visitors are the same, with the same interests and behaviour patterns – and nothing could be further from the truth. Therefore, Faulkner selected a range of performance indicators to supplement the evidence of the raw visitor numbers.

Figure 2.3 Gold Coast resort destination, Queensland, Australia.

Table 2.1 presents six categories of performance indicators, covering business, infrastructure, social, environmental and bureaucracy concerns. These categories and the individual variables within them were either drawn from the literature (Cooper, 1990; Haywood, 1986) or from the CRC research team investigating the Gold Coast. As often happens in actual research, some of the identified variables could not be used because no data has been collected locally on those characteristics. However, in terms of the first four categories Faulkner and his team were able to uncover actual or surrogate measures that could give some indication of the Gold Coast's relative position in respect to certain variables.

In terms of the changing type of visitor the Gold Coast is experiencing, Faulkner (2003: 42) presents evidence from Australia's International Visitors' Survey which shows there has been 'an increased emphasis on "organized mass tourism" within the international market, with all-inclusive tours increasing from 48 to 75 per cent over the last decade'. This he links with the feeling that the Gold Coast 'has become well known, but no longer fashionable', and that hotel occupancy rates have been maintained through 'aggressive price cutting in room rates, which has produced a persistent profit-less volume problem'.

While Faulkner (2003: 42–43) was unable to present firm statistics on the physical state of the Gold Coast's tourism infrastructure, by using customer and local perceptions he felt such personal opinions 'indicated there are pockets of decay that present a real prospect of an "infrastructure time-bomb"'. Furthermore, he warns that 'the destination's heavy reliance on built attractions (theme parks) and the increasing emphasis on the convention sector ... could be cited as symptoms of stagnation according to the literature'. These assessments were verified to a large extent by a parallel infrastructure audit, that found the extensive developments created in the 1970s and 1980s were starting to age and that traffic congestion was building up on local roads (Warnken, 2002).

In terms of the social and environmental impacts, along with the government and bureaucratic responses to the evolving tourist and resident demands on the Gold Coast Faulkner is unable to offer any hard evidence. This is because while social and environmental carrying capacities are simple and relevant constructs they are extremely challenging and argumentative in terms of measurement, as outlined in a later chapter. So it has become a slow process to come up with effective measures that can be applied easily. Likewise, relevant administration questions and measures are in their infancy with respect to the institutional environment. Some attempt has been made to overcome these deficiencies in the Gold Coast planning through the measurement of its social impacts

Table 2.1   Indicators of stagnation and their potential relevance to the Gold Coast

Area of destination performance/indicators

1. Changing markets
   - Growth in low-status, low-spend visitor and day visitors.
   - Over-dependence on long-holiday market, and lack of penetration of short-stay market.
   - **Emphasis on high-volume, low-yield-inclusive tour market.**
   - **A decline in visitors' length of stay.**
   - **Type of tourists increasingly organized mass tourists.**
   - A declining proportion of first time visitors, as opposed to repeat visitors.
   - Limited or declining appeal to overseas visitors.
   - High seasonality.
2. Emerging newer destinations
   - **Competition from emerging newer destinations.**
   - **The destination is well known, but no longer fashionable.**
3. Infrastructure
   - Outdated, poorly maintained accommodation and amenities.
   - Older properties are changing hands and newer properties, if they are being built are on the periphery of the original tourist areas.
   - **Market perceptions of the destination becoming over-commercialized, crowded and 'tacky'.**
   - **Tourism industry over-capacity.**
   - **Diversification into conventions and conferences to maintain numbers.**
   - **Large number of man-made attractions, which start to outnumber the more natural attractions that made the place popular in the first place.**
4. Business performance
   - **Declining profits of major tourism businesses.**
   - Lack of confidence in the tourism business community.
   - A decline in the elasticity of advertising (lower return in terms of increased visitors per advertising dollar investment) and an increase in process elasticity.
   - Lack of professional, experienced staff.
5. Social and environmental carrying capacities
   - Visitor levels approaching or exceeding social and environmental carrying capacities.
   - Local opposition to tourism as the resort's residential role increases.
6. Institutional environment
   - Local government reorganization (amalgamation) diluting the political power of resorts in larger authorities.
   - Demands for increased operational efficiency and entrepreneurial activity in local government.
   - Short-term planning horizons in local government owing to financial restrictions and a low priority given to strategic thinking.
   - Shortage of research data.

Note: Indicators in bold apply to the Gold Coast on the basis of existing data.
Source: Faulkner (2003: 41–42).

(Fredline, 2002). Fredline found that the majority of residents were positive in their feelings toward local tourism, but had some definite concerns with traffic congestion, crime and illegal drug use.

Despite these hardships in developing a robust measure of the Gold Coast's position on the evolutionary destination development curve, Faulkner and his associates considered they had developed a sufficiently clear picture to place the Gold Coast in its appropriate stage at the beginning of this millennium. Using a combination of raw visitor numbers, statistics from various sources relating to identifiable stage characteristics, interviews with local industry and government personnel Faulkner (2003: 43) concluded:

> the Gold Coast is a mature destination showing some early signs of stagnation, paralleling the experience of coastal tourist resorts elsewhere in the world.

With this assessment in hand Faulkner and his team turned toward the management implications, and argued there was a need to move from a destination marketing orientation to a more comprehensive destination management approach. Their first task in this regard was to assist the destination in developing a vision for its future, via a vision project as outlined in the remainder of Faulkner's work (Faulkner, 2003) and that of Fredline (2002) and Warnken (2002)

Questions

1 What is the purpose of theory and how can it help in the management of resorts?

2 How can resort management apply the Family Life Cycle theory in today's market with respect to new life cycle cohorts like 'single adult households' or 'same sex couples'?

3 Why is environmental scanning particularly well suited to tourism management in general and resorts in particular?

4 One of the principal problems for management wishing to operate on a sustainable development basis is to find a simple technique that can assist their strategic planning in this direction. Does Elkington's 'Triple Bottom Line Audit' offer an adequate answer to this problem?

5 Porter's theory of 'Competitive Advantage' lists three primary factors. Is it possible for a resort to lead in all three and if not where would you place your emphasis?

6 Butler's theory of 'Destination Evolution' has been criticized for being more of a category descriptor than a theory. Explain the difference and comment on whether this is an important distinction for a resort manager.

7 The PLC predicts a rather dismal ending for most products. How can resorts resist this fate and become more sustainable?

References

Berry, L.L. (1995). *Great Service: A Framework for Action*. New York: Free Press.

Butler, R.W. (1980). The concept of a tourist area cycle of evolution: implications for management of resources. *The Canadian Geographer*, **24(1)**, 5–12.

Butler, R.W. (ed.) (2006). *The Tourism Area Life Cycle*, Vols. 1 and 2. Clevedon: Channel View Publications.

Butlin, Sir B. with Dacre, P. (2002). *The Billy Butlin Story 'A Showman to the End'*. London: Robson Books.

Carter, B. and McGoldrick, M. (2005). *The Expanded Family Life Cycle: Individual and Social Perspectives*, 3rd edn. New York: Pearson.

Consenza, R.M. and Davis, D.L. (1981). Family vacation decision making over the family life cycle: a decision and influence structure analysis. *Journal of Travel Research*, **20(2)**, 17–23.

Cooper, C. (1990). Resorts in decline – the management response. *Tourism Management*, **11(1)**, 63–67.

Daft, R.L., Fitzgerald, P.A., and Rock, M.E. (1992). *Management*, First Canadian Edition. Toronto: Dryden Canada.

Dwyer, L. (2005). Relevance of triple bottom line reporting to achievement of sustainable tourism: a scoping study. *Tourism Review International*, **9(1)**, 79–93.

Elkington, J. (1999). *Cannibals with Forks: The Triple Bottom Line of 21st Century Business*. Oxford: Capstone Publications.

Faulkner, B. (2003). Rejuvenating a maturing tourist destination: the case of the Gold Coast. In *Progressing Tourism Research – Bill Faulkner* (L. Fredline, L. Jago and C. Cooper, eds), pp. 34–86. Clevedon: Channel View Publications.

Fredline, L. (2002). *Social Impacts of Tourism on the Gold Coast*. Gold Coast Tourism Visioning Project 3.3. Brisbane: CRC for Sustainable Tourism.

Gordon, J.R., Mondy, R.W., Sharplin, A., and Premeaux, S.R. (1990). *Management and Organizational Behavior*. Boston: Allyn and Bacon.

Haywood, K.M. (1986). Can the tourism area cycle of evolution be made operational? *Tourism Management*, **7(3)**, 154–167.

Hudson, S. (2006). Ski resorts: enjoyment versus environmental responsibility – does there have to be a choice? In *Cases in Sustainable Tourism* (I.M. Herremans, ed.), pp. 123–142. New York: Haworth Press.

Iansiti, M. and Levien, R. (2004). Strategy as ecology. *Harvard Business Review*, **82(March)**, 69–78.

Kimes, S.E. (2003). Revenue management: a retrospective. *Cornell Hotel and Restaurant Administration Quarterly*, **44(4)**, 131–138.

Lieberman, W.H. (1993). Debunking the myths of yield management. *Cornell Hotel and Restaurant Administration Quarterly*, **34(1)**, 34–41.

Matzler, K., Hattenberger, G., Pechlaner, H., and Abfalter, D. (2004). Lifestyle segmentation, vacation types and guest satisfaction. In *Creating Tourism Knowledge* (C. Cooper, C. Arcodia, D. Solnet and M. Whitford, eds), pp. 127–137. Referred Proceedings of the Council for Australian University Tourism and Hospitality Education's Brisbane Conference.

Michael, E.J. (2007). *Micro-clusters and Networks*. Oxford: Elsevier.

Murphy, P.E. and Murphy, A.E. (2004). *Strategic Management for Tourism Communities: Bridging the Gaps*. Clevedon: Channel View Publications.

Murphy, P.E. and Price, G.G. (2005). Tourism and sustainable development. In *Global Tourism* (W.F. Theobald, ed.), 3rd edn, pp. 167–193. Amsterdam: Elsevier Butterworth Heinemann.

Nationmaster.com (2005). Encyclopedia: Butlins. http://www.nationmaster.com/encyclopedia/Butlins. Accessed on 14 August 2005.

Normann, R. (1991). *Service Management*. Chichester: John Wiley and Sons.

Parasuraman, A., Zeithaml, V., and Berry, L.L. (1985). A conceptual model of service quality and implications for future research. *Journal of Marketing*, **49(Fall)**, 41–50.

Pigram, J.J. (1990). Sustainable tourism policy considerations. *Journal of Tourism Studies*, **1(2)**, 3–9.

Porter, M.E. (1985). *Competitive Advantage: Creating and Sustaining Superior Performance*. New York: Free Press.

Porter, M.E. (1998). *On Competition*. Cambridge, MA: Harvard University Press.

Ritchie, J.R.B. and Crouch, G.I. (2003). *The Competitive Destination: A Sustainable Tourism Perspective*. Wallingford, Oxon: CABI Publishing.

Stahl, M.J. and Grigsby, D.W. (1992). *Strategic Management for Decision Making*. Boston: PWS-Kent.

Stoner, J.A.F., Freeman, R.E., and Gilbert Jr., D.R. (1995). *Management*, 6th edn. Englewood Cliffs, NJ: Prentice-Hall.

Thomke, S. and von Hippel, E. (2002). Customers as innovators: a new way to create value. *Harvard Business Review*, **80(April)**, 74–81.

Vesper, K.H. (1996). *New Venture Experience*. Seattle: Vector Books.

Warnken, J. (2002). *Tourist Facilities and Infrastructure Audit.* Gold Coast Tourism Visioning Project 2.2. Brisbane: CRC for Sustainable Tourism.

World Commission on Environment and Development (1987). *Our Common Future.* Oxford: Oxford University Press.

Zeithaml, V. (1988). Consumer perceptions of price, quality and value: a means-end model and synthesis of evidence. *Journal of Marketing,* **52(3),** 2–22.

Part
B

External challenges for resort management

3

Changing market and competitive conditions

Introduction

We have seen in Part A how resorts have existed for a long time by responding to new consumer demands and adjusting their product through the use of new technology and marketing techniques to serve those new demands. Resort vacations are no longer the privilege of the wealthy elite, they have become an option for many in the general development of mass tourism. Over time this mass tourism has splintered into a wide range of special interests, leading to a variety of resort types and emphases. However, consumers now have many different ways to spend their discretionary time and income. When individuals do consider vacation options within their discretionary time and income parameters they now also face the widest range of choices ever, and among these choices are resorts competing with all sorts of vacation and recreation experiences.

In order for resorts to sustain their market share of the growing vacation pie they need to examine their global and task environments, to determine what consumer trends and other changes they can take advantage of and how to integrate them into their current resort business and destination package. Helber (1995: 105), a resort development consultant based in Hawaii, notes established resorts should give more attention to establishing 'new products which cater to emerging growth markets' than to internal matters such as infrastructure improvements, environmental cleanups and cosmetic upgrades. So it makes sense for resorts to focus first on changing demand profiles, then on how they can relay the message to relevant interest groups that they are now catering to these new demands.

This chapter demonstrates the need for resorts to respond to ever-changing market conditions, by emphasizing the importance of monitoring global demand trends, and matching supply circumstances with those trends that a resort can and wishes to meet. All this occurs in an ever-changing competitive market for the discretionary time and wealth of a global population. There has been tremendous growth in the discretionary income of developed economies over the past 60 years but even this is being overshadowed by the more rapid changes in China and elsewhere in Asia over the past 10–20 years, where a middle class of many millions has emerged as a major global market force. To ensure that resorts maintain or increase their share of this growing global discretionary spending, they will have to compete with both other tourism and non-tourism products.

Global demand trends

The rise in incomes and living standards throughout much of the world has resulted in more discretionary time and income, which as Maslow (1970) predicted are the conditions needed to pursue the goal of self-determination. This has translated into an era of special interest demands that in turn have created a global market for specialized niche resort products. This process has been gaining momentum as tourists not only become wealthier and more experienced, but also have become more demanding and daring. A current example is the new millionaires who have paid a fortune to be shot into space, soon to be followed by a larger number of wealthy middle class tourists who will take advantage of Richard Branson's plans to develop *Virgin Galactic* into a regular short sub-orbital flight operation. Whatever the motivation is for the new vacation and recreation interests, the resort industry will need to monitor emerging consumer trends and determine whether they can be accommodated within the present resort structure or within yet another modification of the old system.

Some of the recent major consumer trends that are being adopted by resorts around the world are presented below.

New skills

An increasing number of resorts have sought to accommodate the rising interest in acquiring new skills or enhancing existing ones by linking a vacation with such options. This is most common in terms of sport-based resorts, where guests come to learn from the experts – the 'pro's', on how to develop their skills. In addition to the classes and individual clinics there is ample opportunity to practice in the resort facilities, which may include international level facilities that have been exposed extensively through the media. Some resorts help children and families develop new activity skills in a less formal setting, as part of a family holiday.

Adventure and danger

In this increasingly regimented and cosseted world some guests are keen to break out of the mold on occasion and wish to challenge themselves with new and unusual experiences, possibly creating an adrenalin rush in the process. These adventurous guests are drawn to resorts offering the type of hard adventure tourism they seek, either directly or through links with local adventure tourism companies.

Rest and relaxation

In this increasingly busy and complex world many people seek rest and relaxation when they go on holiday, and resorts have always emphasized this as one of their prime service functions. What has changed is the increasing number of ways one can be pampered. The pampering starts with the high level of staff attention and extends to their skills regarding services like special cocktails, cordon-blue meals and massages. The facilities should offer the latest entertainment, gymnasium and spa experiences, the latest styles in room and bathroom fittings, and an attractive setting for a relaxed stay.

Excitement and entertainment

Excitement and the search for something unusual can be found in many activities, apart from that provided by adventure tourism opportunities.

Guests seeking some excitement and entertainment are being drawn to casino resorts, where gambling provides a major activity and for some an adrenalin rush, but in many resorts gambling is now being supplemented with fine dining and top class entertainment. Las Vegas epitomizes this type of market and is now being imitated around the world, but it has been noted that 'some (Las Vegas) casinos now get less than half of their revenues directly from betting' (The Economist, 2004a: 69). The same article notes that other changes could be in store for this type of resort as gambling goes global and onto the Internet, which would undoubtedly force some form of defensive response from the big resort destination like Las Vegas, Macau and Sun City. This process may be underway already, with the recent US Congress bill to 'stop banks and credit-card companies from processing payments to (mainly international) on-line gambling companies' (The Economist, 2006: 77). Yet another sign of how resorts need to continually adjust to changing global circumstances.

Health and wellness

As the populations of western societies age they are becoming more aware of their health. Most existing government health programmes involve reactive therapy, providing consultation, diagnosis, treatment and surgery if it is needed; they are generally not proactive or preventative in scope. As a result, it has fallen to the private sector to assist with elective surgical procedures like cosmetic surgery, and to provide many of the general health and wellness programmes that more people are seeking. An important player in this regard is the resort. Health tourism has become an important feature of international tourism to Southeast Asia, where Thailand, Singapore and now Malaysia are building a reputation for inexpensive yet quality surgery. Many international health tourists to these countries spend some of their time in associated resorts as they recuperate under medical supervision and enjoy the weather and culture of these locations. The town of Spa, Belgium, that was discussed as a case in Chapter 1, opened a new thermal centre in April 2004 and within its first year had exceeded its visitor target (Mawet, 2005). Even in single facility locations like a resort hotel spas have become a requirement not an extra. In the words of one hotel and spa owner, today's five star resort hotel needs a spa like it needed to offer a swimming pool in the old days. This does not mean all guests will take advantage of the spa, but if it is not available at the resort fewer will consider it a viable option.

Cash rich and time poor

As the global economy developed and discretionary incomes rose some experts were predicting the rise of a 'leisure society', where working hours decreased and more time was devoted to leisure. However, for many of us it did not work out that way. Instead, many people found themselves working extra and frequently unpaid hours to keep up with the growing demands of their jobs, and in families both adults were needed to work in order to maintain the lifestyles they were expecting or had been promised by the 'consumer society' marketing. As a result many people in developed economies feel they now live in a 'cash rich and time poor' society, where they have accumulated the financial resources to buy consumer goods but have little opportunity to enjoy them because of the increased time commitment needed to obtain them.

The resort sector has recognized these time pressures on the travelling public and attempted to accommodate them in their offerings. They have emphasized the opportunity they present for families to get together in fun environments, to reconnect with each other while they enjoy the leisure and learning experiences of the resort. They have emphasized their suitability for short-break getaways, whether they be weekend vacations or mid-week business meetings and retreats. This has been an emphasis of many resorts that have easy access to major population centres, as evidenced by the family focus of Centre Parcs in the UK.

Environmental awareness

As the world population becomes more urbanized and evidence of environmental degradation and its impact on global warming increases, more people have become conscious of and concerned about our natural environment. Many resorts are either located in major beauty spots or are associated with world heritage sites or national parks, so they have an opportunity to facilitate and profit from this increased environmental awareness. They also have a responsibility to relay the conservation message and to educate the public concerning their individual responsibilities. It will not be an easy task to balance recreation and leisure with education, but if the environment is to be sustained resorts will need to play their part. They will certainly need to enhance their education and interpretation efforts in this direction, as the public has become more knowledgeable through the increased media coverage of environmental and heritage topics.

Personal investment

Many more people are active in the stock market today as one way to prepare for their future retirement, either directly or through pension and insurance companies, and many leisure and real estate stocks include resorts within their portfolio. Some people have used resorts as a direct form of individual investment, by purchasing their real estate offerings. More people are buying second/retirement homes within resorts that are seen as a financial investment as well as preparation for their golden years. These units can often be leased back to the resort's accommodation management organization, thereby adding to the local rental pool and providing a revenue source to the unit owner.

Mobile resorts

Many people have become restless these days because the global media has made them more aware of the wonderful sights and experiences this world has to offer. As a result old habits of returning to the same favourite holiday destination have given way to a need to explore new locations and opportunities. In terms of resort style vacations the search for something new can be handled through independent travel, membership in an international timeshare association or having a mobile resort take you from one exotic destination to another. The cruise ship, which is little more than a floating resort complex, takes passengers from one attractive location to another, often while they sleep. In this type of resort the guest can combine the secure environmental bubble of the cruise ship, along with an exploratory interest in foreign lands and cultures. Even when guests step ashore they can take advantage of the cruise ship's vetted tours and multi-lingual tour guides and so maintain their sense of security with their sense of adventure.

Benefit segmentation

One of the best ways to identify these special interests and the way in which guests will bundle them together, either as an individual or as a party, is to use benefit segmentation. Benefit segmentation is the process by which customers are grouped into specific clusters based on the personal benefits they are seeking in a product. In terms of cars such benefit clusters as luxury, speed or fuel efficiency have been identified and used to draw customers to the appropriate model for their needs. Morrison (1989: 154) considers benefit segmentation is powerful because 'people buy a "package" of benefits when they buy a service', and this is certainly the case with resorts. However, unlike the relatively simple situation with cars, resorts can and do offer a wide range of benefits and activities some of which will change with the seasons. What is needed is a determination of the principal benefits sought by a resort's actual and potential guests and ensuring the resort meets and satisfies those major interests.

Kotler (2001: 148) considers that value adding companies have figured out ways to create benefit bundles to win buyers' preferences. He feels 'they can offer one or more of the following benefits to win the customer's business:

- Customisation
- More convenience
- Faster service
- More and far better service
- Coaching, training, or consulting
- An extraordinary guarantee
- Useful hardware and software tools
- A membership benefits program'.

Although he goes on to illustrate these benefits with mainly manufactured products they all apply to resorts.

Taking just the first and last identified benefit segmentations as illustrations for the resort industry one can make the following observations. Since resorts are well advised to target those specific market segments they can satisfy, they should customize their products and service to match the benefits their target market is expecting. Is the guest looking for an active or passive experience? Perhaps it is both over the length of the stay, so both must be provided and to avoid conflict they should be separated by zoning or screening within the resort. In terms of membership benefit programmes more resorts are offering loyalty rewards, especially the chains. These types of programmes encourage repeat visits to a single resort or visits to other resorts within the chain. Such programmes are 'an effective way to win, keep and grow customers by rewarding them for being customers' (Kotler, 2001: 157).

While benefit segmentation is an important tool in analyzing resort demand it should be viewed as one of several segmentation processes. In an article on resort vacationer profiles Morrison et al. (1996) found they could develop distinctive group profiles for different types of resort experiences. Utilizing socio-demographic profiles, trip planning characteristics,

71

activity profiles and benefits experienced they could distinguish between visitors to oceanside beach resorts, ski resorts, summer country resorts and casino resorts. In terms of the benefits sought 'the beach resort vacationers were relatively active', the ski resort vacationers were looking for 'physically demanding' experiences, the summer country resort vacationers participated in the greatest range of activities and the casino vacationers looked for 'excitement' plus relaxation, fun and enjoyment.

Supply considerations

To adjust to the changing market conditions over time the resort sector of the tourism industry continues to monitor the preferences of its potential guests and how best to accommodate them. As indicated above, the benefit segmentation emphasizes focussing on the changing benefit demands of customers and guests in order to maximize their satisfaction and encourage either their return or a strong recommendation to others. While demands have changed so has technology and management experience, which permits resorts to respond to these observed demand changes more effectively.

Market segmentation

The most important lesson has been to target resorts to particular market segments – those who the resort can reach and satisfy. Successful market segmentation requires that the selected targets are:

1. *Identifiable*: The group possesses tourist characteristics that are sufficient to justify it with a separate classification and marketing thrust.
2. *Measurable*: It is possible to measure how many potential tourists are in the segment group.
3. *Substantial*: The segment is large enough to justify independent attention and marketing.
4. *Accessible*: The segment can be reached through existing promotion and standard distribution systems.
5. *Exploitable*: The distinguishing features of the segment can be exploited in such a way as to be profitable.
6. *Durable*: The distinguishing features will remain with the segment even as people age and interests evolve or with newly arriving demographic cohorts, so it is not simply a temporary phenomenon.
7. *Competitive*: The resort should have a competitive advantage to serve this market segment.

If resorts can identify a viable and reachable market segment they should start adjusting their product and service to better cater to this desired group.

Changing transport technology

Assisting resorts in this regard have been improvements in transport technology and access. Good airline connections are vital to those international and national resorts that rely on large market areas. The development of larger and more efficient hub-to-hub commercial airlines has helped to keep down the price of air travel and this is expected to continue with the arrival of the Airbus A380. Likewise, some resorts not close to a major international gateway or domestic hub airport have been able to take advantage at times of the developing point-to-point airline offerings. These have been led in the main by budget airlines, like Southwest in the United States, Ryan Air and Easy Jet in Europe, Virgin Blue in Australia and Air Asia in Malaysia. By linking secondary airports these airlines have brought travellers directly to coastal, country or mountain areas that had to rely previously on transfer flights from major hub airports or lengthy drives from the nearest international hub. In the process this has led to cheaper and quicker travel so that the tourist's range of options has extended dramatically, even for short getaway trips.

Internet marketing

An important aid in reaching targeted segments has been the development of the Internet. The Internet has allowed resorts to get their sales message out to the customer directly and with the integration of web-cams can provide instantaneous views of its offerings. These attractive images and sales promotions are being converted increasingly into direct sales, sales that do not require payment of a commission. Furthermore, direct control over this form of communication and marketing allows for more flexibility in pricing and revenue management.

Evolving product technology

Technology advances have permitted resorts to offer more and better activities in a variety of settings. Major beneficiaries of technological advances have been the ski resorts, which have benefited from snowmaking technology and the development of high-speed multiple seat lifts. Those resorts dependent on the attractions of the sea have benefited from technological advances in scuba diving and in the case of Australia's

Great Barrier Reef the development of high-speed pleasure craft to take visitors out to the reef. Likewise, spa and health resorts have benefited from advances in medicine and health diagnosis, along with modern machines to supplement traditional equipment.

Management skills

To make such technical advances work successfully for the guest and the resort has required a concomitant advance in management skills. Management and technical education has helped management to get the most out of their technological investments and to integrate them successfully with their other traditional facilities. Marketing and revenue management concepts have helped to integrate the Internet opportunities into the existing marketing and sales management. Environmental planning has shown how careful use of the environment can occur in tandem with conservation measures to provide sustainable development. Building technology has been modified to minimize the environmental impacts of new developments, so as to integrate modern customer expectations with the environmental constraints of a resort setting. It is these and other management techniques that will be discussed in more detail in Part C of this book.

For resorts to be successful in the ever-changing leisure market they need to focus all their technical advances and management skills on meeting the expectations of their selected target market(s). To do this they should not only offer the value of quality products and service, they need to differentiate themselves from the rest of the travel industry by offering something 'special' and to compete effectively with the growing number of alternative outlets for consumers' discretionary time and income.

Competition

The competition for consumers' discretionary dollar is another area that has changed and grown over the years, so it is recommended that resorts place their offerings to compete with other tourism and non-tourism competition. To examine the challenges and opportunities this presents it is helpful to employ the environmental scanning and competitive advantage theories of the previous chapter. Examination of the societal–global environment reveals consumers have a wider range of leisure options than ever before, some of which will favour resorts while others will not. One way of tackling these challenges is to work on the basis of what competitive advantage resorts may have over competing options for people's discretionary spending.

In terms of tourism competitors the wider societal and global environment reveals some general trends that can benefit resort development, including a generally prosperous world that has permitted steady increases in travel, associated with an aging population that is now looking for creature comforts in association with their special travel interests, and a growing interest in security. A rising middle class in Asia appears to be repeating the disposable income expenditure patterns of Europe and North America after World War II, namely a growing interest in local – followed by regional – and then international travel. The number of potential resort customers in this case will be enormous, but their interests and priorities for resort travel should not automatically be equated to previous western traits because of different cultural and political circumstances. Chow and Murphy's (2007) preliminary study of Chinese tourists' international travel preferences has revealed China should not be viewed as a single homogenous market. They note that significant differences can occur in travel preferences depending on tourists' place of origin, and international travel experience.

As we have seen the world's population is aging, and those who have discretionary income are increasingly spending it on travel and resort destinations. This comes about because of resorts' appeal as a real estate investment and a growing source of health and retirement living. Plus resorts can offer a sense of security, thanks either to the physical barriers of a gated or security ringed community, or to the fact that a community of like-minded individuals adds a sense of security.

Although the general trends appear positive for resorts there are some issues within those trends that are going to have a mixed impact on resorts and will require careful strategic management in order to minimize the negative impacts and to maximize the potential benefits. On the negative side the rising price of oil in recent times has sent waves of anxiety throughout the tourism industry and resort sector. The global price of oil reached a record of $75.00 per barrel during 2006 and its impact on resort growth will be significant since customers need to travel to resorts and once there they do not expect to economize on the use of electricity or the local forms of transport that are often powered by oil. Strategically, resorts need to determine the relevance of oil prices to their business and their short-term and long-term response to this changing global situation.

In terms of oil's relevance resorts should not panic. As Alan Greenspan, then US Federal Reserve Chairman, noted when the recent oil price rise first started, 'Oil averaged $35.24 a barrel in 1981 after the second oil shock, the equivalent of more than $70 a barrel today' (Maiden, 2004: 8). Thus in real terms the price of oil has not changed much over the past 15 years, and its real costs must be considered in relation to other costs. If it is felt advisable to reduce oil costs due to the recent rise in price or anticipated future increases then a resort could adopt the following short-term responses. It could switch to alternative lower-price fuels, it could arrange more common carrier options to replace private car visits and it could encourage guests to be more conservation oriented by doing more than placing small environmental advice cards in their rooms. In the long term it could link up with transport forms that are more efficient in delivering guests, such as the budget airlines offering point-to-point service using the latest fuel-efficient airplanes, and by reconfiguring its layout and product to minimize future fuel needs.

Two other global trends that can have a bearing on future resort development are special events and the rise of the home as an entertainment centre. The increasing use of special events to raise the profile of resorts, especially outside of the high season, means resort managers need to find the best ways to leverage business from them. The events themselves will create spikes of demand, leaving management with a decision over how to handle such opportunities.

One example of managing the opportunities developed through special events occurred in Victoria, BC, a resort destination in Western Canada, in 1986. The manager of a major hotel in Victoria had to judge the impact of an international exposition, to be held in nearby Vancouver, on his 1986 summer business. He faced two possible outcomes. On the positive side was the declared promise of extra FIT business as this international expo drew more people to the province and the more distant visitors (especially from the US) were expected to use the expo as a reason to see more of the province. On the negative side was the possibility that visitors to the province would use the expo as their sole reason to visit BC and therefore the more distant travellers would use it simply as their turnaround point.

The decision that needed to be made was whether to believe in the promoted positive outcome for satellite destinations and allocate more beds to the higher paying FIT market in the summer of 1986, or to be pessimistic and allocate more beds to the tour market, which would guarantee room sales but produce less revenue per room. The manager's decision was to increase the number of spaces allocated to tour groups for that summer, and he had to commit to this decision 18 months ahead of the event in order to be placed on the tour itineraries.

He was right! While the 1986 Expo was a phenomenal success for Vancouver, which experienced wonderful summer weather that year and had 'no vacancy' signs up everywhere; from the perspective of the province's regional areas it was a 'black hole', sucking dry the anticipated interregional and international FIT market, who often returned home immediately rather than seeing the rest of the province. So by spreading his risk to the guaranteed but poorer returns of the tour market, this manager was able to maximize his hotel's return from Vancouver's 1986 Expo.

Resorts not only face competition from other resorts and tourism businesses, they increasingly find themselves in competition with non-tourism outlets for consumers' discretionary time and spending. One of the biggest challenges in this regard is to compete with the family home. To become a traveller of any sort an individual must first leave home and in certain societies and circumstances this is becoming more difficult, as the building and electronics industries create homes that are becoming 'mini-resorts' in themselves. Whether it be home renovation, an exercise room, gardens, a recreational facility like a swimming pool or tennis court, or an entertainment room we are creating more reasons to stay at home rather than spend money on travel away from home. McDonald (2006) notes that in Australia, a nation famous for its outdoor recreation and athletes, people spend approximately 4 hours per day on home leisure activities, which represents half their total leisure time.

In Australia, as elsewhere, homes are now viewed as entertainment and recreation centres, not just as a shelter. The construction of 'Mc Mansions' that contain large entertainment centres to mimic the effects of the cinema and rooms or galleries offering multiple personal computer hookups for the whole family has reduced the need to go out and meet people, shop, or go to the cinema and theatre. The amount of money spent on gardening is increasing, even though the average lot size may be decreasing. In Australia the amount spent on garden goods and services was estimated to be A$722 million in 1988/1989 which increased to A$1780 million by 1998/1999, a 146.5 per cent increase over 10 years (Veal and Lynch, 2001). In that same financial year of 1998/1999 Australian households spent an additional A$2824 million on swimming pools and landscaping (Veal and Lynch, 2001). In addition to building a new home many people have been encouraged to modernize their existing homes to accommodate these new features of modern living. In 1999, 58 per cent of Australian home owners had renovated their homes over the previous 10 years, of which 27 per cent of the renovations had occurred within the last 2 years (McDonald, 2006).

The reasons for these large expenditures on the home are varied and powerful, but they all leave the consumer with less money to spend on other activities. Some people place a premium on security and wish to 'cocoon' themselves from the real and imagined dangers of living in their part of the world. Others see it as a good investment to renovate and upgrade, or build on a grand scale, because housing prices have been escalating around the world. Still others do it because it is fashionable and they feel it is what their families need or want. The result is a more inward looking society that has less motivation to look outwards to the world and explore its various forms and wonders.

However, resorts have always faced competition for the consumers' discretionary income and in the past have survived through adaptation and innovation, so if they are to compete in today's market they must continue to search for opportunities and synergies. One such synergistic opportunity may be emerging in the area of transportation, which seems to be moving towards extra-terrestrial possibilities.

The race is on for the next tourism innovation and it looks like one will be space travel. Several wealthy individuals have booked rides on national space programme launches. The US company behind 'SpaceShipOne' has won the prize for the first commercial and rapid turnaround space flights. That company has been joined by Sir Richard Branson, who plans to introduce 'Virgin Galactic' to take tourists into space on regular scheduled flights. Branson 'is offering seats on his flights for $210,000 . . . Virgin Galactic expects 3,000 rich people to sign up' (The Economist, 2004b: 62). But having got away from it all at considerable expense, what are these extra-terrestrial travellers to do?

If the past is any guide, the transport companies will provide them with an attraction to visit – a resort in space. The new railway companies that were opening up the 'final frontier of the Old West' in the western states of North America built resorts in association with their rail lines, in order to attract high spending human traffic as well as freight. Examples of this can be seen in the origins of some of the most famous western national parks, like Yellowstone and Banff. An equivalent opportunity is already in position in space and awaiting further development – the underused multi-national space station.

Summary

This chapter has shown that resorts can expect to see constantly changing business conditions. Demand will be heavily influenced by economic and social–political situations, and resort management will need to adjust to such changes by utilizing both technological change and emphasizing their quality product and service. To compete in the global environment they will have to stand out in terms of their distinctiveness, their value for money and how they can satisfy the targeted market. Since resorts often are associated with beautiful places they must ensure they make a contribution to growing environmental awareness.

This chapter will conclude with two cases concerning adjustment to new conditions. Billy Butlin's initial holiday camps now represent an old style of resort, where people's leisure was highly regimented through various scheduled programmes. In order to survive the changing social habits and market preferences Butlins has had to re-invent itself and create a new image and product out of the old one. The cruise ship market is a relatively new resort option, but that too has been required to adjust to changes, as it shifted from an elite market to a mass market with various niche products.

Case studies
Butlins' Changing Markets

When you are one of the original resorts for the mass market and that market changes in form and interests you need to change with it or die. This has been an important lesson for Butlins Holiday Resorts, which first opened in 1936 and now 70 years later faces an entirely different competitive environment. In the process the company went from a privately owned business operating one resort to a public company operating nine resorts, to becoming part of a public leisure company conglomerate, *Bourne Leisure*, that now operates three Butlins resorts within its stable of different leisure businesses.

When Butlins was under the control of Sir Billy Butlin, first as a private business and then as head of a public company, the original concept underwent steady refinement and change. Butlin's original idea or vision was:

> ...to open a holiday centre for the great mass of
> middle-income families for whom no one seemed
> to be catering, where they could have a good holiday
> irrespective of the unreliable British weather.
>
> (Butlin and Dacre, 2002: 29.)

At the time these were pioneering concepts and the success of the resorts proved Butlin had identified a key unserved market. The resort concept up to that time was essentially associated with the wealthy elite, not for the mass market. Although many appreciated the vagaries of the British summer weather, few had designed their resorts to accommodate such fickle conditions.

Even with a successful product Butlins felt obliged to watch and listen to its clients and to note changing tastes and preferences. Sir Billy Butlin claims 'I have always studied the behaviour of people in relation to their surroundings before making a big decision. This practice has played a major part in my success' (Butlin with Dacre, 2002: 73). Evidence of this can be seen in the development of the Redcoats, who were and still are, the ambassadors for the brand and friendly coordinators of guests and activities. Further evidence can be seen in the establishment of 'campers' committees through which criticisms and suggestions could be channeled' (Butlin with Dacre, 2002: 209).

Over the 70-year lifespan of the Butlins Resorts there have been several notable adjustments to changing market conditions. By the 1970s Butlins had started to tone down the 'enforced-gaiety-atmosphere of the camps' as guests became more sophisticated and wished to do their own thing at their own pace (Butlin with Dacre, 2002: 163). Part of this increased sophistication came from growing and varied holiday experiences, part from the growing number of holiday options which led to wider choice for the consumer and growing competition for Butlins. In tourism, like all businesses, one person's success leads to copycat operations, so over time consumers had a wider range of resorts from which to choose. Furthermore, new options came with improved technology and reduced travel restrictions, as demonstrated by the rising popularity of Mediterranean tour packages that could take the British to assured sunspots. Butlins response to this has been to adjust to a shrinking traditional market, by reducing its number of resorts and taking its three remaining resorts at Skegness, Minehead and Bognor Regis upmarket.

Today the Bourne Leisure group has branded their three Butlins venues as 'Family Entertainment Resorts' (Butlins, 2003). The resorts emphasize activities and entertainment opportunities for all age groups. Activities range from recreational pursuits to learning opportunities in various classes and clubs. Humour is still important within the entertainment realm. Each resort now has an entertainment hub that is located under a 'baby millennium dome' called a 'Skyline Pavilion' (Figure 3.1). Each of these pavilions house stages, bars, restaurants, shops and a variety of entertainments. As the seasons change so does their décor, with festivities to celebrate events such as New Year and Halloween. Entertainment under these pavilions ranges from current pop stars to comedians, dancers and street theatre, with appearances by characters such as Bob the Builder, Angelina Ballerina and Fireman Sam. Close to the pavilion in each resort is a sub-tropical 'Splash Waterworld'. This water play area offers a variety of water features such as swimming pools, water slides and wave machines that offer a complementary or competitive activity focus to the nearby beach (Figure 3.1).

A major component of Butlins' resource base is its accommodation offerings. These now have a new look, with upgraded chalets and apartment blocks to luxurious hotel accommodation (Figure 3.1). The hotel has been designed to look like a cruise ship and all rooms have balconies that offer views of the sea. Their internal design and furnishings offer space and luxurious living. Residential dining has been upgraded too, with more variety, à la carte menus, more flexible dining times and the introduction of self-catering options.

All-in-all Butlins has had to re-invent and re-brand itself several times over the past 70 years, as market conditions and consumer tastes have changed dramatically. But if one looks at the present branding emphasis one can still see the origins of Sir Billy Butlin's original concept. It is still about providing value for money to those British families who wish to take their annual holiday or a short-break vacation in England; where they can be sure of a range of activities and entertainment that will satisfy everyone in the family group. All the opportunities for a fun-filled holiday are there, but it is now up to the guest to determine how much they avail themselves of these opportunities.

Figure 3.1   Butlins Resort, Bognor Regis, England.

The Cruise Ship Market

Cruise ship holidays have become very popular over the past 30 years or so, and the ships themselves can be viewed as floating resorts. They offer a range of inclusive vacation options, from budget to luxury, with various activities on board and occasional port-of-call stops during the journey. Passengers or guests can find everything they need on board, from accommodation, meals, entertainment and exercise. If they wish to break free from the temptations of shipboard life they can disembark at various ports to sample the culture and sights of different locations. In this regard they function like resorts, providing all that is needed on-site, but offering controlled explorations of the outside world should a passenger/guest so desire. What started out as an expensive and stately form of travel for a few has become a more extensive and varied form of tourism for a far larger clientele. In the process cruise ships have become true resorts and real competitors for the more traditional land-based resorts.

The similarities between a cruise ship operation and a resort are numerous. The guest pays a significant amount upfront for an all-inclusive package of transportation, meals and accommodation, and can often have an enjoyable stay without any additional major expenditure. However, both the resort and cruise ship offer tantalizing extras to give their guests extra things to do and opportunities to spend. Berger (2004: 8) notes cruise ships' extras include:

1. *Tours at visited ports-of-call.*
   These are often pre-booked on board via the ship's travel agency, which provides the cruise line with additional commissions.
2. *Alcoholic beverages and soft drinks.*
   The bar is one of the major social gathering points on any cruise ship, and now there are soft drink bars for the young.
3. *Gambling.*
   Berger estimates that only a third of the passengers he observed gamble, but many others watched.
4. *Art auctions.*
   Berger notes these were constant and popular on the cruise he took, and represent just one of the retail opportunities where you have a wealthy and 'trapped' audience.
5. *Photographs.*
   Continuous photo opportunities are covered by professional photographers who offer their souvenir products for sale.
6. *Beauty salons and spas.*
   These are very popular options as the cruising environment provides both the time and motivation to 'scrub up'.

In addition to Berger's observations one could add certain recreation activities like swimming, skeet shooting, golf driving and rock wall climbing, health and fitness via gymnasiums, massage and yoga.

Moving to the supply side we see many similarities. Cruise lines are famous for the quality and quantity of their meals, yet Berger (2004: 5) points out they are able to 'offer such elaborate dining because of economies of scale and because little waste occurs'. But the rigid schedules and formal nature of cruise ship dining is changing to the more relaxed and flexible form of land resort dining as a 'freestyle cruising format' takes a greater hold (Miller, 2002).

More cruise lines are placing their branding emphasis on the type of journey they offer, rather than on the destinations visited. In addition to the *Norwegian Cruise Line* emphasizing its 'freestyle' style of travel which is meant to represent 'relaxed yet upscale' cruising; *Carnival* has become the largest and most successful cruise company by emphasizing its 'Fun Ships' and 'Million Ways to Have Fun' marketing campaign; while *Royal Caribbean* has promoted an adventure theme, including a rock-climbing wall on every ship, as part of its 'Get Out There' campaign (Kwortnik, 2006). The level of personal service on the smaller cruise ships is especially high with specific crew members assigned to your table and cabin, and in the larger vessels 'hospitality training (has been) introduced to encourage crews to treat cruisers as "guests", not as passengers' (Kwortnik, 2006: 293).

One result of these trends is to see how the cruise lines can now be differentiated along similar lines to resorts. Kwortnik and the Cruise Lines International Association (CLIA, 2006) have identified four basic market products within the very competitive cruise ship market which can be compared with land-based resort differentiation (Table 3.1). All of the identified categories emphasize a focus rather than a clear difference from all other categories, as can be seen in the overlap between prices paid for each cruise category. For some categories the emphasis is on the type of experience being sold within the cruise ship or resort, such as the luxury and premium categories, where the emphasis is on old resort values, like dressing up for dinner and personal service. For others the emphasis is on the cruise ship's destination, whether that be a trip up the Amazon or a re-enactment of the Northwest Passage through Arctic waters. In between these two extremes is the mass market which wishes to experience a little of both worlds, some luxury and pampering with some activities and famous sights; but the challenge becomes one of branding the product to position each cruise line in the individual consumer's perceptual space of what this market has to offer.

Table 3.1   Cruise line and resort brand positioning

Cruise line	Features	Resorts
Luxury (Cunard, Crystal and Silversea)	Traditional and exclusive ($400–$900 per person per day cruises).	Chateau resort style hotels in Canada and major national park lodges.
Premium (Princess and Celebrity)	Fine dining and sophisticated atmosphere, abundant entertainment ($250–$450 per person per day cruises)	Upmarket resorts often associated with major destination and sport championship sites.
Contemporary (Carnival, Disney and Norwegian)	Mass market floating resorts, good food, plenty of activities ($150–$300 per person per day cruises)	Major family-based resort chains.
Destination (Windstar and Lindblad)	Special destination and activity attractions (wide range of prices)	Beach, ski and culture resorts.

Source: after Kwortnik (2006: 288).

While the two types of vacation have many similarities there has been a distinctly different growth pattern between resorts and cruises. Land-based resorts, as the older and more established form of tourism, have experienced a far slower growth rate over the past 40 years than cruising. 'The birth of the modern cruise industry can be traced to the 1960s, in the wake of the first Boeing 707 flight from New York to Europe in 1958. With a rapidly shrinking transatlantic passenger base, opportunistic shipping companies repositioned their service from transportation to vacation travel' (Kwortnik, 2006: 287). According to Berger (2004: 3) 'in 1970 approximately 500,000 people took cruises, in 2001, 9.8 million people took cruises . . . The International Council of Cruise Lines estimates that by 2010 almost 21 million will take cruises'. While such rosy figures may appear optimistic at first glance there is no doubt that cruising has become a major market segment and a new form of resort attraction, and it is on target for that 2010 goal. In 2005 the CLIA reported that its members carried 11.18 million passengers, a 6.9 per cent increase over its 2004 results (Karantzavelou, 2006b). According to Morrison et al. (1996: 16) the CLIA is an American-based business association that accounts for approximately 80 per cent of the world's cruise business, so in total one could say the 2005 cruise market was

Table 3.2 Overview of cruising markets

Location/type	Comment	Supply/markets
River, canal and lake cruises	Several markets according to location.	Small, shallow-draft vessels, often domestic markets, cabotage limited.
Special interest, such as sail, education or exploration	Worldwide markets, high differentiated.	Often purpose-built vessels, specialist crews, a degree of monopoly through differentiation.
Long distance ocean cruises, including RTW cruises	Single world market.	Large vessels, often relying on 'tradition' and luxury, resources acquired internationally.
Extended ferry 'mini-cruises'	Usually domestic or between country pairs, especially in Western Europe.	Joint product with car ferry services.
Short ocean cruises	World market, but heavily dominated by US demand. Differentiated by location, dominated by the Caribbean.	Mostly large vessels, usually purpose built for mass market cruising.

Source: Bull (1996).

almost 14 million passengers and if it maintains the 7 per cent growth rate the prediction for 2010 is within reach.

While evidence of this growth is everywhere, with the CLIA offering 1800 different ports-of-call, 150 ships of varying styles and a whole new generation of cruise ships between 2000 and 2006, when 68 new cruise ships were introduced to the market (Karantzavelou, 2006a), most data and attention focuses on just one aspect of the cruise market – the short ocean cruises. However, as Bull (1996) illustrates in Table 3.2 there is a wide range of cruising markets and cruise/resort styles. River and canal cruises are a feature of the European market, where its major rivers like the Rhine and Danube have relatively large and fully equipped cruise ships traversing large sections of these beautiful and historic waterways; and its substantial canal remnants from the early industrial revolution era provide for self-catering holidays along the backwaters of Britain and France. A small but growing segment of the cruise industry are the small explorer cruise ships, such as in the *Lindblad Line,* which traverse the Arctic waters or penetrate upstream in major water systems to commune with nature and the indigenous peoples found in these isolated systems.

A consumer survey in 2006 of the cruise market reveals it has moved from the old elite product to a more balanced market that has many similarities to the resort market:

> Today's cruisers are younger and more affluent than ever.
> The 2006 study found that the average age of all cruise
> vacationers fell to 49 . . . Average income for the first time
> exceeded $100,000 at $104,000 . . . cruising has the highest
> percentage of extremely satisfied customers (45%),
> outpacing all-inclusive resorts (42%) and visiting friends
> and relatives (40%).
>
> (Karantzavelou, 2006c)

The study noted further that only 17 per cent of the US population had so far taken a cruise, leaving plenty of room for future growth in this market.

Given that the cruise market and resort markets have become so similar, they now form an important competitor to the land-based resorts, and provide an excellent example of the ever-changing competitive environment. Resorts can choose to either compete or collaborate with this new form of moving resort. In terms of competition resorts can duplicate some of the features of cruise vacations that have proved to be popular with the consumer:

- Greater convenience and ease of planning through more use of the Internet and travel agencies.
- Providing virtually totally inclusive package prices, so the final bill is not a shock.
- Programmes for children, so the adults can rest in the knowledge that their children are in a secure environment under the instruction or supervision of trained staff.
- Provide opportunities to visit local sights and destinations with a minimum of inconvenience, by providing escorted tours for international visitors or simply local directories and maps for domestic tourists.
- More diversified products to explain local culture and sense of place.

(Based on Morrison et al., 1996: 17.)

Collaboration opportunities can exist with a market sector that is experiencing the highest growth rates in the current tourism market. Its growth can expose cruisers to the associated benefits of land-based resorts, especially as some cruise lines have either linked up with resort destinations or built their own island resort bases to provide more extensive activity-based opportunities. As cruisers come into favourite ports-of-call they can be convinced to set down roots in such spots via timeshare or second home agreements with local resorts. Some forms of collaboration are underway already; *Club Med* has built its own luxurious sail oriented cruise ships, Raddison Resorts have linked up with *Diamond Cruises, Disney* has developed its own Florida-based cruise line and the Royal Caribbean Cruise line and Hyatt International have developed shared customer mailing lists (Morrison et al., 1996).

Questions

1 Discuss the identified global demand trends and develop some strategic resort responses for two of them.

2 Compare and contrast the concepts behind benefit segmentation with today's emphasis on creating value.

3 Examine ways in which Internet marketing may be enhanced in a resort setting, paying special attention to market segmentation's operational requirements.

4 Discuss how today's entertainment advances (plasma television, computer graphics and simulations) place pressure on how resorts will need to present their special events *or* local 'sense of place'.

5 Take a mature resort (50 years or older) in your area and discuss how it could evolve to meet changing social conditions and market trends.

6 Given that cruise ships are now the fastest growing element within the resort sector, would you advocate competition or collaboration with them? Explain the reasons for your choice and illustrate its benefits with some rationalized concrete proposals.

References

Berger, A.A. (2004). *Ocean Travel and Cruising: A Cultural Analysis*. New York: Haworth Hospitality Press.

Bull, A.O. (1996). The economics of cruising: an application to the short ocean cruise market. *Journal of Tourism Studies*, **7(2)**, 28–35.

Butlins (2003). *Butlins Student Information Pack*. Bognor Regis: Butlins Information Centre.

Butlin, Sir B. and Dacre, P. (2002). *The Billy Butlin Story 'A Showman to the End'*. London: Robson Books.

Chow, I. and Murphy, P. (2007). Travel preferences for foreign destinations: evidence of Chinese outbound tour group tourists traveling to Australia.

In *Tourism – Part Achievements, Future Challenges*. Refereed Proceedings of the Council of Australian Tourism and Hospitality Education (CAUTHE) conference, Sydney 11–14 February, CD Rom.

Cruise Lines International Association (2006). Cruise industry trends for 2006 – Cruise lines International Association. *Travel Daily News*, January 16, 1–4. www.traveldailynews.com. Accessed on 17 October 2006.

Helber, L.E. (1995). Redeveloping nature resorts for new markets. In *Island Tourism: Management Principles and Practice* (M.V. Conlin and T. Baum, eds), pp. 105–113. Chichester, UK: John Wiley.

Karantzavelou, V. (2006a). Cruise industry trends for 2006 – Cruise lines International Association. *Travel Daily News*, January 16, 1. www.traveldailynews. com. Accessed on 17 October 2006.

Karantzavelou, V. (2006b). CLIA member cruise lines to see growth in 2005. *Travel Daily News*, March 16, 1–2. www.traveldailynews.com. Accessed on 17 October 2006.

Karantzavelou, V. (2006c). A great potential for cruises. *Travel Daily News*, April 11, 1–3. www.traveldailynews.com. Accessed on 17 October 2006.

Kotler, P. (2001). *Kotler on Marketing: How to Create, Win and Dominate Markets*. London: Simon and Schuster.

Kwortnik Jr., R.J. (2006). Carnival cruise lines: burnishing the brand. *Cornell Hotel and Restaurant Administration Quarterly*, **47(3)**, 286–300.

Maiden, M. (2004). Economy unlikely to rescue Latham. *The Age*, October 18, 8, 12.

Maslow, A.H. (1970). *Motivation and Personality*, 2nd edn. New York: Harper and Row.

Mawet, J.P. (2005). Director, Aqualis Spa, Belgium. *Interview*, September 27.

McDonald, S. (2006). *Metropolitan Parks in Melbourne: A Critical Analysis of Factors Affecting Visitation by Regional Victorians*. Unpublished M.A. Thesis, School of Sport, Tourism and Hospitality Management, La Trobe University.

Miller, L. (2002). Freestyle cruising: a clear alternative. *FIU Hospitality Review*, **20(2)**, 41–46.

Morrison, A.M. (1989). *Hospitality and Travel Marketing*. Albany, NY: Delmar Publishers.

Morrison, A.M., Yang, C.-H., O'Leary, J.T. and Nadkarni, N. (1996). Comparative profiles of travellers on cruises and land-based resort vacations. *Journal of Tourism Studies*, **7(2)**, 15–27.

The Economist (2004a). Gambling goes global. *The Economist*, October 2, 69–71.

The Economist (2004b). Virgin territory. *The Economist*, October 2, 62.

The Economist (2006). Busted flush. *The Economist*, October 7, 77–78.

Veal, A.J. and Lynch, R. (2001). *Australian Leisure*, 2nd edn. Sydney: Pearson Education Australia.

4

The seasons

Introduction

Seasons are a fact of life for both nature and humans. They have their growing phase, their climax, their decline and dormant periods expressed so eloquently in classical music by Vivaldi's *The Four Seasons* and Tchaikovsky's *Symphony Pathetique*. For resorts designed to accommodate various forms of human activity, often in changing natural settings, it becomes of paramount importance to recognize these seasons and to integrate them into their offerings. This chapter will focus on three ways resorts can and have blended their product to meet the changing seasonal conditions and humans' activities within them.

It starts with one of the more obvious seasonal relationships between humans and the natural environment through sport and recreation. There was a time when each sport had a definite seasonal period, which was largely fixed by environmental conditions. For example, in the UK autumn and winter meant it was football season and in the spring and summer tennis and cricket. In North America it was football in the fall, ice hockey and basketball in the winter and baseball in the summer. Although the development of professional sport and the commercial power of television have distorted these seasonal patterns the core of the seasonal association is still present, and it remains a factor for those resorts which cater to specific sports and related recreational pastimes. It has developed into a situation where sport resorts are influenced by both natural and commercial seasonal cycles that will require careful management in order to maximize their business opportunities. An example of this occurs when ski resorts sometimes have some of their largest snowfalls in the spring, but guests have their minds set on the next sport or recreational activity of the calendar year.

Next this chapter turns to the general issue of tourism seasonality that has a particular significance for those resorts that specialize in outdoor recreation and leisure. By focussing on a particular sport or range of sports a resort has to invest heavily in providing the infrastructure and support facilities for those particular activities. If all goes well the result is excellent business volumes during the season followed by a dramatic decline in visitation when the season is over. This calls for a variety of management strategies that are designed to extend the season in some way or to facilitate a smooth transfer to another sport or business focus.

Finally, the chapter examines seasons as they apply to humans passing through the different phases of their life cycle, and how resorts are taking these changing human conditions into account. A major component of resort marketing has been to align their various leisure products to major and profitable market segments; but with aging populations new non-leisure market opportunities are emerging. More people are considering resort locations in terms of retirement living, more people are looking for alternative forms of medical assistance or cheaper and quicker surgery, more health insurance companies and governments are looking for more efficient ways to deliver health services; one result of these trends is the beginning of new partnerships between real estate, medicine and the resort sector. This section, therefore, pays specific attention to the health and wellness features of resorts, plus their growing role in the provision of health care and retirement in certain countries.

Seasons and sport

Sport primarily involves competitive recreation activities that many engage in for pleasure and some as a professional business career. These activities are generally seasonal and many have received increased attention as a result of the growing media sports exposure. To meet the demand for such sports some resorts have committed to their provision and development, which in turn has committed them to the seasonal cycle of their selected sport. In the cooler and more temperate zones of the globe this has led to distinctive seasonal patterns of winter sports followed by summer sports, but in the warmer latitudes it is possible to develop year-round sport activity in such 'summer sports' as golf and tennis. An example of the growing interest in the resort-sport link is presented in a special issue of *Tourism and Hospitality Research* (Butler, 2006) on Golf Tourism in the Algarve region of Portugal.

Resorts that specialize in a particular sport need to make a massive investment in the appropriate infrastructure, support facilities and services for that sport if they wish to compete on a national or international level. For ski resorts, this means the clearing of vegetation to establish a range of runs, some of which need to be challenging in nature while others should be more suited to beginners. In these times of global warming more resorts need to augment nature's snowfall with snow-making equipment. This requires a secure water supply, extensive plumbing and distribution, leading to snow guns placed strategically along the resort's principal runs. To deliver skiers to the top of their chosen runs requires chair lifts, which need to be fast and safe to move thousands of skiers on busy days. To make sure the runs are at their best requires regular grooming, which usually takes place at night so as to be ready for business at first light in the short winter days. To extend the time on the slopes some slopes will be provided with floodlit illumination. To ensure skiers get the most out of their experience or newcomers learn the basics, there needs to be a staff of professional ski instructors available to teach at a variety of levels. In case of accidents there needs to be some form of medical assistance available at the ski resort. This type of investment and commitment is duplicated in many golf and tennis resorts.

To obtain the greatest exposure for the resort and its facilities many have joined various professional tours, to become one of the competition event stops during the sport season. Beaver Creek and Vail, Colorado host the US Freeskiing Open; Pebble Beach, California, is a key event on the US Professional Golf Association tour; and St Andrews, Scotland hosts the British Open Championship at the Links – the home of golf; while the Hyatt Regency at Coolum in Queensland hosts the Australian Professional Golf Association's national championship. These tour events reinforce the symbiotic relationship between the sport professional and their public, bringing the two together in the setting of accommodating sports tourism resorts.

The growing economic significance of sports tourism has not been lost on the larger destinations. Melbourne, Australia has attempted to differentiate itself as an event city and in the three-month period of January to March, 2006 hosted the Australian (Tennis) Open, the Formula 1 Grand Prix and the Commonwealth Games. Scottsdale, Arizona has built its resort reputation on the sports of golf and tennis. If offers 174 golf courses, world class resorts and spas, many of which also provide tennis courts and coaching, and it regularly hosts professional baseball spring training camps – all under the well publicized sunny skies of the region. The Gold Coast, Australia plays host to a variety of events throughout the year in order to diversify its market appeal and to spread its season. These include 'hallmark events' such as the Gold Coast Indy, Australian Surf Life Saving Championships and the Gold Coast Marathon.

In Honolulu, Hawaii there has been a conscious decision to pursue a sports market in order to diversify the area's tourism market and to boost out-of-season visits. 'Our superb climate and year round outdoor playing season, and our central location in the Asia-Pacific region, make Honolulu a natural venue for national and international sporting events' (Harris, 2004: 129). To build on this potential Honolulu has developed a number of facilities such as the Waipio Pennisula Soccer Complex, and the Central Oahu Regional Park Tennis and Baseball Complex. These modern and comprehensive facilities attract national and international events that bring the tourists, and also provide 'excellent athletic facilities (that) could be used by Oahu's families throughout most of the year' (Harris, 2004: 129). In short they are seen as dual purpose investments – economic stimulants for the tourism industry and a social investment in the health and welfare of local citizens.

Sport tourism resorts are not restricted to national and international level destinations, because there is considerable business opportunity in serving local athletes. Children and teenagers are involved in sports that lead to championships, and they bring their supporters (family and friends) to these events. Even more lucrative sports markets exist with the growing number of 'seniors sports events', where retired professionals or keen amateurs come together with friends and family to relive old times and to have fun. Some communities and resorts have established themselves as tournament destinations to attract these types of events and their mix of socializing and sport.

Resort seasonality

Weather is a major determinant of travel and recreation patterns because most tourist and sport activities require optimal conditions to create guest satisfaction. These have been described as the 'physical factors' of seasonality by Butler and Mao (1997). They form only a part of the *push* and *pull* factors that lead to seasonality within tourism. Their influence is modified by the 'social and cultural factors' that impact on guests' choice of vacation. Both sets of factors are shown in Figure 4.1.

Figure 4.1 shows the physical and social/cultural factors operating on tourists at their home (generating area) and with regard to their anticipated holiday destination (receiving area). In the case of a beach resort the push factors encouraging guests to consider a beach holiday are the poor weather conditions at home; the pull factors include knowing that

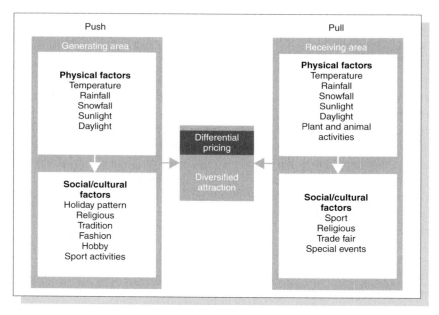

Figure 4.1 Seasonality factors for tourism (Butler and Mao, 1997: 10).

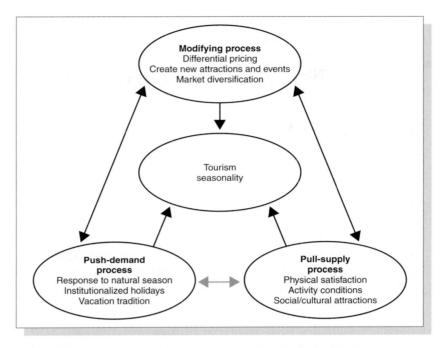

Figure 4.2 Management strategic for seasonality (Butler and Mao, 1997: 14).

the resort destination's weather conditions are likely to be much better. The actual dates selected for the holiday often will be determined by social and cultural push factors such a School holidays or traditional statutory holidays.

How resorts can attempt to influence these regular seasonal travel patterns is shown by Butler and Mao in Figure 4.2. The original push and pull features have now been labelled demand and supply processes, and their impacts on seasonality have been joined by the modifying process of resort management. Among the principal management strategies that Butler and Mao identified are differential pricing, creating new attractions and events, and market diversification.

■ *Differential pricing.*
   A common strategy is to apply the economic rules of supply and demand, so that if people wish to visit in the high season when resources are at full stretch they will pay a premium. If visitors come in the shoulder season they will pay a more competitive rate because there is some spare capacity and more choice. If they come in the off-season they will receive a heavy discount because the resort is looking

for business to maintain its core staffing, and in recognition that some of the local activities will be closed down.

■ *Out-of-season attractions and activities.*
If the prime resort attraction is highly seasonal, like skiing, then the resort will need to develop alternative attractions outside of the high season. These can either be other outdoor activities such as golf, hiking, mountain biking, and nature watching; or new indoor activities such as festivals, conferences, or workshops. The goal is to spread the high season into its surrounding shoulder seasons, and possibly into a four-season situation.

■ *Market diversification.*
In developing different products the resort will be opening itself up to different markets. These market segments may be able to use and appreciate the same type of facilities as used by the high season visitors, but more often they have their own distinctive needs that the resort will need to accommodate.

One study into offsetting seasonality has revealed a combination of strategies is often the most desirable management response. Owens (1994) reports on the results of a survey of 59 Canadian and 59 US 'all-season' resorts. All-season resorts in Canada experienced their largest percentage of sales during the summer months (44 per cent) and their lowest sales in the winter (17 per cent). The figures for the US resorts were 39 per cent and 25 per cent respectively. In addition to differential pricing many of the resorts attempted to offset the low season business lulls by diversifying into a multi-recreational product. A ski slope becomes a water slide in the summer or indoor activities are created at summer resorts for inclement weather use. More resorts are placing stronger emphasis on soliciting convention and corporate meetings, especially those close to major metropolitan areas. However, 'both Canadian and US respondents strongly agreed that "service excellence" will be the most important competitive opportunity for resorts' (Owens, 1994: 30).

On a related theme Fernandez-Morales (2003: 944) has examined the impact of market diversification in Spain's *Costa del Sol*, where the 'tourism product is based on sun and sea, so the industry is seriously affected by seasonality', but its various resort destinations have different levels of seasonal peaking. He reports that local policies to diversify the coastal market into golf and rural tourism have had minimal impact, whereas the inland centre of Granada which can offer a combination of sun and nearby beaches along with ski- and cultural-tourism has had greater success in reducing its seasonal variation. However, he feels the growing significance of the seniors market along with the continuous off-season social tourism market holds promise for less extreme seasonality among coastal Mediterranean resort destinations in the future.

Before management can begin to implement any of the above options it should have a definite idea of how extreme its seasonality is, and how to approach this issue. As accountants love to point out, you cannot manage something unless you can measure it, because only then will you have an accurate idea of the problem's scale and how well management strategies are improving the situation.

Seasonality in economic terms is a peaking issue that creates inefficiencies within a system. Richardson (1971: 104) shows that any peaking situation can be measured by examining its load factor. The load factor is the ratio of average load to peak load and illustrates the relative usage efficiency within a system. The formula is:

$$\text{Load Factor} = \frac{\text{Average number of visitors per month}}{\text{Number of visitors in peak month}} \times 100$$

It has been calculated to be as low as 33 per cent for urban transportation systems due to their twin rush hour peaks, and as high as 75–80 per cent for electric power transmissions, where some peaking can occur within a generally consistent pattern at meal times and during events like the Super Bowl half-time break.

The author has illustrated the utility of this measurement in terms of highly seasonal ski resorts within Australia to his resort management students. Using published data and local knowledge he has derived load factor scores of 25–30 per cent. This is not surprising when over a five-year period one resort reported receiving an average of 250 200 visitors over the four-month ski season, and only 133 000 over the remaining eight months. Such results portray the frantic activity of the high season and near ghost town conditions at stages in the long off-season, and confirm the urgent need to make these resorts more efficient through the introduction of non-snow products and attractions.

In terms of how to approach the seasonality problem Jang (2004) has offered one option that combines the long-term objectives and risk tolerance features of an investment portfolio. The long-term objective for resort seasonality management is to find the right combination of products that will provide the best overall annual return. To do this management should set an annual revenue target that reflects the level of risk they are prepared to accept, then seek out product combinations that are likely to produce this targeted revenue. Using an established dataset Jang illustrates how the application of the Markowitz financial portfolio model can identify different seasonal markets to meet different risk-taking objectives. In the case of a high risk strategy such as filling the greatest number of available bed-nights the investment and risk is far higher than for a low risk strategy, such as attracting more day-trippers who are mainly sightseeing and shopping which requires relatively little extra investment.

Resorts and human seasons

Resorts have recognized that humans have their seasons too, as they pass through the life cycle they age and take on different vacation priorities. Resorts focussing on a particular sport know that individual sports appeal to specific age cohorts and they need to examine demographic trends, such as age pyramids, to ensure there are sufficient numbers in their target age cohorts coming through the system. Age, of course, is not the only determinant of demand but in terms of high physical impact sports and recreation there is a strong correlation. One resort sport feeling the demographic pressure today is downhill skiing. This activity has blossomed with the Baby Boomer cohort, but as those individuals enter retirement, fewer are able to maintain such a physically demanding sport. Therefore, ski resorts are attempting to find new markets like international visitors or snow boarders and are diversifying into new products such as year-round attractions and real estate.

When resorts invest in a sports tourism or recreation product they need to make three choices. Where the sport focus is on a specific activity and age cohort it will need to establish a brand identity in that particular field. Such a strategy will help to differentiate the resort and provide it with a top-of-mind awareness for future interested individuals, as the original group passes through its age cycle onto other activities or products. Another strategy would be to broaden the appeal of the resort's core activity attraction by providing complementary activities for guests and their families, as has been done at the Hyatt Regency Coolum (Case Study) and Mt Buller ski resort in Australia. Mt Buller has supplemented its downhill and free-style skiing with snowboarding and such simple snow activities as tobogganing, snowball fights and snowmen building. Do not forget in Australia snow only falls in the mountains, so for many

Australians a mountain visit is the only way to experience such things. A third strategy is to diversify into a number of different sports that can accommodate a wide range of age groups. This is a common practice with resort destinations, which attempt to use their facilities year round by appealing to different age groups. The city of Kamloops in the BC interior can depend on reliable sunny weather and by using its central location in the province along with good transport connections has promoted itself as a 'tournament city'. It offers tournaments for children, adults and seniors in a wide range of sports, depending on the money spent by the participants and their supporters to drive much of its tourism revenue.

There comes a time when even the fittest and most enthusiastic sports person begins to find their body is calling out for more 'tender loving care' in order for them to continue or to help them ease into a new activity. As people get older the pampering and repair work of health spas becomes more appealing, and as western populations have aged the demand for this type of resort activity has exploded. The Munich Institute for Leisure Economics (2004) illustrates this trend with respect to Germany. It reports that the German health-related tourism market in 2003 consisted of 1.6 million people taking 2.5 million short or long trips. This large market has already developed into four recognizable sub-markets. Of these the 'health care holiday' group is the largest with 1.4 million trips in 2003, followed in descending order by 'wellness holidays' (800 000 trips), 'beauty holidays' (200 000) and 'anti-aging holidays' (10 000). Large though these numbers may appear, they are expected to increase by 70 per cent by 2010 because of Germany's aging population, and will make health tourism 'the most dynamic growth market of the future'.

According to Morrison (2005: 48) 'One trend that looks set to stay is the holistic spa treatment combined with western medicine. Doctors are on hand to help combat health problems, working alongside alternative practitioners to aid mind, body and soul'. Such spas or wellness centres are becoming an important component of five star resorts, focussing on health as well as beauty and spiritual treatments. They have become as necessary as swimming pools used to be for five star hotels, but the challenge is to staff and run them profitably.

One Australian resort that has used its spa and health tourism as a clear differentiator is the Daydream Island resort in the Australian Whitsunday Islands. 'After making his fortune selling vitamins, Vaughan Bullivant (the current owner) set about realizing his dream of what a resort should be – A\$75 million later, he thinks he's got it right at last' (Scott, 2004: 17). That dream is to rebuild this resort's fortunes around the concept of health tourism, combining the provision of spa pampering and medical assessments with the usual outdoor activities and healthy meal options, to send guests home feeling fitter as well as rested. The Daydream rejuvenation spa emphasizes its links with the local waters and the life of the nearby Great Barrier Reef to promote its focus on rejuvenation – a gentle process of assessment and correction. It does this through the provision of naturopathy, aromatherapy, hydrotherapy and massage, along with beauty therapies. It offers 16 individual treatment rooms, many with private balconies and sea views, located in the quieter northern end of Daydream Island.

The growth in spas and wellness centres reflects an aging population's concern over their health and how to maintain an active lifestyle as long as possible. In some parts of the world this has been a long-standing reason for visiting resorts. In Japan the traditional onsen baths have been a focal attraction of many resorts. There are some 3000 onsen hot spring areas in Japan, with approximately 137 million people using onsen accommodation each year. One of the foremost onsen resorts is at Kusatsu in the Gunma Prefecture. It has a field of hot springs in the centre of town (Figure 4.3) where 'a number of wooden chutes carry the hot water, which is an extremely hot 55 degrees Celsius when it comes out of the ground, to various ryokan inns in town, cooling along the way' (Kusatsu, 2005).

The growing health orientation of many resorts is preparing some of them for a move into general health care and surgical procedures. In Thailand resorts are playing a role in the globalization of health services, as more international visitors are drawn to the country because of its growing reputation, especially for its dental and cosmetic surgery. The number of international visitors who have travelled to Thailand for surgery has risen from 540 000 in 2002 to 1.1 million in 2004. The appeal is quality care, cheaper prices than home, speedier attention than at home and the cultural-resort type of experience. A spokesperson for Thailand's Ministry of Health, which is encouraging this medical tourism, claims that in addition to offering quality medical treatment:

> We also focus on health promotion and spa treatments. We sell our difference, our Thai culture, our Thai-ness. We differentiate from Singapore (Thailand's principal Asian competitor in this area) in that they are more western, here we have a holistic approach of Thai and Western medicine.
>
> (Levett, 2005: 6)

Part of that Thai approach is to offer extra value, such as complimentary gum massage after dental surgery, another is to make surgery a part of the

Figure 4.3 Kusatsu hot springs and summer festival.

vacation, so patients can relax and recuperate quicker than if they had to return immediately to home and work. Thailand is just one of several Southeast Asian countries pursuing the growing health care market. Henderson (2004: 111) reports that Malaysia, Singapore and Thailand 'have taken the lead in developing this sector', with each country playing to its particular strengths. Malaysia focusses on medical screening and hospitalization; 'several hotels arrange packages incorporating check-ups and subsequent hospital referrals . . . Sunway Medical Centre, in collaboration with Sunway Lagoon Resort Hotel, advertises a 'medical holiday that's packed with relaxation and fun' (Henderson, 2004: 114). Singapore's government is striving to 'retain its status as the "healthcare hub of Asia"' by setting a 'target of 1 million foreign patients by 2012' and spa tourism is being developed (Henderson, 2004: 114). Thailand is linking its cosmetic surgery and resort destinations' reputations, 'developing healthcare centres in Chang Mai and Phuket, in the north and south of the country, respectively, as well as in Bangkok (the central capital and international gateway)' Henderson (2004: 115). In this survey of health tourism in Southeast Asia Henderson (2004: 117) notes 'cosmetic and non-essential surgical procedures have been united with time spent at resorts, and alternative therapies are becoming accepted options for tourists on vacations'. As waiting lists for surgery at home lengthen and the costs to government increase both parties are exploring resort alternatives, which now include essential surgery and procedures. See the Roompot case at the end of this chapter.

Aging and retirement offer other opportunities for guests and resorts besides attempting to slow the ravages of nature and gradual decline of one's physical and mental abilities. A key factor in many resort plans has been the retirees growing interest in 'downsizing and moving to somewhere nice'. Those living in metropolitan areas have experienced a major capital gain in the rising price of their home and many see this as a natural and financial opportunity to move, permanently or seasonally, to resort destinations where they can enjoy the facilities and amenities with the occasional visit from friends and relatives. Resort destinations around the world are catering increasingly to the retirement market, which has been portrayed as a new form of international migration. An example of this is presented by Gustafson's (2002) investigation of Swedish retirees who have chosen to spend their summers at home and their winters in Spain. This sociological study reveals these new nomads are neither tourists nor immigrants, but are akin to the seasonal migrant worker – both welcome and unwelcome at the same time. If the resorts and host communities are to practice their duty of care and get the most out of such markets they will need to develop new approaches and products for these retirees, who represent a new type of guest and market segment.

Summary

This chapter has illustrated the strong association between resorts and seasons. It is not merely the seasonality of resorts brought on by the weather and traditional institutional arrangements, like national holidays, it is also linked intimately to the seasons developed by humans for their play and enjoyment and to the seasonal nature of their own lives. Sport has become such an important part of life that its seasons have been expanded and glorified, to the extent that some resorts have banked their future on a core sport and its continuity. As people pass through the age cycle their needs can be met by resorts along an almost cradle to grave continuum – from nursery slopes, to junior camps, to adult participation and competition, and finally on to body maintenance and repair. All provided in attractive settings with professional staff to make the triumphs as memorable as possible and the pain as bearable as possible.

The following three case studies are presented as evidence of the above trends and as indicators of what is and can be achieved by matching resorts to the natural and human seasons.

Case studies
Sport Tourism – Hyatt Regency, Coolum, Australia (www.coolumhyatt.au-hotels.com)

The Hyatt Regency resort in Coolum, Queensland is a resort that has featured sport as a vehicle to capture business and enhance its reputation. It views sport as a succession of activities and events throughout the year. It has taken this approach because vacationers have a lot of choice and it needs to provide people with reasons to select the Hyatt Regency resort year round. In addition, major events raise the profile of the resort which leads to top of mind awareness and additional bookings. Since the vast majority of its market is domestic a good differentiator in the Australian market is sport. The resort also features major concerts, like the recent Michael Crawford (star of Phantom of the Opera) event, which serve the same purpose.

The Hyatt Regency resort is located in a popular destination region within Queensland – the Sunshine Coast, an hour or so northeast of Brisbane. Being a five star resort within a popular destination it needs to stand out in the minds of vacationers and to draw them throughout the year. It does this by emphasizing its core sports of golf and tennis, which are available year round, and its hosting of the Australian PGA championship which provides it with high–top-of-mind awareness amongst the country's many golf enthusiasts. The high profile event for tennis is the annual 'Australian Festival of Tennis' where celebrities and professionals engage in a week-long tournament.

To draw and please golf enthusiasts the resort offers everyone a chance to play on the championship course, with its 'natural waterways, challenging characteristics and magnificent environment'. But in addition it provides a 'golf improvement centre' that consists of 'a 260-metre all-weather driving range, a chipping green with an adjoining practice bunker'. Plus it provides an impressive clubhouse and golf shop, along with professional lessons in 'golf and playing' and its daily complimentary group golf clinic lessons (Figure 4.4).

For tennis enthusiasts the 'Tennis Centre' offers a centre plexicushion court with six adjacent grass courts. All courts are floodlit for evening play. Partners for singles and doubles can be arranged via their local grading system. Social tennis is available throughout the week, as is professional coaching.

To provide activities for others or when the golfers and tennis players need a change of routine the resort makes further use of its site, which stretches from a Pacific Ocean beach to the rainforest base of the local Mount Coolum monolith. On the coast is its Beach Club that offers changing facilities, a swimming pool and access to the resort's patrolled surf beach, surf fishing, beach volleyball and general sun-baking. In the rainforest is a nature walk and in the centre of the resort is Camp Hyatt. This is a centre for children up to 12 years of age, who under the care of qualified childcare professionals can engage in a range of group activities such as arts and crafts, kite flying, archery, canoeing, music and beach activities. This leaves mum and dad with the opportunity to pursue their sport interests during the day and to catch up with the children's adventures over dinner at night.

A further key attraction of the Hyatt Regency is its Sun Spa. This Spa is intended to 'luxuriate and pamper' the customer, leaving fitness and hard work-outs to the gym. It consists of a 25-metre heated pool, aquacise pool, fitness centre, aerobics and yoga studio, hair and beauty salon and squash courts. Its professional staff offer massages, aerobics,

Figure 4.4 Hyatt Regency Coolum, Australia (Courtesy of Hyatt Regency Coolum).

yoga, crosstraining, pilates, tai chi and chi energy. Eighty per cent of its business is massages and beauty treatments, with exotic treatments like mud baths being fringe activities.

In addition to its outdoor sport emphasis the Hyatt Regency at Coolum has developed its conference and meetings appeal, because if people can have multiple reasons to visit it makes the room charges more bearable and it is a good way for the resort to help counter the seasonal lows. Forty-five per cent of its business is now meetings – conference related, ranging in size from 5 to 600 attendees. The resort is gaining recognition from large corporations that can reserve the whole resort and with its wide range of conference facilities plus sport and relaxation attractions, keep everyone on-site rather than loose some to the attractions of a metropolitan centre.

To make this sport and relaxation package work the Hyatt Regency at Coolum needs to spend a lot on maintenance and professional staff to ensure it offers what is expected in a five star resort – the best. The grounds need to be immaculate and require a staff of around 50 permanent staff along with casuals at specific times (events and seasonal activities). Given the large size of the resort and its emphasis on golf and other outdoor activities 300 vehicles (trucks, vans, buggies, bobcats) are on-site and require three full-time mechanics (Holland, 2006). Many other professionals are required to interact directly with the guests in a sports resort, particularly in the areas of coaching and spa treatments. These individuals need to be highly qualified in their field and to have good public relation skills. In some cases a resort will outsource such personal training and body care to professionals on a contractual basis that allows them to operate their own business within the resort using resort facilities.

All of this helps to present a sports-oriented resort that offers something for the whole family year round.

Weather Seasonality – Wickaninnish Inn, Canada, (www.wickinn.com)

The Wickaninnish Inn is a four star resort hotel and Relais & Chateaux property on the west coast of Vancouver Island, near Tofino, BC (Figure 4.5). On this western edge of Canada the high season is from March to October, as visitors come to see the grey whales migrating to the Arctic and enjoy the summer activities provided by fishing the Pacific waters and enjoying the natural wilderness of nearby national parks and rugged landscape. The low season of approximately four months in length,

Figure 4.5 The Wickaninnish Inn, BC, Canada.

depending on the severity of the winter season, and is a major challenge to the outdoor emphasis of the region.

This was the situation faced by Charles McDiarmid whose family owned a waterfront property just south of Tofino. They, along with a group of Tofino residents, built and opened the Wickaninnish Inn in 1996, first the 46-room Pointe building then the Beach building of 30 rooms and suites was added in 2003 (McDiarmid, 2005). The Inn's Pointe building is located on a rocky promontory and is surrounded by Pacific Ocean views on three sides, with an old growth forest as a backdrop. The buildings utilize indigenous materials and are designed to complement the local scenery. The Inn's primary market is those seeking 'a luxurious yet rustic getaway', and it markets itself as offering 'Rustic Elegance on Nature's Edge'.

Until recently most of the up-market properties in Tofino closed for the winter, especially for January and February when the weather could be particularly wet and rough. But such a shutdown and the associated low season volumes would hinder an adequate ROI, especially for a new venture. Therefore, McDiarmid (2005) set about turning a problem into an opportunity.

In the construction of the Wickaninnish Inn's Pointe, the building was placed on the rocks in such a way as to provide maximum exposure to the winter storms. All the rooms were provided with reinforced picture windows and fireplaces, so guests could sit in comfort and watch the Pacific storms roll in unimpeded, to crash on the rocks below them. To ensure they receive the full impact of nature's wrath there are microphones positioned outside to bring all the sound and fury into the main restaurant; while each room has a balcony door opening to the sea. In this way Charles McDiarmid and his Wickaninnish Inn created a new high season within the low season – a storm watching season.

The storm watching season has created a popular season where none existed before and has made a major contribution to the success of Wickaninnish Inn and the local community. Instead of closing over the winter months of January and February the Inn remains open placing its winter months on a par with Spring rates but still behind its occupancy rating for August. In addition the publicity generated by this unusual feature and its approach to nature in up-market travel magazines has led to more extensive awareness and interest. Plus it has encouraged other high end coastal resorts in the area to join the move to a storm season focus, but none have the advantage of site and purpose-design that the first-mover – the Wickaninnish Inn possesses.

Health Tourism – Roompot Vakanties, Netherlands (www.rpholidays.nl)

Roompot Vacations in the Netherlands is a family focussed resort chain which offers vacations in cabin and chalet accommodation at its coastal and country parks throughout the Netherlands. It has been in operation since 1965 and has witnessed many changes in Dutch society and its leisure market over that period. One of the more recent changes has been the Dutch government's new health care policy, which in an attempt to be more efficient in its use of national funds has set up a coupon system, whereby citizens are allocated a set amount of money for their health care each year and they are free to find the best value (quality and price) care from any approved medical facility within the Netherlands. Roompot resorts intend to become one of the popular options for the Dutch people seeking health care (Versluijs, 2005).

Roompot has 30 facilities scattered across the Netherlands and has been operating a dialysis treatment service in some of its resorts for the past five years (Versluijs, 2005). This medical treatment option was attractive to the resorts because it helped to use surplus capacity, since dialysis is required several times a week it presented a steady demand for the converted facilities. The government and insurance companies support such a partnership because to provide these services within a resort environment costs less than via the traditional hospital structure. Plus, patients prefer the home-like atmosphere of the resort, which goes hand-in-hand with the professional medical treatment, where family can drop-in and meals are either provided or self-catered.

The dialysis experience and the government move to a coupon system for health care has encouraged Roompot to consider expanding its health care options and move into new resort locations. It has created a new development strategy design to integrate health care into its traditional leisure market (Table 4.1). Roompot sees this aspect of its resort offerings as a leisure-care-cure package for short-term stays. It does not want to negatively impact the leisure focus of its resort parks, so the plan is to use only a few health bungalows in each park and to select ones that are located in quiet peripheral areas. But it wants to expand beyond dialysis treatment into eye surgery, plastic surgery and hip replacements – all common ailments for an aging population, and by 2010 many of the Dutch population will be over 50 years of age. To achieve this Roompot will create a medical team for each resort, in partnership with a local hospital, where the actual surgery will take place and the patient brought to the resort upon progressing from intensive care.

Table 4.1   Roompot development strategy units

Approach	Traditional	Current	Future
Focus	Hospitality	Therapy	Surgery
Theme	Leisure and accomodation	Care	Cure
Components	Hotel	Total body check	Laser surgery
	Apartment units	Sports fitness	Dental care
	Care units	Spa	Plastic surgery
	Restaurants	Sauna	Cosmetic surgery
	Conference facilities	Special diets	Orthopaedics
	Swimming	Therapy	Radiology and X-ray
	Sauna	Acupuncture	Physiotherapy
	Outdoor recreation		

Source: After Versluijs and Nourens, Roompot Resorts, Internal Report.

Part of the care process is to teach patients how to take care of themselves and to use medication appropriately. In this regard other important clients will be insurance companies and pharmaceutical companies, which have a particular interest in helping people overcome the difficult weeks after surgery and to become self-reliant in terms of applying medication. The expectation being that a less institutional setting in a happy place, supported by family and health professionals, will lead to a higher cure rate than usual.

Questions

1   Seasonality has been presented in this chapter as a 'curse', but it also has some positive aspects for resorts. Discuss what these positive aspects are and how these features could be maintained within a four-season resort strategy.

2   Using a well-known resort-based sporting event, examine how that resort translates its short-term media exposure into an annual business.

3   Justify 'differential pricing' to yourself, as a resort business, and to your customers, the resort guest.

4   Critically analyse the seasonality strategy of any resort known to you, and assess which aspects of that strategy have worked the best and why.

5 Review your household's vacation history in terms of the Family Life Cycle theory. Analyse how well your history fits with the theory and examine the opportunities presented for 'out-of-season' resort vacations by your household's vacation history profile.

6 Given the growing interest in health tourism, how would you position an international or local resort to take advantage of this trend?

7 Relate Jang's (2004) use of the Markowitz financial portfolio model to the three case studies of this chapter and assess its relevance to their individual strategies.

References

Butler, R. and Mao, B. (1997). Seasonality in tourism; problems and measurements. In *Quality Management in Urban Tourism* (P.E. Murphy, ed.), pp. 9–23. Chichester: John Wiley and Sons.

Butler, R. (ed.) (2006). Special issue on golf tourism. *Tourism and Hospitality Research*, **6(3)**, 167–238.

Fernandez-Morales, A. (2003). Decomposing seasonal concentration. *Annals of Tourism Research*, **30(4)**, 942–956.

Gustafson, P. (2002). Tourism and seasonal retirement migration. *Annals of Tourism Research*, **29(4)**, 899–918.

Harris, J. (2004). *The Renaissance of Honolulu: The Sustainable Rebirth of an American City*. Hawaii: City and Council of Honolulu.

Henderson, J.C. (2004). Healthcare tourism in Southeast Asia. *Tourism Review International*, **7(3/4)**, 111–121.

Holland, M. (2006). General Manager, Hyatt Regency Coolum Golf Resort and Spa. *Interview*, January 4.

Jang, S. (2004). Mitigating tourism seasonality: a quantitative approach. *Annals of Tourism Research*, **31(4)**, 819–836.

Kusatsu (2005). *Kusatsu Onsen in Japan*. Kusatsu: Tourist and Commerce Section of Kusatsu Town Hall.

Levett, C. (2005). Keep smiling. *The Age*, October 29, 6.

McDiarmid, C. (2005). Managing Director, The Wickaninnish Inn. *Interview*, September 5.

Morrison, A. (2005). Spa report – to infinity and beyond. *British Airways High life Magazine*, October, 46–54.

Munich Institute for Leisure Economics (2004). Health care and wellness tourism of Germans until 2010. *Travel Impact Newswire*, 25 March, 3. imtiaz@travel-impact-newswire.com.

Owens, D.J. (1994). The all-season opportunity for Canada's resorts. *The Cornell Hotel and Restaurant Administration Quarterly*, **35(5)**, 28–41.

Richardson, H.W. (1971). *Urban Economics*. Harmondsworth: Penguin Books.

Scott, L. (2004). Fanatasy Island. *The Weekend Australian Magazine*, June 26–27, 16–21.

Versluij, C. (2005). Director Roompot Holidays, Netherlands. *Interview*, September 28.

5

Governance

Introduction

Governance involves the setting of policy and the exercise of authority to ensure that policy is followed. The significance of policy and procedure on tourism businesses has been recognized in the tourism literature (Elliott, 1997; Michael, 2006), but with an emphasis on politics. While such works confirm the vital importance of political governance to many aspects of development and management they do not discuss corporate governance to any great extent. This chapter will broaden the concept of governance to include consideration of corporate governance and its impact on resort development and management issues, in addition to the important political elements of governance.

An important issue for any resort development and management is the question of who owns the business and who possesses the governance authority for their area and its particular relevance to their operations. In western societies such lines of responsibility tend to be defined clearly and allow for disputes to be resolved through the courts. Sometimes different grants or subsidies can be obtained from various levels of government in order to build or operate a resort in certain regions. Permits from different authorities will always be necessary in order to build and operate a resort. The legal ramifications associated with development permits and operating licenses are significant and to disregard them can lead to major penalties.

A related issue involves ownership of the land on which a resort is to be built, for there are important status and legal differences when a business occupies leasehold land as opposed to freehold ownership. If the resort is to be built on crown land or publicly owned land, then the issue of governance becomes a particularly sensitive one, because the resort will need to meet the land owners' expectations and requirements over and above the commercial considerations of its operations. Those owners of public land will not only be the appropriate government, but the public in whose name the land is held in trust; so many stakeholders will be involved. Another key factor in this relationship will be the length of lease obtained and the procedures, if any, to account for land improvements made over the life of the lease. If the resort sits on private land and is owned outright, the owner has greater operational freedom, but must still respect the wishes of shareholders and the general planning and legislative requirements of its local and higher levels of government. At either extreme and in all situations in between resort planning and management must consider the opportunities and limitations provided by the various types and forms of governance.

Corporate governance

Most businesses have to consider corporate governance rules and expectations, public companies have obligations to shareholders and private companies have obligations to banks, while all have responsibilities to tax departments. One major issue in the area of corporate governance that has particular relevance to the resort sector is the growing separation between ownership and management control of either the whole resort or of particular businesses within it. As resort businesses have grown into publicly traded corporations and international ventures, a new type of investor has emerged in the form of institutional investors like investment and pension funds. These are placing major investments in resorts to provide the steady long-term revenue returns they will need for their members. This creates a situation where the resort management annual priorities may not coincide perfectly with the owners' long-term objectives. For example, resort management may wish to raise the quality and satisfaction of the vacation experience, necessitating investment in product technology and staff preparation. While such objectives may lead to a more successful tourist destination and higher profile for the resort, such investment may only have marginal impacts on inventors' interests in real estate sales or long-term asset values. On the other hand, more removed ownership may be better placed to assess the true value and merit of maintaining a resort business and could be better placed to find alternative uses for the land and assets.

The problem of governance through various levels and types of ownership has been examined in the business literature via a collection of theories. Dalton et al. (1998) report that resource dependency theory and stewardship theory have been used with good effect to identify potential ownership links to deliver mutually beneficial returns. Daily et al. (2003) have convened a special examination of various ownership options such as different stock options, repurchase programs and international ownership choices.

Much of the governance literature in tourism relates to the western free-market philosophy of government, which supports a policy of minimum interference in the economy. However, some resorts will not be located in such regimes and will need to prepare for different circumstances and rules. Michael's (2006) book on public policy clearly demonstrates the link between business and government in all political economies, but the level of overlap is determined by the current political philosophy of those in charge. The ascendant philosophy in the western world right now is a belief in the efficient delivery of services and products through the free-market system of capitalism. Some countries attempt to provide a safety net for those people and 'key industries' that are unable to provide sufficient revenue to support themselves, and are referred to as social or welfare political-economic systems. Others believe the state is in the best position to deliver a fair distribution of resources and rewards to the people, which links them with the central planning philosophy of communism.

Naturally, as politicians come and go, either through the ballot box or revolution, these three political-economic systems absorb features from each other and do not remain pure. The biggest political-economic system in the world – China, is now going through such a process of adjustment, and can be described as a 'transitional economy'.

China's tourism and resort appeal is growing in line with its dramatic economic development. Pine (2002) has noted that since China adopted its 'Open Door Policy' in 1979 it has raised its annual visitor number to 31 million and is predicted to reach 130 million by 2020. By 2000 there were 10 481 hotels within China and the top three operators were the national corporation of Jin Jiang International, followed by the international corporations of Bass Hotels and Resorts (now known as Six Continents Hotels) and Shangri-La Hotels and Resorts. Within this growth Pine (2002: 63–64) observes that 'state ownership is still the dominant mode of ownership, accounting for 63 per cent of all hotels and rooms. The chief problems occasioned by (this) state ownership are the failure to separate hotel management and ownership and effective monitoring of the state's assets'. But according to Tang et al. (2006) the problem goes further than this, and is an issue of corporate governance. Tang et al. (2006: 185) consider 'A consensus of both industry researchers and practitioners has found that almost all state owned hotels (in China) are struggling with complicated ownership and internal systems, unclear responsibilities and obligations, and incomplete market operations'. Some hotels continue to be political toys, established to be symbols of political success, used to reward politicians and bureaucrats, while others have tried to respond to tourism market demands but have difficulty adjusting to changing market conditions because they need to explain their needs to non-business oriented owners. Due to the unclear objectives and responsibilities present in the corporate governance of these hotels many have become bankrupt and are now in the hands of state banking systems, which is adding yet another layer between management and the true owners of the business – the state. 'Briefly speaking, the complicated relationships among ownership, decision-making power, controlling rights, and the rights for residual claims have fundamentally confounded the possibility of any proper corporate governance' (Tang et al., 2006: 187).

Corporate social responsibility

Corporate social responsibility (CSR) is a growing concept that reveals the overlap between business and political governance is considerable, even in nations with a declared minimal interference in economic matters. CSR indicates business has wider social and environmental responsibilities than simply making a profit; and regardless of whether this policy has been generated internally or as a response to public criticism and government legislation, it means business responsibility needs to extend beyond its internal environment to incorporate local (task) and national/international (societal–global) responsibilities. CSR has its roots in stewardship, environmental scanning, community tourism, triple bottom line accounting and sustainable development concepts to name but a few; but it has placed social responsibility alongside financial responsibility as a central corporate governance concern.

CSR has evolved as an important corporate governance issue due to the growing need for business 'to stay abreast of the public's evolving ideas about corporate roles and responsibilities' (Zadek, 2004: 125). As the public has become more informed about global economic, human rights – and deteriorating environmental – conditions it has reacted negatively to those businesses that have been linked with such problems. Zadek has reviewed the experiences of Nike and other companies and feels there is a definite path to corporate responsibility, that has much in common with Howatson's (1990) earlier observations on how Canadian firms were responding to growing concern over their environmental impacts. Zadek (2004: 126–127) feels CSR is part of an organizational learning process, where companies go through a five stage learning process:

1. *Defensive*: Defend against attack to their reputation by denying practices, outcomes or responsibilities.
2. *Compliance*: To mitigate losses and litigation risks adopt a compliance approach as a cost of doing business.
3. *Managerial*: To achieve longer-term gains by integrating responsible business practices into daily operations by embedding societal issues into the core management processes.
4. *Strategic*: To enhance economic value in the long term to gain first mover advantage by aligning strategy and process innovations with societal issues.
5. *Civil*: To realize economic gains through collective action by promoting broad industry participation in corporate responsibility.

'The trick is for companies to be able to predict and credibly respond to society's changing awareness of particular issues' according to Zadek (2004: 127), and this is as relevant for the resort business as any other.

For resorts CSR is a means to update and integrate previous environmental and social concerns into a more central policy and governance role. However, if a company is to adopt such a policy it must be credible, and fully integrated into its strategy and operations. The public and media will be on constant alert to claims of CSR, and resorts can expect to be held to account over such claims. One watch-dog in this regard is *Tourism Concern*, which has already noted some resort shortcomings with respect to CSR claims, according to a report in the eTN *Travel Wire News* (2006).

Various levels of political governance

Due to their size and significance resorts regularly come under the jurisdiction of several levels of political governance. The different levels of responsibility often overlap, such as in the case of labour laws or planning authority, but the senior levels of government generally set the eventual parameters. Where there is confusion or actual conflict between different policy levels the courts can be called upon to settle jurisdictional disputes. In order to demonstrate the different emphasis of each level of political governance this chapter will divide what is an overlapping continuum of government responsibilities into three separate categories, before proceeding to illustrate their multiple concerns and impacts on resort management.

National governments

National governments have become involved with resorts, either directly or indirectly, because of their growing significance within tourism and their increasing role in regional development. This involvement extends through a wide range of governance responsibilities, several of which are outlined below.

Resorts are playing a larger role in *national tourism plans* because they have the capacity to attract and hold both international and domestic tourists. International visitors have long been of interest to national tourism plans because of their high yield and the hard currency they bring into a national economy. International visitors to developing economies can be tempted to resort vacations that offer international standard facilities, security and reasonable prices. Good examples of this can be seen in Cancun, Mexico and Phuket Island, Thailand; where two isolated coastal regions have been developed around international resort markets for the benefit of the host nation as well as the host region. National governments also recognize the potential quality resorts have to keep domestic tourists at home. In today's less secure and more expensive global environment a domestic vacation at a national resort can appeal to more family budgets and reduces the leakage of funds to other countries.

To reach international visitors and domestic users national governments need to *market their major resorts*, and this is often done in partnership with state and industry organizations. The types of resort included in international and national campaigns are the major resort destinations like the Gold Coast (Australia), Las Vegas (USA) and the Mediterranean coast (Europe). Such marketing is often linked with special events, such as a sport tournament or a festival, to provide the visitor with a special reason to spend several days at the destination. Others can be included as part of a national tour as happens with the Uluru (Ayers Rock) resort, which often forms an important stop on tours of Australia.

International gateways determine the entry point of the high yield international visitors, so resorts with good *access* to international airports have a distinct advantage. This was a prime reason for the Australian government's investment in the Cairns International Airport, to serve the growing tourist region of Northern Queensland and the Great Barrier Reef. Airports are vital to the success of international and national vacation travel patterns because air travel has become the mode of choice for long distance travel. Any resort located close to an airport will gain considerable competitive advantage due to increased access to more distant markets.

There has to be a comfortable and convenient road system to bring visitors to the doors of a resort. The most influential type of road for any long distance trips is the limited access divided highway, usually referred to as a freeway or toll highway, because it is easier to drive and ensures quicker travel. Any resort close to an entry point on such a road system will have a distinct locational advantage, similar to that noted with proximity to an airport. Lundgren (1983) demonstrates how this process favoured certain ski resorts in the Laurentian mountains, when old railway and road systems were supplemented by a freeway system linking the region to Montreal, the region's principal market.

National governments have long accepted the conservation of *outstanding natural and cultural assets* as part of their mandate, and where this has occurred it creates a major attraction for resorts. The presence of national parks that take many days to explore and enjoy is a big attraction, but also a dilemma because of their dual mandate – designated for conservation and recreation. As a result resort destinations must locate either outside of the park, like Gatlinburg on the edge of the Great

Smoky Mountains National Park (USA), or within a small demarcated area inside the park, as in the case of Banff township within Banff National Park (Canada). Likewise, the positioning of resorts with reference to cultural icons must be handled with care. They need to provide views and access, but should not disturb the aura of the cultural attraction.

An example of national tourism planning using resort development, resort marketing, access advantages and national attractions to draw both international and domestic visitors can be seen in the development of Sentosa Island in Singapore. Few people realize that the small city nation-state of Singapore has set aside an island to be a principal recreation area for its people, and this Sentosa Island is now undergoing a major transformation that includes resorts which will appeal to international travellers as well as local residents. This transformation is part of a general realignment of Singapore's economy, as it faces growing competition from Asian nations with lower industrial labour costs. To prepare for this competition Singapore is attempting to diversify its economic base and is moving strongly into service areas such as education, health and leisure, hoping to become the regional centre of such services.

A good indication of this move to become more competitive in the service economy is Singapore's vision for a rejuvenated Sentosa Island. Leisure revenue generating activities are spread throughout the island via a physical zoning plan. Unlike normal planning zones these are not exclusive, because all contain various elements of the island's leisure activities, but like normal zones each has its own distinctive emphasis. On the south side of the island is a 'Beach Zone' offering relaxing beach and outdoor recreation activities, that also includes the Shangri-La Rasa Sentosa Resort Hotel with its attendant facilities. Along the spine of the island is the 'Green Zone' proving a home for the area's historic structures and two championship golf courses amongst the secondary rain forest, as well as acting as a buffer to separate the other zones. To the east is the residential zone of 'Sentosa Cove', which will offer up-market waterfront residences upon completion. On the north side, closest to the city, is the 'Entertainment Zone', which includes a theme park, various forms of entertainment for all ages, a waterfront village and speciality retail shops and restaurants.

One addition to the revitalized Sentosa Island offerings is the proposed casino. In April 2005 the Singapore government approved the building of two casinos in Singapore, one of which is to be located in the entertainment zone of Sentosa Island. The casinos are viewed as a way to continue the reinvention of Singapore, creating a vibrant and dynamic city for tourism and business, and helping it reach its goal of doubling the number of international arrivals to 17 million and tripling receipts to S$30 billion in the next 10 years (Henderson, 2006).

State governments

State governments are close partners with national government planning and marketing objectives because the two are in a symbiotic relationship – what is good for one is often good for the other. Whether the goal is to attract international visitors and domestic visitors; to provide an economic rationale for the conservation of natural or cultural resources; or bring more business and amenities to regional areas; the two highest levels of national government find plenty of common ground and opportunity to collaborate. An example of this was the creation of the 'Travel Industry Development Subsidiary Agreements' in Canada during the 1970s. These tourism development projects were jointly funded by the federal and state governments; and one outcome was the start of the Whistler Resort Municipality and its international ski resort, that will be hosting the 2010 Winter Olympics (Montgomery and Murphy, 1983).

States are particularly keen to support national policies when they match their individual aspirations for development, and resorts have been viewed as one path to regional development. As people and business converge on a nation's large cities there is a need to redress this imbalance, and one way is to develop rural and regional areas as recreation and retirement areas (Christaller, 1964; Peet with Hartwick, 1999). Given the labour intensity of tourism and health services, resorts and other service sector activities could be developed as local growth poles, stimulating other industries and the development of amenities that would keep more people in these regional areas. This has been the underlying economic rationale behind many successful regional resorts around the world, such as Cancun in Mexico (Inskeep, 1991) and Languedoc – Roussillon in France (Klemm, 1992).

State marketing often supports national marketing campaigns, especially where those campaigns encourage visitors to see the whole country and states have an opportunity to highlight their individual attractions. In many cases this provides a chance to promote both well-known resort destinations and to showcase new resort ventures. To build on the awareness level generated by such joint campaigns, states are developing 'one-stop-shopping' contact details where customers can acquire follow-up details and make reservations. But it is in the development of its regional infrastructure that state governments can most influence the development of the resort sector.

The development and location of infrastructure has a major impact on the viability of resort development. The cost of developing the individual resort product is sufficiently taxing for most developers that they rely on state assistance to help bring customers to their door and to provide them with the basic services of power, water and waste disposal. State road systems are needed to bring visitors to the resort entrance, and the more safe and scenic the better. Tapping into power and water grids is far less expensive than providing a self-sufficient service, as is the ability to use approved large scale waste disposal facilities.

One very successful resort operator always ensures it has state and national government support, including infrastructure systems before it commits to the actual building phase of a project. The Disney organization did not convert its purchasing options into actual purchases in central Florida until it had signed agreements with the Florida legislature that supplied a major entrance interchange on Interstate I-4 and entitled it to create its own autonomous municipality, to control the local land use planning and building codes along with other local government responsibilities (Zehnder, 1975). The success of these negotiations was repeated when Disney moved its theme park resort concept to France. As the Disney model for resort development has grown the need for partners has increased, and in France national and state governments were willing to become active partners. 'The land was artificially valued at $5,000 per acre, its value as agricultural land in 1971, and that value was guaranteed for 20 years ... The French would improve the highways to the site and extend the TGV express train at their own expense ... The French government would loan Disney as much as $770 million for the project at an artificially low interest rate of 7.85 per cent, with no repayments for the first five years' (Flower, 1991: 208). All this because of the Disney name and reputation, in the hope that Euro Disneyland (now called Paris Disneyland) would provide the same positive economic boost to a declining rural economy, as it has in central Florida to the previously quiet service town of Orlando.

State interest in resort development can be seen in other ways, including recognition of its ability to create a more positive and hospitable investment environment. A task force was put together by the British Columbia government to 'promote resort development in British Columbia through the identification and elimination of barriers to investment, development and expansion' (BC Resort Task Force, 2004: i). As a result of its inquiry and deliberations the Task Force proposed a province-wide resort strategy that would provide:

- increased business certainty within the economic climate for resort development;
- increased clarity of access for potential resort developers;
- a more predictable investment environment;
- increased exposure in the international tourism market;
- reduced conflict between previously competing users of Crown Lands;
- expanded (four season) use of existing facilities.

(BC Resort Task Force, 2004: 7)

In these and other ways state levels of government are seen as important 'behind the scenes' partners in developing the resort potential of their jurisdictions, especially when it involves linking that development with the general economic and social development of rural areas.

Local governments

Local governments have the responsibility to apply national and state policies, as well as develop their own policies to reflect local conditions and sentiments. 'The essential character and atmosphere of a resort is very much in the hands of local government through the way it influences the activities of the private sector' according to Hughes (1989: 15). Three areas where local government governance has a regular impact on resort development includes, but is not restricted to, local building codes, local liquor licensing rules and gambling laws.

Basic building codes reflect national and state requirements, which set general expectations for safety and security. They cannot be expected to anticipate every individual building situation, so in addition to ensuring existing building codes are followed local councils usually have the right to allow variances to those codes if they do not fit a particular situation, as long as such variances do not negate the objective of the original code. Local liquor laws and hours of operation are a local government responsibility in many parts of the world, with important ramifications for entertainment–recreation complexes like resorts. Some areas still retain a prohibition against the sale of alcohol, which would be a major social and economic blow to many resorts and their budgets. Others have restrictive hours of operation that may require regular appeals for extensions of serving hours, particularly on weekends and public holidays. It all requires resort management to determine the exact local liquor laws and how they may impact business.

Laws regulating gambling are set generally by high levels of government, but their control over this activity is being challenged as local acceptance levels change and global competition develops. Nations which have been opposed to legal gambling for a long time are now reversing their stand as social mores change and the leakage of revenue to illegal gambling or adjacent national systems is proving too strong to resist (Henderson, 2006). At the global level is the growing availability of Internet gambling, which is proving difficult to regulate and is expected to impact customer commitment to casinos by the regular gambler. At the local level authorities have the right to specify operating conditions, such as hours of operation and caps on payouts, but the biggest factor in the US has been the provision of gambling on indigenous native reserves. The hope has been that the development of native reserve casinos, many with associated accommodation, meals and entertainment, would provide employment and revenue for the local tribes people; but according to Hsu (2003: 229) the 'debate continues about the costs and benefits of Native American gaming within tribes, and about the legitimacy of gambling as a Native American enterprise'. What is beyond doubt is that such developments have increased the competition in the gambling market and will intercept some of the travel to major gambling resort destinations.

Multiple levels of governance

As should be apparent from the above discussion of the three major levels of jurisdictional governance, although each level has its prime responsibilities and aspirations for resort development there is considerable overlap in these areas. This becomes evident when considering the development of major resort destinations, either those that have evolved over time or have been planned major developments. An example of the former is Hawaii's involvement with Honolulu and the Waikiki Improvement District regarding Waikiki's role within that state's tourism ambitions. An example of the latter would be South Korea's development of Kyongju as a heritage centre for a nation promoting its cultural roots.

Hawaii's 2005–2015 tourism plan (www.hawaii.gov/tourism/program_planning.html) is a shared vision for Hawaii's tourism future, representing a joint effort from the visitor industry, community, the Hawaii

Tourism Authority (HTA) and other government agencies (HTA, 2004). It recognizes the importance of tourism to the state economy, but notes that after 30 years of steady growth it has now entered the stagnation phase and needs to develop a more coordinated planning approach if it is to 'create the right balance between achieving economic objectives and sustaining Hawaii's natural, physical, cultural and human resources' (HTA, 2004: 4). To achieve this objective its vision is that by 2015 tourism in Hawaii will:

- honour Hawaii's people and heritage;
- value and perpetuate Hawaii's natural and cultural resources;
- engender mutual respect among all stakeholders;
- support a vital and sustainable economy;
- provide a unique, memorable and enriching visitor experience.

(HTA, 2004: 6)

This vision is to be brought about by the cooperation, collaboration and participation of all stakeholders, with the state and country authorities playing a key role. To ensure the strategic plan stays on track several key performance indicators will be monitored. Known as 'measures of success' they will involve regular measurement of visitor satisfaction, visitor spending, state and country tax receipts and resident sentiments.

Waikiki's role in this state-wide strategy is substantial given it is the major tourist destination in the state and frequently acts as a staging post for visitor excursions throughout the island of Oahu and to other islands. In terms of the state's tourism vision the city and county of Honolulu has undertaken a complementary path to a sustainable tourism future, where a renewed and redirected planning focus plays an important role on behalf of the Waikiki resort destination. If we take the five vision targets in order, Waikiki's current and planned contributions to the state plan consist of the following, as drawn from the condensed observations and words of former mayor Jerry Harris (2004):

1. *Honour Hawaii's people and heritage*
   As part of the rebirth of Waikiki, the families of the ancient Hawaiians whose *iwi* had been disturbed came together to plan a memorial site where their ancestors' bones could be respectfully re-interred and honoured appropriately. To teach more visitors about the history of Waikiki and its people, bronze surfboard markers with historic information have been erected at selected sites throughout the peninsula (Figure 5.1).

Figure 5.1 Heritage tours and markers in Waikiki, Hawaii.

2. *Value and perpetuate Hawaii's natural and cultural resources*

   Wai is the Hawaiian word for freshwater. One way to ensure that we don't use more water than is being recharged is to conserve water and reduce consumption and waste. To accomplish this goal, an array of conservation and reuse programs have been established. As a result of these creative initiatives, Oahu's daily water consumption today is 20 million gallons less than earlier demand projections.

   Tourism needs to promote and celebrate the host culture and provide support and resources for its perpetuation. To provide opportunities for more cultural events in Waikiki, a hula performance mound was created under the historic banyan tree. Now visitors can enjoy local dance and music performances every night at Kuhio Beach.

3. *Engender mutual respect among all stakeholders*

   Over the last six years, we have worked to empower the people of this island to be active participants in creating and realizing a shared vision of their future. The results of this experiment in grass roots democracy have been remarkable, sometimes stunning successes and sometimes disappointing defeats; but what emerged from the messy democratic process was a new community-based vision for the future of Honolulu. The real legacy of the 21st Century Vision for Oahu is an empowered citizenry, knowledgeable about sustainability, and dedicated to improving the quality of life on this island.

4. *Support a vital and sustainable economy*

   We need to diversify our visitor industry into (various) niche markets, and eco-tourism provides us an opportunity to do so sustainably. By attracting visitors to our island to enjoy unique environmental experiences, we can grow our visitor industry as we protect and enhance our environmental assets. There is no better example of this principle than the story of Hanauma Bay, where a flooded volcanic cone produces a rich sea life that was in danger of being overwhelmed by visitors until ecological controls were implemented.

5. *Provide a unique, memorable and enriching visitor experience*

   People travel from around the world to experience the Hawaiian culture and enjoy our pristine environment. Yet in developing tourism, development was destroying the very things visitors were coming to experience. Honolulu's pristine environment was being damage. The unique cultural experience people were coming to enjoy was cheapened and mass-produced. Visitors seeking authenticity found only parody.

By the 1990s, Honolulu had lost its 'Hawaiian sense of place'. Years of inattention to urban design, landscaping, and cultural heritage had turned Waikiki into 'Anywhere USA'.

To plan for Oahu's economic recovery required several initiatives. The first step of the plan was to bolster our core economy by revitalizing Waikiki. The second step was to diversify our tourism base so that visitors would come to our island for more than the Waikiki experience. The new visitor markets the city targeted were sports tourism, eco-tourism and cultural/edu-tourism.

From architecture and urban design culture and arts programs, the Hawaiian sense of place is returning to Waikiki.

Inskeep (1991) in his comprehensive text on tourism planning makes reference to the multiple levels of government involved in the planned conception and growth of several resort destinations, that were intended to generate regional development and other objectives from the start. One that involved multiple layers of governance is the Kyongju area in South Korea. 'The Kyongju project which involved various central government agencies and the Kyongju tourism agency, with some World Bank involvement, includes the city of Kyongju, Bomun Lake, and ruins of 14 historic sites, including some royal tombs' (Inskeep, 1991: 201). Here the objective was not only to improve the economy of an isolated rural area, but to 'build an international resort city based on the ancient Korean culture of the Shilla Dynasty' (Inskeep, 1991: 201). In the process a small domestic tourist destination has been transformed into a major regional resort environment that provides both an economic injection to this rural part of South Korea and a tribute to national pride – as evidenced by the large number of school groups who visit the area. Such a dual function within government supported resort development is common, especially in terms of conserving the environment while profiting from it.

Dual mandate situations

Dual mandate resorts and situations are most common in terms of national or state park systems. Governments have a responsibility to conserve the natural environments of these public properties, while providing recreation access to the same areas. It is a management challenge of

monumental proportions because the goals of conservation and access are in perpetual conflict: resulting in 'pro-development' versus 'no development' factions bombarding various levels of government, as the owners-in-trust, with their respective cases. The situation is becoming more tense as natural landscapes disappear under the pressure of global population increases and growing demands for resources, including space. Resorts have been part of the problem or answer, depending on one's development stance, since the early days.

When the railways opened up the western states/provinces of North America in the nineteenth century, they saw the attraction of their wilderness areas and the economic potential they held for tourism. As a consequence magnificent resort hotels were constructed in the newly created national parks of Banff and Yellowstone, and elsewhere (Stern, 1986). This association between resorts and parks has continued around the world, from the game reserves of Africa to the 'social tourism' of state park resorts in the US and other countries. But such an association has been fraught with debate and rancour.

Some authors in North America have argued that wilderness reserves should be larger and left to nature's development cycles rather than managed along the lines of a plantation or farm, with their zoning and multiple use strategies (Chase, 1987). Others suggest that if people do take up their right of public access to the national parks they should do so on the same self-reliant terms as the pioneers, and not expect creature comforts to be provided or their walking paths to be made smooth (Sax, 1980). But even though North America is still blessed with such space and spirit these dreams are proving hard to achieve in this age of fiscal and personal accountability. Not even the US can afford to freeze resource assets in its wilderness and national park areas, as demonstrated by the regular encroachment of oil drilling in Alaska and forestry and mining in the western states. Nor can one turn back the clock to the pioneer days and tell visitors they are 'on their own' once they have been admitted to a park, because there is the 'duty of care' responsibility that comes with admittance. Failure to uphold such a responsibility is punished severely in the courts, as will be discussed in the later chapter on 'Risk Management'.

Resorts will need to be part of national park dual mandate planning because as the early railway development showed, they can be a viable partner in such a management situation. They can provide the appropriate 'duty of care' within their zoned area, appealing to the type of guest who has come to appreciate and support the conservation efforts of the park. Such guests are willing to pay for the privilege, which in turn helps to provide some financial support for the conservation objectives of the park. Resorts accept that under these conditions there will be restrictions placed on their development options, but as long as there is sufficient latitude for them to operate at a profit (if it is a commercial venture) or to break even (if it is a government venture) then most are able to operate within the guidelines and to form valuable and positive relationships with the parks' other goals.

An example of the governance challenges facing governments and resorts in park situations can be seen with the government planning for alpine resorts in Australia. After an extensive period of consultation with a wide range of stakeholders the Victorian state government has drawn up a development strategy for its alpine resorts that demonstrates many of the issues and opportunities mentioned above (Victoria, 2004).

The Victorian Alps bioregion is land above 1200 metres in altitude and extends approximately 3000 square kilometres along the Great Dividing Range. Within that large area are six peaks or high plateaus where snow sports are possible and most of that land is Crown land, held in public ownership. Historically, each resort has been managed by a different agency, but in 1997 the Victoria state government proclaimed the Alpine Resorts (Management) Act which established an Alpine Resort Management Board for each resort. The functions of these boards include, but are not restricted to, the following:

- preparation and implementation of a Strategic Management Plan for each resort;
- to act as a committee of management for crown land within the resorts;
- to develop a tourism and marketing strategy for each resort;
- to collect fees for the resort;
- to attract investment for the resort.

(Victoria, 2004: 45)

The vision for the six alpine resorts within Victoria, Australia has been built around six broad and common issues. These are presented below in terms of the *issue* and their associated goal *response*.

Climate change issue: Global warming is an issue for all snow resorts, but especially those in Australia where the mountains are relatively low and the snowfall unreliable.

Response: Resorts, especially those at higher elevations will remain committed to a snow tourism industry and proactively plan for the impacts of climate change. This includes more investment in snowmaking equipment and the provision of a variety of snow activities for a nation that can only experience the delights of a day in the snow at such rare locations within Australia.

Resort use and visitation patterns: They are primarily focussed on a few short winter months, leading to crowded and expensive facilities when it snows.

Response: The resorts will provide high quality recreation experiences and safe access for both winter and non-winter seasons. This involves the development of a four-season approach to the resorts' management, attempting to highlight mountain attractions outside of the snow season and creating an alternative to the magnetism of Australia's beaches.

Development directions issue: Resorts need to be distinctive and appealing, with a continual respect for the natural regions within which they are situated.

Response: Resorts will be expected to enhance their visitors' experience by 'providing attractive, ecologically sustainable mountain townships that have local character and a distinct sense of place in the landscape'.

Vibrant economic entities issue: The alpine snow resorts 'contribute an additional A$129 million and 3740 jobs to the Victorian economy', but most of this happens over a few hectic weeks and the rest of the year they are quiet backwaters of the tourism industry.

Response: Each resort needs to develop an investment strategy that identifies their specific opportunities and will encourage them to build on their current levels of economic activity. Some have started to emulate the real estate model the North American ski resorts, others are attempting to build an education–sport–culture base.

Environmental management issue: The pristine environment is what distinguishes these mountain areas from their surrounding forestry and agricultural regions and that needs to be protected through careful management.

Response: Resorts should be developed and managed within an ecologically sustainable framework. This will include careful water

131

management as investment in snow-making increases and the head-waters of the local river system need to be protected against overuse and pollution.

Stewardship of public land issue: The government responsibility for public land and the need to make it available to a variety of users, some of who will have conflicting interests, requires a direct 'on-site' approach to management, rather than relying on broad-based policy directives from the capital city.

Response: The creation of the Alpine Resort Management Boards to provide a local body of government and user stakeholders are expected to implement government policies with a local perspective and touch. They are instructed to embrace the stewardship role and to work collaboratively with local communities and interest groups.

Within this system of governance lies the key issue of land ownership. Even in public land regions like the Victorian Alps in Australia there are areas under private ownership, and within the resort area crown lands there are people and businesses that have secured long-term leases of up to 99 years. Where these incursions into public land have occurred the government's rights and obligations take on a different tone.

Land ownership and leases

Whether a resort has complete or partial control over its land ownership will strongly determine its development options. As has been stated above, even when a resort has clear title and absolute ownership of its land it is restricted in its development options by various government laws and guidelines. But the situation becomes much more constrictive if a resort is simply leasing the land. A common leasehold situation arises when a resort is located on crown/public land. That land is owned by the people through its government and there are often strict conditions on how it can be used and how long a business like a resort can have guaranteed access to it.

Access and use is determined by the length of lease that grants the resort monopoly control over the allocated land for a set period of time. The time period can range from 25 to 99 years. The longer the lease period, the more time the resort has to amortize its initial investments and a greater chance to obtain an attractive return on investment. Plus, the longer the lease the more saleable is the business, should the original developers wish to move on. But whether a resort is on a short or long lease there is always a shut down period when the lease enters its final years, and there is little attraction in enhancing or buying a facility that is due to be handed back to its original owner.

Access to public land via a lease is just part of the negotiation process when a resort deals with a government property, because there are often associated development conditions and restrictions. This is particularly true with respect to environmentally sensitive areas such as national or state parks, and also in the case of cultural attractions. If the resort is to be located in such high profile tourism areas it can expect strict restrictions on its development and activity profile, which can impact its potential revenue return. Common restrictions include limits on a resort's size and height that reflect its footprint on the sensitive environment; the type of building style that will maintain its harmony with the surrounding environment; the type of activities that are considered appropriate to the local environment and society.

Summary

This chapter has examined the issue of corporate and political governance and their considerable influence on the development options for resorts. In terms of corporate governance major investments like resorts need to answer to a variety of business stakeholders, and as public companies become more involved the growing separation between investors and operators throws up additional challenges. One area where governments can have a great influence on resort development is in relation to publicly owned land like national parks, which increasingly need more private investment to help deliver their dual mandate.

Given the growing significance of the 'experience economy' and resorts' potential role within it, more levels of government are enacting permissive legislation to encourage resort development, especially where the traditional economic structure is struggling to compete in the global economy. The government policies and financing that has aided resort development show resorts can be used as modern agents of change, to create centres of employment and amenity that can stimulate local growth and confidence. The case of the Singapore government's renewed interest in its Sentosa Island opportunities presents an example of this approach and thinking.

To conclude this chapter on governance and policy it would be instructive to illustrate the machinations that can emerge from such entanglements. It is reported in *The Economist* (2004) that the ski resort town of Killington, Vermont, USA is considering seceding from its home state and pledging its allegiance to the neighbouring state of New Hampshire. The reason is a variation of the old war cry 'taxation without representation', in this case an angry town 'which gives the state $21M a year in taxes, but receives only one-tenth of that back'. *The Economist* points out there is a well-known local precedent for such a move, but notes it will be difficult to achieve in this case because 'the mountain whose ski slopes provide the town's main revenue is owned by Vermont' – in other words it is a public good which has provided the revenue in the first place.

Case study

Victoria's Alpine Resorts

The State of Victoria in Australia has developed an *Alpine Resorts 2020 Strategy* (Victoria, 2004) after considerable consultation with various stakeholder groups and the national science research group (CSIRO) in terms of the impact of global warming on the sustainability of skiing in these alpine regions of Australia. This document and its directives concerning the future development of ski resorts in this fragile area confirm the state's extensive powers through its designated agencies – the Alpine Resorts Coordinating Council and Alpine Resorts Management Boards. A level of authority that far exceeds the ski resort experiences in Europe and North America according to Tomsett's (2006) assessment in Figure 5.2. That composite figure reveals Australian government agencies have

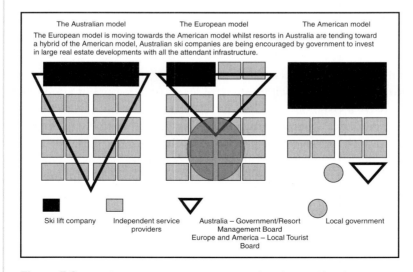

Figure 5.2 Various governance patterns within the world's ski resorts (Tomsett, 2006).

far more control over the actions of the ski companies and other resort service providers than is experienced in either Europe or North America, so it is important to see what level of progress such central planning and control can produce.

The Alpine Resorts Coordinating Council's primary role is to coordinate the individual Alpine Resort Management Boards' operational approaches to the plan, to ensure the implementation of its strategy. It is the management boards, made up of government appointees, which are responsible for the development of each individual resort. These resorts compose only small sections of intensively developed land, representing only 3.5 per cent within the alpine bioregion, but can leave a much bigger footprint on the whole region. Thus it is felt that their individual efforts need to be monitored and coordinated by the council in order to retain control over the entire bioregion and to present a unified alpine marketing image.

In terms of meeting the recreation interest in this part of Australia the principal strategic objective of the strategy is to create four-season, vibrant and sustainable alpine resorts (Victoria, 2004: 5). The CSIRO research indicates the large high altitude resorts will remain viable for snow-based recreation through to 2020, with the continued help of artificial snow-making, so the challenge is to make these resorts more appealing. To achieve this the resorts will need to provide high quality experiences to compete for the tourist dollar and will need to create a summer appeal that is capable of diverting some of the traditional Australian beach traffic inland to the mountains.

In terms of its conservation objectives the strategy proposes both improved environmental management and stewardship. The environmental management encompasses important areas like maintenance of the region's flora and fauna, which has already brought it into conflict with the cattlemen who have traditionally grazed their stock in these areas; and water management which involves maintenance of the headwaters that supply the farms and towns of the surrounding lowlands and are susceptible to drought. In addition there is the overall responsibility of stewardship for these lands, because 'the alpine resorts (and surrounding land) are owned by the Crown and managed for and on behalf of all Victorians' (Victoria, 2004: 34). Thus, the state government is duty bound to ensure these assets are available for future generations.

To pay for these recreation and conservation objectives will require a lot of money, but the strategy says little about where this money will come from and leaves it to the ingenuity of the various Alpine Resort Management Boards to 'attract investment for the resort' (Victoria, 2004: 45). However, senior government and the private sector are starting to come together in order to provide the capital needed to achieve the strategic objectives, by emphasizing the potential synergies that exist within the dual mandate. One of the catalysts in this process is the Tourism and Transport Forum (TTF) of Australia. It is encouraging the exploration of public–private partnerships (PPPs) to bring about new and quality resort development in or adjacent to national parks that can meet the objectives of both sides of the dual mandate. Through its *Natural Tourism Partnerships Initiative* TTF hopes 'to enhance the economic capacity of park agencies to conserve our natural efforts' (www.ttf.org.au). More discussion of this growing interest in PPPs can be found in Chapter 6.

Questions

1 Consider the frictions that could develop between corporate and political governance in a resort situation and discuss ways in which these frictions may be turned into positive partnerships.

2 Examine the stewardship theory of environmental management and discuss how relevant that has been and may continue to be for the resort sector.

3 Take a developing national economy of your choice and examine how the government of such an economy could create tourism development policies that would encourage sustainable development and management for its resorts.

4 If government policy is to be 'government for the people by the people', how can governments share their responsibility for public lands with the private sector?

5 Although it is often local government which is at the coal face of resort development it has the smallest level of resources to manage such businesses. How would you suggest a resort manager and local council approach this situation if they wish to develop an harmonious partnership of interests?

6 Consider the length of lease would you negotiate for a local or national resort, and explain your reasons and priorities for such negotiations.

7 Critically assess the Victoria government's *Alpine Resorts 2020 Strategy* in terms of Australia's love affair with summer beach holidays.

References

BC Resort Task Force (2004). *Recommendations of the B.C. Resort Task Force.* Canada, Victoria, BC: Minister of State for Resort Development.

Chase, A. (1987). *Playing God in Yellowstone.* San Diego: Harcourt Brace Jovanovich.

Christaller, W. (1964). Some considerations of tourism location in Europe. *Papers and Proceedings of the Regional Science Association,* **12**, 95–105.

Daily, C.M., Dalton, D.R. and Rajagopalan, N. (2003). Governance through ownership: centuries of practice, decades of research. *Academy of Management Journal,* **46(2)**, 151–158.

Dalton, D.R., Daily, C.M., Ellstrand, A.E. and Johnson, J.L. (1998). Meta-analytical reviews of board composition, leadership structure, and financial performance. *Strategic Management Journal,* **19**, 269–290.

Elliott, J. (1997). *Tourism: Politics and Public Sector Management.* London: Routledge.

eTN (2006). Hilton's claims of responsible development are a 'greenwash'. *Travel Wire News,* 1–3. news@travelwirenews.com. Accessed on 26 July 2006.

Flower, J. (1991). *Prince of the Magic Kingdom.* New York: John Wiley and sons.

Harris, J. (2004). *The Renaissance of Honolulu.* Honolulu: City and County of Honolulu.

Hawaii Tourism Authority (HTA) (2004). *Hawaii tourism strategic plan: 2005–2015.* http://www.hawaii.gov/tourism/program-planning.html. Accessed on 8 August 2005.

Henderson, J. (2006). Betting on casino tourism in Asia: Singapore's integrated resorts. *Tourism Review International,* **10(3)**, 169–179.

Howatson, A.C. (1990). *Toward Proactive Environmental Management: Lessons from Canadian Corporate Experience.* Ottawa: The Conference Board of Canada.

Hsu, C.H.C. (2003). Social impacts of Native American Casino Gambling. In *Legalized Casino Gaming in the United States* (C.H.C. Hsu, ed.), pp. 221–232. New York: Haworth Hospitality Press.

Hughes, H.L. (1989). Resorts: a fragmented product in need of coalescence. *International Journal of Hospitality Management,* **8(1)**, 15–17.

Inskeep, E. (1991). *Tourism Planning: An Integrated and Sustainable Development Approach.* New York: Van Nostrand Reinhold.

Klemm, M. (1992). Sustainable tourism development: Languedoc–Roussillon thirty years on. *Tourism Management,* **13(2)**, 169–180.

Lundgren, J. (1983). Development patterns and lessons in the Montreal Laurentians. In *Tourism in Canada: Selected Issues and Options* (P.E. Murphy, ed.), Western

Geographical Series, Vol. 21. Canada, Victoria, BC: University of Victoria, pp. 95–126.

Michael, E.J. (2006). *Public Policy: the Competitive Framework* Melbourne: Oxford University Press.

Montgomery, G. and Murphy, P.E. (1983). Government involvement in tourism development: A case study of TIDSA implementation in British Columbia. In *Tourism in Canada: Selected Issues and Options* (P.E. Murphy, ed.), Western Geographical Series, Vol. 21, pp. 183–209. Canada, Victoria, BC: University of Victoria.

Peet, R. with Hartwick, E. (1999). *Theories of Development*. New York: The Guilford Press.

Pine, R. (2002). China's hotel industry – serving a massive market. *Cornell Hotel and Restaurant Administration Quarterly*, **43(3)**, 61–70.

Sax, J.L. (1980). *Mountains without Handrails*. Ann Arbor, Michigan: University of Michigan Press.

Stern, R.A.M. (1986). *Pride of Place – Building the American Dream*. Boston: Houghton-Mifflin.

Tang, F.F., Xi, Y., Chen, G. and Wang, R. (2006). Ownership, corporate governance, and management in the state-owned hotels in the People's Republic of China. *Cornell Hotel and Restaurant Administration Quarterly*, **47(2)**, 182–191.

The Economist (2004). Snowballing to freedom: A ski resort's revolution against taxation. March 13, 37.

Tomsett, P. (2006). *Stakeholder Analysis of Tourism Strategies: Case Study of Victorian Alpine Resorts*. Unpublished Ph.D. Thesis. School of Sport, Tourism and Hospitality Management, La Trobe University, Melbourne, Australia.

Victoria (2004). *Alpine Resorts 2020 Strategy*. Melbourne: Department of Sustainability and Environment.

Zadek, S. (2004). The path to corporate responsibility. *Harvard Business Review*, **82**, 125–132.

Zehnder, L. (1975). *Florida's Disney World: Promises and Problems*. Tallahassee, Florida: Peninsula Publishing.

Part
C

Internal challenges and
strategies for resort
management

6

Planning and financial management

Introduction

Resorts as businesses must take control of internal matters and challenges at the earliest opportunity, if they are to fulfil their original vision and become sustainable financial enterprises. The link between planning and finance has been made clear by Gee (1996: 91), who in the opening sentence to his planning and development chapter states:

> The process of resort planning and development is basically an economic one, and all other goals – social and environment – must be subordinated to, yet integrated with, the economic objective.

Hence this opening chapter of Part C will start with an examination of the planning process and how this crucial first stage often sets the scene for a successful or disastrous financial future.

The planning process in this context refers to the generic nature of planning – a scheme of action or procedure for the future. As such it incorporates the dreaming that leads to a vision; the conceptualization that creates the physical form and environmental setting for that vision; the business management strategies that are designed to produce the maximum effectiveness and efficiency from an often considerable investment; while either accepting imposed corporate social responsibilities or setting new and higher standards of sustainable development. These are not necessarily separate and independent stages within a planning process, for in a business situation the financial implications and possibilities will need to be considered at each stage. They are, however, universal components of the planning system and should operate at all levels, be it for a single resort hotel facility, an integrated resort complex or a broader urban resort destination.

The financial discussion within this chapter is equally generic, referring to the management of expenditures and revenue throughout the development of a resort. It attempts to set the big picture rather than enter the domain of modern accounting principles and procedures. It highlights the length of time some resorts take to reach the fulfilment of their vision and how different financial priorities will arise with the various stages of development.

Planning process

It should be appreciated that the planning process will differ in detail with each resort development. Major differences include whether it is a greenfield site or part of an urban complex, complete with neighbours who have existing rights and expectations; whether it is a privately owned or leased property; and the governance system operating at the resort site. However, within each situation a generic planning process still applies.

The development situation can vary from the isolated and undeveloped conditions of a greenfield site in rural regions to a central and developed site within an urban region, or anywhere in between. The various development situations will involve different cost structures regarding the provision of infrastructure, construction and labour. In times of economic growth and optimistic outlooks it is tempting to let the dream overwhelm the financial realities of a development situation. During Australia's major resort development in the 1980s, many resorts 'were funded on unrealistic expectations of the strength of resort demand and poor understanding of resort investment principles' (Ernst and Young,

2003: 7). As a result 'ego investments, dumb planning and boosterism have led some developments that were never going to return a profit' into receivership according to Chris Brown, CEO of the Tourism and Transport Forum of Australia (Ernst and Young, 2003: 3). In Australia and elsewhere, it is often the second or third owners who turn such resort dreams into profitable businesses by applying more realistic financial yardsticks and/or revising the market emphasis of the previous owners.

It is not just the developers and owners who are involved with the planning process of resorts, for there are generally other stakeholders involved. Among these are members of local communities, be they the neighbours and residents in an urban area or the neighbours and indigenous owners of wilderness areas and traditional sites. They will generally welcome the employment and business opportunities that a resort can bring, but will expect a sensitive development that integrates with the local landscape and culture. There are operators of core and secondary businesses within the resort, who will need to conduct sufficient business to pay their annual leases and meet their corporate obligations, such as joint marketing campaigns. There is always the government that is keen to enlarge its tax base, even on a deferred basis, to support the growing expectations and responsibilities of society around the world.

It becomes the responsibility of the planner to attempt to meet the needs of stakeholder groups in a manner that meets the profit objectives of a resort business, within the expectations and constraints of a variety of concepts and policies. To achieve this, planners have adopted three types of planning tools to create 'a strategic vision for an area which reflects a community's goals and aspirations, and implementing this through the identification of preferred patterns of land use and appropriate styles of development' (Dredge, 1999: 774). The three types of planning tools are – process, functional and normative, and each is discussed below.

Process tools

Process tools are concerned with the nature of the planning process and focus on the steps involved in providing a comprehensive coverage of the issues involved. In terms of resorts there have been two principal contributors in this regard, Inskeep and Gee. Inskeep (1991: 202) provides a comprehensive road map for the planning of resorts which contains some of the points this chapter is emphasizing (Figure 6.1). The first step is to conduct a *market analysis* for the type of resort product under consideration.

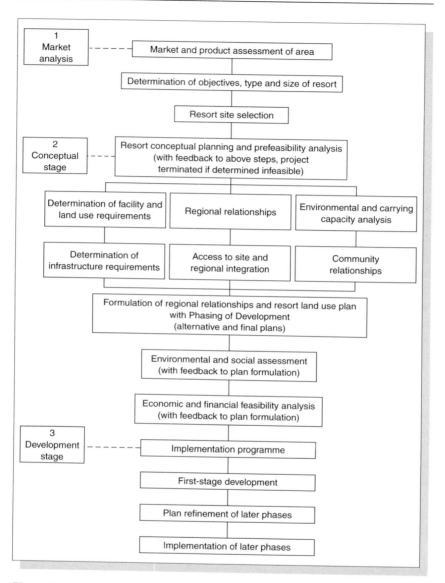

Figure 6.1 Resort planning process. (After Inskeep, 1991: 202)

If there is no or limited consumer interest in the resort developer's dream it should end there. At the *conceptual stage* regional business and community relationships need to be explored and the resort plan drawn up with the appropriate consultation of key stakeholders. This is followed by a phased *development*, which in bigger projects usually requires set stages of development during which various forms of financing are secured and various types of revenue generation pursued to maintain debt repayment and cash flow. Given the length of time development can take, it is quite possible that the original plan will require some modification and later phases may be quite different from the original vision.

Walt Disney's plans for Walt Disney World are a good illustration of the need for flexibility. In the original plans EPCOT was intended to be the 'Experimental Prototype Community of Tomorrow', which incorporated a combination of Disney engineering and forward looking planning to produce a utopian city of the future. Unfortunately Walt Disney died before this phase of the resort project could be developed, so it lost its champion. Instead of the envisioned EPCOT the Disney management took advantage of a new opportunity, developing its second theme park within Walt Disney World as a continuous International Exhibition. By partnering with major corporations and a selected number of countries Disney has created a technology and travel theme park with minimum direct investment. Walt Disney's initial EPCOT dream has not been forgotten and has since emerged in the form of 'Celebration' – a new town planned from scratch that attempts to create an ideal urban environment.

Gee presents the resort development process as five distinct but overlapping phases (Figure 6.2). The first phase is *conceptualization, planning and initiation*. He mentions that the original idea for a resort can come from a wide range of sources, including hotel management companies, public or quasi-public agencies and special interest groups as well as developers and property owners (private or public). These initiating groups will not always have the same objectives and images for the resort, so considerable negotiation will be needed at times. For example, 'long-range investment thinking often conflicts with a strong cash-flow orientation (including cash dividends to stockholders); some parties have long-term tax shelters in mind while others prefer to sell the project upon completion. Problems frequently arise as to whether an owner and/or developer's wishes should override those of professional planners and designers' (Gee, 1996: 95).

Gee emphasizes the long time span required for this first phase, an investment in time and resources that many do not appreciate because it is invisible to the public. Given the complexity of developing a modern resort, which can include the size and component parts of a small town, the planning process requires a project flow chart showing each step in logical sequence with its component parts in place before the first paying

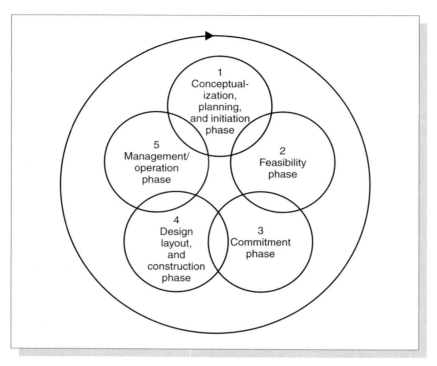

Figure 6.2   Phases of the resort development process (Gee, 1996: 95).

guest arrives. For large projects it is best to obtain the necessary land either as an option to buy or lease and on the condition that the final plan is accepted by the local government authorities. Better to lose thousands of dollars in failing to convert options into purchases by the assigned due dates, than to loose millions on a project that is doomed to failure because planning permission has been withheld.

The second phase of *feasibility analysis* helps to make the judgement on proceeding with the project or backing out. It is obviously linked with phase one but has been placed second because there has to be a preliminary product plan and targeted market segment in place, before an assessment can proceed. The tangible aspects of the proposed plan (supply side) and market (demand side) should be analysed by a reputable third party, so as to obtain arms-length objectivity to the dreams that have driven the project to this stage. If the feasibility results are disappointing this should lead to a modification of the initial plan or the withdrawal from taking up land options and conditional agreements.

The third phase is the *commitment* stage, when everything becomes public. Formal agreements and legal documents are signed and registered. The assembled land is acquired, the land use plan is submitted to local authorities and more committed financing is put into place. It is at this stage that the project must submit environmental impact statements for approval along with seeking additional permits for shoreline management, water rights and waste disposal where applicable.

The fourth phase involves the actual *design, layout and construction* of the resort. Local environmental conditions and the desired image determine the design to a large extent. The spatial layout of the resort, working with local zoning and building codes, is used to group co-habitable activities together and to separate conflicting activities. Construction needs to be of a high quality to entice guests and the buyers of condominiums and to maintain appearances when large numbers visit the site.

The fifth phase is the *management and operation* stage that occurs prior to the actual opening and during the resort's operation. It involves an aggressive sales and marketing campaign, the recruitment and training of staff and the finalization of contracts with suppliers and partners like transport companies. It is at this stage when 'both management and employees alike must operate the resort the way it was intended to operate' (Gee, 1996: 121), bringing to life the earlier visioning and planning so that a distinctive and attractive resort is created.

With the amount of detail to be considered in the development process of a resort it comes as no surprise that it is often a long process, frequently involving several detours and actual changes. Along the way negotiations regarding land and other costs, rights, access, variances and financing will close some doors of opportunity while opening others. One can be almost certain that the final product will be somewhat different from the original dream and definitely certain that a lot of money will be spent before the first paying customer arrives. A good example of this process occurred with the development of Walt Disney World in Florida.

A fascinating account of the resort development phases is provided by the development experience of Disney World, as related by Zehnder (1975). He provides a detailed description of the development and opening of what has become one of the world's most successful resort destinations; but all of this was born out of secrecy and last minute negotiations before the physical development took place and the new Disney show piece was opened. Walt Disney was looking for a second theme park site closer to the purchasing power of the eastern and mid-west states, plus he wanted land to buffer his creations from the type of parasitical development that had grown up around his original Disneyland theme park in California. This was why in comparison to the 230 acres (93 hectares) at Disneyland, he assembled a property of 27 400 acres (11 089 hectares) in Florida, an area approximately the size of San Francisco at that time.

Most of the land was poor quality grazing land including a considerable area of swamp, which was selected primarily for its location and price. The location near Orlando in central Florida was away from the expensive coastal real estate but at a prime crossroads, linking central Florida with the northern states and Miami and the Florida Keys to the south, plus the east and west coasts of Florida. The marginal farmland close to Orlando was 'acquired at an average price of less than $200 per acre' (Zehnder, 1975: 14) which was presumably its true agricultural value at that time. It was only possible to achieve agricultural prices by purchasing it piecemeal through dummy companies, in order to conceal the identity and purpose of the real purchaser and have the price raised in anticipation of the land's created value. This process took 18 months, before any public announcement of the Disney project was made, but of course there was growing speculation about the 'mystery industry' coming to Orlando.

The official announcement of the Disney plan was made on 15 November 1965; but the project was still not guaranteed to proceed. The Disney corporation then made it known they would require state and local cooperation before they would proceed with their grand plans for the area. Before they could open they needed highway links to the interstate system, 'because 80% of the tourists who visit Florida came by automobile Disney World was impossible without them' (Zehnder, 1975: 48). To convert central Florida scrub and swamp land into an attractive setting for its initial Magic Kingdom theme park and EPCOT, plus provide surrounding support facilities, the Disney Corporation required the creation of an autonomous political district. This would enable them to construct the water management, infrastructure and building according to their own high standards and international market levels, but required lengthy negotiations with government. This became a reality in May 1967, when 'after 19 months of conversation Disney World in Florida (became) a reality' (Zehnder, 1975: 108). The autonomous Reedy Creek Improvement District and the developments within it not only could set their own and often higher standards of infrastructure development and building; they could benefit also from more favourable financial assistance through the municipal bond market and could qualify for state municipal grants in areas like low-cost housing grants.

The construction of such a mammoth project was undertaken in stages and is still underway today, 40 plus years on from its original conception. The final plans for the original development stage were made public in April 1969, after months had been spent clearing land, draining swamps, building raised land masses and setting up a water management scheme that would ensure the expensive theme parks and support services would not be flooded during Florida's wet season. The plans called for a 'Vacation Kingdom' to be constructed around a 200 acre (81 hectares) man-made lagoon and a 450 acre (182 hectare) natural lake, five related resort hotels of 500–700 rooms, a transport network of monorail, water craft and land vehicles, golf courses, riding trails and an entertainment centre. Once the resort started to take shape Walt Disney World needed to hire and train '6200 staff (of whom) 5500 were between 17 and 22 years of age' (Zehnder, 1975: 215). So an important facility is the 'casting' centre, where staff are trained in their specific tasks and indoctrinated with the Disney culture or 'magic'. Before the first guests arrived the site had to be prepared for their impact, which included a tertiary sewage treatment plant and solid waste incinerator (Murphy, 1997). When everything was in place and everyone ready to fulfil their role Walt Disney World opened, on 1 October 1971. In its first year of operation 'Disney World attracted 10 712 991 visitors and recorded a gross revenue of $139 million' (Zehnder, 1975: 242). This was after an 8.5-year gestation period and an investment of around $1 billion (1970 dollars) in the project.

Functional tools

Functional tools are the theories and techniques that explain the way resorts develop and function. 'Derived principally from systems theory . . . the more ambitious functional theories attempt to explain the dynamic relationship between human behaviour and structure of settlement forms' (Dredge, 1999: 775). Classic examples of this type of tool are the morphological models of traditional coastal resort development. These show the dual locational attraction of the beachfront and regional access via a railway station or road connection, with the various functional land uses drawn out from those centres to provide the maximum convenience for the customer and maximum return on the land (Pearce, 1989; Smith, 1992). Others include the type of theories discussed in Chapter 2.

An example of the morphological and life cycle approaches in terms of resorts is Jan Lundgren's early work in the Caribbean and Canada. His study of Montreal's Laurentian mountains, to the north of the city, examines the resort changes that have occurred within that city's recreational hinterland. Among Lundgren's (1983) observations are:

- Instead of steady evolutionary growth patterns the Laurentians experienced shifts in development. These were based on 'abrupt' changes in consumer recreation preferences, changing from an early appreciation of relaxing in a winter/summer environment, to more active alpine skiing and snowmobiling. Similar rapid changes occurred with the transport infrastructure, where the rail connection was replaced by country roads and then freeways, each having its own morphological impact on resort locations and success.
- The recreational utility of the Laurentians' natural landscape has changed with the above market and supply conditions.
- The classical recreational land use in intensity and land value gradient has changed over time, spreading outward from the original concentrations around the early railway stations.
- External forces to the marketplace, such as government policies, had a significant impact, as in the case of new parks or sponsored snowmobile trails, and the creation of development zones.
- As the area became more popular ownership moved from private to corporate. 'Private individual ownership is increasingly replaced by corporate and crown land ownership . . . (creating) opportunities for corporate investment, on a large scale, in commercial recreational projects, should profitable opportunities present themselves as the massification occurs' (Lundgren, 1983: 122). Something which has continued with the recent Intrawest investment at Mont Tremblant.

Normative tools

Normative tools 'deal with the generalizable connections between human values and settlement form' (Dredge, 1999: 776), as illustrated in Chapter 2. Normative tools emerge from the theories which attempt to explain and predict the 'norms' of human behaviour, which while being the apex of academic enquiry are often 'more nebulous than the preceding groups (of tools) for resort managers' (Dredge, 1999: 776). Two distinct normative theories and tools have particular relevance for resort business and management.

Christaller (1964), one of the founders of central place theory which explains the spacing and hierarchy of urban places, discussed the logical outcome of such a theory on recreation and leisure. In order to maintain a national demand for the goods and services of urban centres some way needs to be found to generate income in rural regions; and Christaller suggests a key way to prime this pump is to use the recreational assets of rural regions. In this way he envisages a continual circulation of income, with rural region's spending their recreation and agricultural revenues in the major urban centres, to buy the products and services they need. This has certainly been the thinking of many central and regional governments. They are attempting to stem the outward migration from their rural regions by bringing new industries and activities to rural areas, to provide the employment and amenities that will keep more locals at home and encourage new visitors and residents.

In many jurisdictions a key feature of such policies has been the development of resorts and associated real estate and support industry investment. In effect using resorts as growth poles. Canada pursued this policy with its Travel Industry Development Subsidiary Agreements (TIDSA) (Montgomery and Murphy, 1983), and Wales with its South Pembrokeshire Partnership for Action with Rural Communities (SPARC) (Sharpley and Sharpley, 1997: 38–39). The State of Victoria in Australia has been encouraging tourism development outside of Melbourne in order to spread the benefits of this industry throughout the state, and an important aspect of that is the opportunity for resort development. Under its 'product development' objectives Victoria wants to develop 'product that meets the needs and expectations of priority markets and helps to dispense visitors geographically and seasonally' (Victoria, 2002: 93). Among the state's identified 10 primary product segments are:

- Food and wine
- Nature-based tourism
- Alpine/ski
- Golf
- Events.

All of which can be accommodated in resort environments.

By bringing resorts into regional economic development as development nodes or growth poles, resorts can provide the critical mass needed to stimulate consumer and investment interest in the recreational opportunities of rural regions. In this way they can help to complete the income circle envisaged by Christaller, linking the rural and urban economies into a mutually beneficial economic partnership.

Another normative approach to tourism development has been at the level of actual resort development and planning, by creating a systematically planned 'vacationscape'. The pioneering work of Clare Gunn through the various editions of his book *Vacationscape* has provided a comprehensive description and prescriptive model of resort development, one that incorporates the human, physical and business needs of an ideal resort experience. Gunn (1997: 67) views resorts as destinations, which in turn are collections of elements or zones (Figure 6.3). These include:

- *Attraction complex(es)*.
  These form the 'backbone' of the resort destination. They are the reason guests will come and must be accorded the most sympathetic and supportive planning and development. Whether the resort has a single or multiple attraction cluster(s) they 'should be planned to make outstanding use of resources and enrich visitors while supporting profitable business' (Gunn, 1997: 60).
- *Focal community(ies)*.
  Focal communities can be either planned accommodation and support clusters and/or existing service communities in the area. They should offer a range of accommodation and services such as restaurants and entertainment, suitable for the targeted guests. Furthermore, the life needs of staff should be considered in this context. Only when 'development policies consider the visitors' needs alongside those of residents, will destinations be able to fulfill their functions more efficiently and beautifully' (Gunn, 1997: 63).
- *Linkage corridors*.
  Corridors are needed to tie the various attraction complexes and focal communities together. These must be effective and attractive for the visitor and sensitive to the natural environment. They will need to be engineered to complement, rather than overwhelm, the local setting. One of the challenges in this regard is signage, which should be present when needed – but not too bold or intrusive in appearance.
- *Transport and access*.
  Access to the resort destination from the national or international transport grid should be seamless. Whether guests first arrive by plane or boat, they are most likely to enter the resort by car or bus. The design for their ease of access 'must go beyond structural engineering and include greater consideration of travelers' functional needs and visual impressions along the way' (Gunn, 1997: 63). This would involve concern over the safety and ease of access regarding collection points at airports, stations or seaports. It will involve the same at the drop-off points within the resort and their links with registration and accommodation. It requires planning for guests' personal needs,

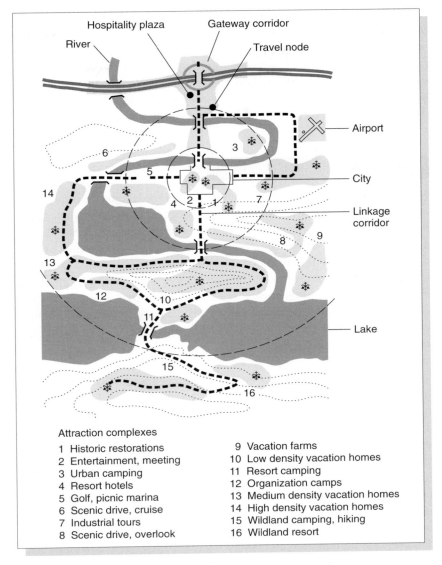

Figure 6.3 The destination zone concept (Gunn, 1997: 67).

including information about the attraction complexes and how to reach them.

In conclusion Gunn feels 'when tourism is treated as a system of inter-locking parts, progress toward desired goals (on the part of the guest and resort) is much more feasible' (Gunn, 1997: 104).

This is the same point made by Dredge (1999) who in her article recommends the development of integrated destinations, which link the nodal structure of communities with various attraction systems via a range of different travel patterns. She demonstrates that such an integrated approach can be applied to a single node destination (resort hotel), a multiple node destination (integrated resort complex) and a destination region such as an urban or coastal conglomeration.

Planning and financial feasibility

Naturally the three tool groups identified by Dredge are more points of emphasis rather than truly independent categories and no single tool can be applied to all situations. 'Planners employ a variety of these tools at different stages to define the planning process, to describe and explain the problem under investigation, to generate attentive solutions and to identify the preferred option' (Dredge, 1999: 776). However, given the business emphasis of this book there is one factor that needs to be present at every phase of the development process and in the application of every tool, and that is the financial feasibility and expected consequences of what is being proposed.

The standard approach to evaluating a proposed business development would be to accept that several alternative levels of expected income streams can occur with each major development decision. Therefore a probability associated with the risk should be assigned to each possible outcome. However, calculating the risk and probability with resort investments is complicated by the nature of the product and its development. Resorts sell highly personal and intangible products called 'vacation experiences', so it is difficult for financial institutions to gauge the merit of each individual component of a resort product and how it fits in with the overall consumer experience and satisfaction. The development phase can take a long time, during which both internal factors (target markets and building costs) and external factors (currency exchange rates and economic cycles) may change. If 'an investment appraisal does not allow for the probability of possible administrative delays in moving from a greenfield, inappropriately zoned site to full development approval, it is likely to arrive at an overoptimistic expected net-present value of returns' (Stanton and Aislabie, 1992: 446).

In their assessment of up-market integrated resorts Stanton and Aislabie (1992) have identified three common assessment difficulties:

1. *Uniqueness of resort characteristics.*
   Since each resort is attempting to differentiate itself in terms of product and image, and all will have a different site and setting this 'uniqueness' makes the forecasting of user demand very difficult.

2. *Dynamics of demand and cost of uncertainty.*
   The time lag between initial proposal and opening, plus the uncertainty of the resort's subsequent life cycle complicates calculations regarding cost and revenue projections. 'The longer the construction period, the greater is the likelihood that initial income projections will need revision' (Stanton and Aislabie, 1992: 444).

3. *Locational and institutional influences on uncertainty.*
   The use of greenfield sites increases the level of uncertainty because such locations will have no record of tourism volumes and expenditure. Local government regulations can impose costs, mainly consisting of time delays, plus local charges and minimum standards can vary widely from jurisdiction to jurisdiction. It has been estimated 'that delays alone can add between 5 and 10 percent to the cost of projects' (Stanton and Aislabie, 1992: 445).

Evidence that such difficulties regularly occur can be found around the world, but one of the most detailed accounts of the problems in assessing investment returns has been provided by the global accounting firm of Ernst and Young (2003) in their assessment of Australia's resort market.

Ernst and Young note that external factors which are beyond the control of resort developers take on a particularly significant role when the development and subsequent tourism area life cycle (TALC) phases can take so long to run their course. They illustrate both the negative and positive effects of external factors in relation to Australia's resort investment cycles between 1980 and 2002.

■ *1980s – Japanese led investment.*
   During the 1980s Japan's economy was at its peak. The country was encouraging its citizens to travel overseas, its industrial corporations were busy diversifying and purchasing overseas assets. Among the businesses that attracted Japanese investment was the resort sector, with 'the majority of developments built at a high capital cost, driven by local entrepreneurial developers, backed by foreign (Japanese) capital, motivated by real estate capital gains rather than income

considerations' (Ernst and Young, 2003: 83). In Australia this led to the creation of several luxury international standard resorts such as the Sheraton Mirage Port Douglas, the Hyatt Sanctuary Cove and the Hyatt Regency Coolum; and elsewhere in the Pacific the Westin Kauai Lagoons in Hawaii.

■ *1989 – pilots' strike.*
The Australian pilots' strike in 1989 and the economic recession of the early 1990s particularly impacted isolated resorts, with several going into receivership. 'By default, Westpac, one of Australia's major banking groups, became one of the largest hotel owners in Australia at that stage' (Ernst and Young, 2003: 83).

■ *Mid-1990s to 1997 – Asian investment.*
Overseas investors, particularly from Asia took the opportunity to purchase properties from receivers at a significant discount to their replacement costs. 'Thakral Holdings purchased the Westpac portfolio of hotels in 1994, making it the largest owner of hotels in Australia at that time. Several listed hotel and resort trusts were floated on the Australian Stock Exchange in the mid 1990s' (Ernst and Young, 2003: 83).

■ *1997 – Asian crisis.*
The sudden and dramatic currency devaluation across Asia led many Asian investors to sell off stronger valued overseas investments in order to maintain their home business interests. As a result ownership of many resort hotels and integrated complexes swung into the hands of Australian investors, either through direct purchase or indirectly through trust purchases. 'The 1990s were marked by the acquisition of properties built the previous decade at a significant discount to the initial development cost . . . (and) The second half of the 1990s also saw the rise of the strata titled investments in both capital cities and holiday destinations' (Ernst and Young, 2003: 84).

■ *Post-Olympic blues.*
The Sydney Olympics of 2000 were a great success in terms of many criteria, but such investments often represent a peak of intensity and output. The new supply of hotel accommodation depressed hotel performance in several key markets over the following years, and the impact of terrorist activity was brought home to the Pacific region with the Bali bombing in 2002.

By the end of 2002 the ownership profile of Australia's 20 largest resorts, based on room numbers, revealed the three largest resorts were owned by publicly listed Australian companies. However, the majority of the top 20 resorts still remained in Japanese or Asian ownership, while three of the resorts were strata-titled (multiple ownership) and only one was owned by an individual – Daydream Island.

Of particular concern to the Australia study was what is the state of resort investment returns under such volatile conditions over such a short period? In this regard Ernst and Young's assessment does not make very encouraging reading. They report that some of Australia's major resort assets 'have sold at a significant discount to their initial development cost, attesting to the misperceptions of developers and investors of the previous decades as to the potential of the hotel and resort sector' (Ernst and Young, 2003: 86). This is not a feature unique to the Australian resort market and indicates the need to combine dreams with reality. Part of that reality is to set higher expected rates of return (indicative yields) for regional hotels and resorts to reflect their higher risk profile. Ernst and Young report that while a 'quality CBD hotel' would require yields in the 8–10 per cent range, regional hotels and resorts should plan for 12 per cent plus returns because they are more exposed to market volatility. Having justified such targets, their research found that over the 1995–2002 period Australian resort yields had been only in the 2.7–8.14 per cent range. They draw several pertinent lessons from this evidence relating to the planning and development stages that have been discussed previously.

In terms of resort development and investment Ernst and Young emphasize the following issues that must be addressed at the various planning and development stages, to which additional comments and examples are offered:

- *Site selection stage.*
  Recognize that there are a limited number of 'excellent' sites, those which are both accessible and have strong differentiating features.
- *Market analysis stage.*
  Bring all stakeholders together at the beginning of the project, including governments. Ensure everyone understands the vision and the feasibility analysis. There will be a lack of accurate data on regional visitation patterns and preferences because national and state data sets seldom disaggregate to a local level. This gap needs to be filled for key areas, to supplement state and national surveys. Specific demand trends and future projections remain difficult and expensive to obtain, but a careful media watch and commitment to product flexibility can minimize future shocks.
- *Approvals stage.*
  Anticipate that 'local councils often do not have sufficient resources or expertise to deal with complex planning regimes (and) local

157

communities, particularly retirement communities, may object strongly to a resort development' (Ernst and Young, 2003: 89). New resort developments will need to comply with stringent environmental legislation and local building codes. All of which will require extensive community consultation. Yes, this can be 'time consuming and costly' according to Ernst and Young (2003: 89) but it can also be the most effective way to build goodwill and a local customer base for those off-season periods.

- *The construction stage.*

  Resort development will incur higher construction costs as a result of building more spacious and better equipped units, and meeting the needs of sensitive and possibly remote environments. In greenfield remote sites the cost of providing infrastructure can become prohibitive. The availability of start-up capital can be a major constraint.

- *Operating stage.*

  The time needed to achieve a steady trading state is longer for resorts than for standard hotels, generally ranging from three to seven years.

- *Other issues.*

  Isolated integrated resorts are more susceptible to supply fluctuations, given the small size of the specialized markets in which they operate. They are also a 'derivative' business, dependent on other transport and infrastructure businesses. Such resorts are particularly risky because they cannot stand alone if the infrastructure is removed or transport company fails. With the development of generic strata-title developments there is a danger that the emphasis for some resorts may become more real estate than vacation market oriented, leading to a loss of focus on what makes resorts special and different.

Ernst and Young conclude that given the marginal profitability of many resort projects and the difficult issues and challenges they face it is necessary to concentrate on those features that have led to successful resort ventures and made them special. In their mind the following are *key success factors*;

- a concept which meets market demand;
- a design which reflects the resort's environment and provides a point of differentiation;
- location in a region which has an established demand and barriers to entry for competitors;
- access to transport infrastructure, with airline access being of paramount importance for remote resorts;
- community support for the development;

- control of construction costs;
- partnership with flexible financiers who understand the cyclical nature of resort operations and are prepared to take a long-term view;
- an alliance with complementary facilities, such as national parks and heritage sites, or other attractions;
- creation of economies of scale by developing multi-tiered accommodation catering to different target markets; and
- mixed use development combining land, residential, marina and retail facilities which have the potential to increase the project's viability.

(Ernst and Young, 2003: 91–92)

Let us examine two of their suggestions in more detail. In the case of mixed use development the rise of condominium or strata-titled development has become a significant component of modern resort financing. In the search for partners other sectors of the economy have turned to public–private partnerships (PPPs), which may have some potential for resorts built on government land.

Strata-title financing

The growing link between strata-title real estate and resort development has been gaining strength since the 1980s. Like other successful commercial trends its success is based on meeting the needs of customers, but in this case it has also met the needs of many resort owners by providing a new product with which to diversify and refresh their offerings. The big market for the strata-title accommodation within resorts has been the baby boomer generation. 'Baby boomers are not only earning top dollar at the turn of the millennium; they're also on the receiving end of an enormous intergenerational transfer of wealth . . . demographics predict vacation – home purchases (in the U.S.) will jump from the 3.3 million homes bought in 1997 to 5 million in 2013 . . . (so not surprisingly) ski areas have become amenities to drive real estate sales' (Clifford, 2003: 45).

One who has explored this phenomenon from a financial point of view is Turner (1994), who has examined the condominium market in Canada with specific reference to Whistler ski resort.

The condominium option offers advantages to the investor or buyer and the developer or resort owner. For the *investor* Turner has identified the following advantages:

- *Investment and lifestyle opportunities.*
  Condominiums enable small investors to participate in markets from which they may otherwise have been excluded.
- *Convenience and security.*
  Most purchasers want a property that is worry-free, secure and convenient. They do not want to be bothered with general maintenance duties such as repainting or mowing the lawn.
- *Investment advantages.*
  By making the unit available to a rental pool the owner can share in any operational profits or losses. Tax deductions such as rental and maintenance expenses, real estate taxes, mortgage interest and depreciation for the period in the rental pool can be claimed by the investor.
- *Security of ownership.*
  The investor enjoys the rights of fee simple ownership. S(he) is taxed separately and is free to sell, mortgage, bequeath or rent the property.
- *Tax shelter.*
  Tax shelters in some parts of the world confer significant rental accommodation inducements. In Australia 'negative gearing' enables taxpayers to subtract their operating losses from their tax assessment. So their break-even point does not have to match their mortgage and they can cover the loss with their other taxable revenue.

The advantages for the *developer* are seen as being:

- *Profit margin.*
  Profit is the primary objective and Turner maintains whereas a residential condominium in nearby Vancouver could expect a profit margin of 10–12 per cent, a resort development often produces margins of 20–30 per cent.
- *Competition.*
  Part of the explanation for the lower return on a metropolitan condominium is the presence of competition in the condominium housing market, but in a resort situation this can be moot with one resort owner or controlled access to the development. Whistler, at the time, was dominated by two major firms, and competition was constrained by the high front-end costs, short building season, union job site and limited skilled labour pool.
- *Cash flow.*
  The early infusion of equity capital from condominium unit sales provides greater leverage (with financiers) and diversification opportunities

(seasonality answer and additional attractions) for developers. It can spread their investment risk and make their overall investment port-folio more secure.

■ *Operating profit.*
The development of management contracts with the strata corpora-tions provides an additional revenue stream. The utilization of a 'rental pool' provides extra rooms at no cost and in Whistler an average 40 per cent share of the room charge.

Turner develops several income scenarios for condominium development at Whistler, using a common base of 85 unit sales and local figures and ratios. Turner shows how in a 'hot market' those sales could generate a final value of $21.6 million, in a falling market $15.7 million and in a deferred sellout and rental pool market $18.5 million. Of the three scenar-ios option 3 was considered the most realistic projection because 'while Whistler relies on the major population center of Vancouver for approxi-mately 70 per cent of unit sales, it draws only 24 per cent of its hotel guests from its home province during the high winter season' (Turner, 1994: 31).

Public–private partnerships

PPPs are relatively new. They started in the UK during the 1990s under the title of Private Financing of Infrastructure (PFI) and the idea has now spread to Australia and other nations concerned with upgrading infrastructure and essential services, like education and hospitals, with-out adding to the public debt. The PPP process is 'designed to attract pri-vate investment to what would otherwise be government funded and operated infrastructure and services', with the overall objectives being:

■ to achieve better value for money through efficiencies by involve-ment of the private sector in a long-term relationship, payment for outputs rather than inputs and optimisation of risk allocation;
■ to improve the whole-of-life delivery of the public sector; and
■ to promote economic growth and local industry development.
(Australian Procurement and Construction Council, 2002: 1)

After a decade or so of experience with PPPs in the UK and Australia the Australian Procurement and Construction Council (2002: 2–3) has iden-tified the following advantages and disadvantages of this system:

Advantages
■ improvement in the efficiency and quality of ancillary services provided;
■ facilitating innovation;

- optimizing whole-of-life asset management;
- greater flexibility in development and financing arrangements;
- well structured risk sharing in a 'partnership' environment;
- more timely service provision.

Disadvantages
- a lack of widespread acceptance from key stakeholders, especially among unions and the general community;
- lack of cross-jurisdictional and cross-agency consistency;
- limits future financial flexibility due to the commitments of long-term contracts;
- heavy reliance on financial evaluation such as value-for-money judgements;
- reliability of performance specifications;
- transaction costs and timeframes;
- changing service needs during the lifetime of contract.

The Council concludes in its review of PPPs that results to date have been mixed, but places a significant portion of the blame for this on the evolving nature of the process. It feels that greater experience with this type of infrastructure and service development will result in government objectives being achieved more often.

Others are more critical and prefer the traditional system of government assets and public debt supporting society's infrastructure needs and social programmes. Fitzgerald (2006) addressing the Australian Fabian Society, states there is 'a long list of myths about PPPs'. These include:

- They are the only way to avoid debt.
- They are cheaper.
- They transfer risk.
- They allow a long-term view.
- They allow the state to access skills
- It brings sophisticated risk analysis.

In his view, after evaluating eight PPPs in the state of Victoria, Australia 'I evaluate that all of the benefits resulted from the use of a wrong discount rate. In my assessment the discount rate should have been 5.4% instead of 8.65%. The extra 3% was justified on the basis of "market risk" transferred, in circumstances where I asked for details of this market risk I found nothing of substance.' (Fitzgerald, 2006: 4). Likewise, Sheil (2002: 5) considers 'the magic pudding that fills the cost gap is known as "risk allocation"'. He feels, in fact, that PPPs have become 'an un-holy alliance' where the 'private consortia will always seek to purchase the benefit of a very secure income stream, with risk characteristics similar to a government security, but higher returns' (Sheil, 2002: 8).

Providing a more balanced assessment of PPPs is the work of John Quiggin. He states:

> The adoption of PPP programs by Australian state governments could, somewhat uncharitably, be described as a triumph of hope over experience .... A more favourable assessment would be that governments have learned from past mistakes and are seeking the most cost-effective means of delivering physical and social infrastructure .... Both assessments have an element of truth ... (but) the main conclusion is that the AFI/PPP approach should be adopted only in special cases.
>
> (Quiggin, 2004: 60 and 61).

Quiggin identifies two key issues associated with PPPs, the aforementioned risk allocation and the public sector comparator. He considers that 'risks should be identified explicitly and then allocated to the party best able to manage them' (Quiggin, 2004: 57). In this regard he advocates splitting the risk assessment and allocation in the most effective and efficient way, noting the different risk circumstances of the construction and operation phases, and permitting the unbundling of risk among operators depending on the possible variation in demand. Where variation in demand for a service is expected to be constant or regular, the demand risk should be borne by the public sector. Where it is volatile it would be more appropriate to treat it as a private sector risk. Overall, the costs of producing an infrastructure or service via a PPP should be compared to those using the public sector alone. Such public sector comparators should be transparent and even-handed, however many in the past 'have generally used the cost of risk to the private sector, which is substantially greater' (Quiggin, 2004: 57) and has led to the criticisms voiced by Fitzgerald earlier in this section.

So if we are to follow Quiggin's advice what would make a suitable 'special case' for PPPs? It would have to be an infrastructure and/or social development that would be hard to justify in terms of increased public debt, both on a philosophical and financial basis, yet one where there would be both general economic and social benefits. This book believes such a case exists in the development of resorts that permit a greater use and appreciation of existing national and state parks; resorts that can be built in regional areas to function as growth poles by offering a concentration of economic opportunity and amenity enhancement; or where resorts are beginning to be used as extensions of the health system and can play a significant role in the provision of retirement housing and care for the elderly.

In the first two instances government often owns the land but is unable to fully realize the potential of that land for the recreation, economic and social purposes identified. This calls for a partnership with a private sector that can deliver such objectives in an effective and efficient manner – the resort sector. The last suggestion relates to the global crisis of providing sufficient health and general care for the aging populations of western societies. Governments are desperate to find more efficient ways to provide these health services and to partner with organizations that have extensive operational experience in these areas. What has been presented as examples in Chapter 4 could become more formal and commonplace occurrences under the umbrella of PPPs.

To determine whether such ideas have merit will require the type of objective and transparent analysis advocated by Quiggin, including a fair assessment of risk and its appropriate allocation, plus a comparison with a public sector only provision. Such an approach would provide a useful and logical progression to the earlier forms of partnership identified by Walker (1983) with respect to tourism and recreational property development and Murphy (1985) in regard to social tourism policies around the world.

Financial implications

Gee's five phases of the resort development process each have their own financial requirements, which will need to be managed carefully in order to proceed smoothly through the phases and arrive at the opening in the best financial condition. This is a generalized process that can apply to all types of resort, but all resorts do not necessarily pass through the entire process, especially where management takes over in the later phases – sometimes after the initial owners have been declared bankrupt and have forfeited their business and dream.

1. *Conceptualization, planning and initiation phase.*
   Resorts often require considerable blocks of land and will take a long time to show a positive return on investment (ROI) because of the time spent in developing the original idea. To purchase the block of land outright at this stage would tie up a lot of capital and would be a real risk, as it has yet to be determined whether the dream is a viable business proposition. The answer is to buy an option to purchase, which means the resort developers commit to buy the land at a predetermined price by a set date, and to show their good faith they

provide a non-refundable deposit. In cases where the land is govern-ment owned and not for sale the developers can seek a long-term lease, again using the option route. Given the amount of time taken to secure a ROI and that in this case there will be no chance of increased equity and land value over time except where an asset assessment has been negotiated, the developers should seek leases comparable to their investment and likely returns. Banks will expect leases of 30 years plus, and generally leases of 50–99 years are the most desirable.

2. *Feasibility analysis.*
Feasibility studies should be undertaken on two fronts – the market and supply sides. The hiring of a market research company can become expensive if it requires the solicitation of large samples, some of them internationally based, and sophisticated research designs. Supply side feasibility needs to assess the costs associated with the proposed development and a competitive analysis of alternative local resorts and travel options. Detailed costing of proposed developments needs to be undertaken at this stage and matched against existing price structures and 'willingness to pay' results from the market fea-sibility studies. This will indicate if there will be a sufficient return on the investment and risk needed to convert the dream into a reality. As Huffadine (1999: 7) has observed: 'costs on loans and costs of construction are very high and there is a long payback period with (typically) low cash flows during the first 3–4 years'.

All the above work is likely to take many months and can consume considerable funds, but it is vital to have such an objective assessment and to make it a major part of any business plan placed before a potential financial backer. Such feasibility studies need to be as confi-dential as possible because the potential resort developers do not wish to alert competitors to their plans.

3. *Commitment.*
If the figures from the feasibility studies provide a positive response the resort developer(s) should proceed to the third stage of commit-ment. This will be the stage at which the plans become public and even larger amounts of money are invested in the project. However, it should be noted that feasibility studies are not infallible, not all of them predict the future correctly and their interpretation relies on the reader's perspective on life – is the glass half full or half empty?

The big financial commitment at this stage is to convert the land and lease options into actual purchases and contracts. At this stage and the next the financing should be short-term, covering the acquisition and construction periods, often at a high interest rate. Lenders of short-term capital, such as development banks or venture capitalists, often require the developer to 'make a preliminary commitment to a long-term loan upon completion of construction' (Huffadine, 1999: 8). At that point, when revenue starts to flow, developers are advised to turn to long-term investment, generally for 25–30 years with a lower interest rate. The sources for such financial assistance are varied and can include banks, real estate investment trusts, insurance companies or pension funds. Many of the larger resorts are now owned by public groups, with their shares traded on major stock exchanges (Huffadine, 1999).

4. *Design layout and construction.*

Huge sums will be needed to create the resort before the first guest arrives and starts to contribute to the revenue stream. This is particularly the case with greenfield sites and isolated locations, where the developer will be responsible for a considerable investment in the infrastructure. This can include expenses on a road system, with possible air or water connections, the provision of power and drinking water, the growing demands for electronic communications and the appropriate treatment and disposal of liquid and solid wastes. On top of this will come the actual building and attractions that will be needed to lure the guests. Everything, the infrastructure, the core attractions and support facilities, should fit the intended resort image and should be of quality construction, for it will take many years to recoup the initial development costs.

In large resort projects it is advisable to build in stages to minimize the time lag in welcoming the first guests. This means the site must have sufficient space to allow for several stages of development and to permit later stages to be constructed with minimal impact on the business activities of the earlier stages. In addition it is helpful to have a variety of accommodation types to provide an early cash flow, so increasingly large resort developments are creating real estate options alongside their hotel accommodation.

According to Laventhol and Horwarth, as cited in Gee (1996: 114) the typical development costs for resort hotel rooms (luxury category) in 1984 ran from $150 000 to $200 000, but some rooms (suites) could run to $300 000. When these figures are compared with the cost of building the Hamilton and Hayman Island resorts, where building costs of up to A$1.1 million per room have been cited (King, 1997: 58), you can understand why some of these island resorts have struggled financially. Especially when an industry 'rule of thumb' is that for every $100 000 a room costs to build you have to charge $100 per night (King, 1997: 58). The actual costs of construction have undoubtedly increased since these figures were assembled, but the rule of thumb will explain the current high prices charged for many resort rooms.

5. *Management and operations.*

Given such a protracted gestation period, many resorts undertake a 'soft opening', which means they welcome the first guests before a resort is complete, even in terms of its first stage. The advantages of this are that it brings in a revenue stream at the earliest opportunity, gets the word out about the resort and its potential and permits a shakedown of new staff and systems before the full guest component arrives. The disadvantages are that it presents an incomplete picture to the guest, discount prices applied for an incomplete experience may set future price expectations and may tempt the resort to be less prepared than it should be because it is viewed as a 'dress rehearsal'.

Cash flow is a key issue in resorts where there has been a colossal preliminary investment that needs to be paid off in regular instalments. A major concern under these circumstances is to develop some form of year-round business. This leads back to the problems of seasonality and the growing challenge to survive and prosper on just a few weeks of business.

It is at this stage that resorts often change the source of their lending switching from venture capitalists and banks, who often charge high premiums on their loans, to insurance companies and pension funds which are looking for a more modest but regular return on their loans so they can meet their client obligations.

New resorts will need to make a quick and substantial impact in the competitive resort market which means a major budget item at this stage will be marketing. In addition to the challenge of selecting the most powerful message and appropriate outlets for that message the resort will need to build its distribution channels, to extend its coverage and increase its awareness amongst those businesses that help to sell its product. This will involve the creation of familiarization tours and the development of links with tour wholesalers, carriers and destination marketing organizations. Furthermore, at this stage the resort should be promoting itself as a good community neighbour; using public relations to outline its contribution to the local economy and amenity offerings, with the possible inclusion of local 'mate's rates' for certain functions at set times. In this sense the local community is brought on board as a local partner and champion of the resort.

Summary

This chapter has started the examination of the internal challenges and strategies of resort management by combining the physical planning and financial management considerations. It has done this to emphasize how the two go hand in hand, and set the scene for later success or disappointment. Key features of the planning process are the need for translating a dream into a practical reality, noting the considerable time this will take and the need to work with others. One of those others will be the financial backers. It is vital for resorts to build a solid business plan to present to potential finance sources, one that includes a combination of the resort's vision, objectives and financial accountability.

To illustrate these features the chapter will end with an examination of three cases. In terms of planning, Dubai offers an example of central government planning that includes a resort component in its vision for the future. In terms of planning and finance the example of Huis Ten Bosch in Japan demonstrates the need for careful feasibility studies prior to commitment to a dream. In terms of finances it is naturally difficult to obtain details from private companies and complicated at times to extract the relevant details from major public corporations. However, one small public company, Grand Hotels Bad Ragaz in Switzerland, provides sufficient information in its annual report to show how a successful resort should be run.

Case studies

Dubai, United Arab Emirates

Dubai is a city and emirate within the United Arab Emirates located on the Persian Gulf. Like many of its neighbouring states it is an oil-rich country, but its proven reserves will last for only another 10–20 years at current rates of extraction according to estimates cited by Arlidge (2006: 10) and Jenkins (2004: 4). The situation has encouraged this city–state to embark on a programme of modernization and economic diversification, to prepare the country for a non-oil-based future. Dubai has reduced its dependence on oil substantially over the past few decades. 'In 1985 oil accounted for just under half of the contribution to the Gross Domestic Product, and in 1993 just 24 per cent. In 2002 the contribution was 17 per cent and by 2010 is expected to decline to 1 per cent' (Jenkins, 2004: 15).

An important part of this diversification strategy has been the development of tourism, and within that development resort tourism has been a major component. 'Dubai, in a period of less than 50 years, has developed and transformed itself from a small desert sheikhdom into a cosmopolitan city and a major tourism destination in the Middle East' according to Jenkins (2004: 6); it attracts large numbers of beach tourists from Europe during their winter months, and business and shopping markets from the short-haul markets of Iran and India. It is developing a reputation as a long-haul stopover destination for flights between Europe and Southeast Asia and Australia, linked with its growing and successful Emirates airline 'which is on a flight path to overtake British Airways as the world's biggest long-haul carrier by 2012' and its large modern international airport which has 'connections to over 140 destinations' (Arlidge, 2006: 10). Between 1982 and 2002 the number of hotels in Dubai increased from 42 to 272 and the importance of the luxury market is reflected in the fact that 32 per cent of all hotel beds in 2002 were classified as being in five star hotels or above (Jenkins, 2004; Laws, 1995). Dubai now receives over six million visitors a year, with the leisure tourists focussing on waterfront resort hotels for beach activities or to use as a base to visit the shops and other attractions of Dubai, and it plans to raise its tourist market to 15 million visitors by 2010.

The way Dubai has gone about this transformation is instructive for many resort destinations. Jenkins (2004: 8–11) identifies five key features in Dubai's tourism-related strategy.

1. Make shopping a major draw card for tourists, with the peak promotion being the Dubai Shopping Festival from mid-January to mid-February each year.
2. Create a total resort destination with the construction of iconic resort hotels, attractions and facilities. It has built the first seven star hotel, the Burj Al Arab Hotel, which is designed to resemble a billowing sail and where the most expensive suite costs A$25 000 a night. The world's first indoor ski resort, where visitors can ski slopes offering varying degrees of challenge year round. It is in the process of building Dubailand, which will be 'an enclave of theme parks, villages and shopping malls (and) is the Middle East's answer to Disney World'; and Dubai's new A$12.5 billion 'six-runway airport will be the biggest in the world, handling 150 million passengers a year' (Arlidge, 2006: 10 and 11).
3. Use the all-round quality of Dubai's facilities to add value to specific events, whether these be top international conferences like the International Monetary Fund and World Bank meetings, or major sports events such as The Desert (Golf) Classic.

4. Increase the capacity and variety of the luxury accommodation sector. This has involved the building of apartment hotels, particularly for the Gulf Co-operative Council countries' market, and the well-publicized holiday homes about to be placed on the artificial three Palm Island developments and The World, a collection of man-made islands created to outline different countries of the world. 'Last week the first £4m hacienda-style villas on the Palm Jumeirah were completed and the Beckhams, the first of 70 000 residents, will move in this summer' (Arlidge, 2006: 10). 'The development of a market in real estate with 99 year leaseholds and residence visas available for non-nationals is a first approach to attracting long-stay visitors in the UAE, and is an issue still surrounded by controversy' (Jenkins, 2004: 8).

5. To provide the necessary infrastructure to support these developments has required a major investment in roads, utilities and airport expansion. Such infrastructure supports other economic diversification into areas of higher education (Academic City), health (Medicine City) and finance (International Financial Centre) in addition to tourism facilities. Traditional signs of success and stress are occurring with the late introduction of a light rail system to help alleviate road congestion and air pollution, along with concerns over investment security and guest worker treatment (Arlidge, 2006: 11).

It should be appreciated that Dubai's successful diversification into resort tourism is strongly influenced by some special competitive advantages – some natural and others management generated. The natural advantages that have assisted Dubai include its oil wealth, its welcoming winter warmth and geographic location offering proximity to the major European market and a growing transshipment role for the long-haul flight market. Management decisions that have assisted its progress start with 'the undoubted vision, entrepreneurial flair and commitment of the ruling family' (Jenkins, 2004: 14). Their leadership has put in place an investor-friendly business policy offering tax-free enclaves and strong support for the PPP model, along with the ability to conceive and deliver iconic projects that help to differentiate Dubai as a tourism destination. Together these advantages have created an appealing up-market destination that will ease the transition from an oil-based economy to a mixed service economy and could create a Middle East equivalent to the long-term success of Singapore.

Huis ten Bosch, Japan
(http://english.huistenbosch.co.jp/about/index.html)

Huis Ten Bosch (HTB) was the idea of Mr Yoshikuni Kamichika, who decided 'to build a resort town that combined Dutch city planning with Japanese technology' near Sasebo in the Nagasaki Prefecture of Japan.

The concept was to build on the local area's link with the Netherlands during Japan's period of national isolation (1600–1868), which was conducted through a trade port located on the small island of Dejima. The construction of HTB (Home in the Woods) started in 1988 as a replica of a seventeenth century Dutch town, with numerous copies of historic landmarks from around the Netherlands and located in a restored seafront environment. It was opened to the public in 1992 (Figure 6.4). The total costs of the project were $2.5 billion. Unfortunately, this wonderful dream was not a business success and HTB went into receivership in February 2003. The bank which held the principal loan sold the business to a finance company for one-tenth of the total debt, and that finance company has restructured the financial and management direction of the resort.

The following information is taken from a presentation by Mr Daisuke Takeuchi, CEO of HTB, made to the Asia Pacific Tourism Association's 'Globalization and Tourism Research: East meets West' Conference, held in Nagasaki Prefecture, Japan in July 2004. Mr Takeuchi, as an employee of the finance company responsible for restructuring the HTB business model provided details about what had gone wrong with the original model and how they, as second owners, are planning to put things back on a solid business course.

What went wrong?

Mr Takeuchi stressed that the resort is a beautiful creation and attractive destination, with which the author and his wife concur, but there had been some fundamental business flaws in the original business plan. These included:

- HTB is not really a theme park. It has no rides, it is mainly a reconstructed Dutch town with attractive gardens and water features. Hence, it is difficult to categorize and market this particular resort concept.
- The resort is isolated with respect to Japan, being located on the southern island of Kyushu, and commands a local market population of only six million compared to the 30 million for Tokyo Disneyland.
- Transport connections with Japanese and overseas markets involve several transfers. For example, the author's visit from Australia involved arrival at Narita, Tokyo's international airport, a two-hour bus transfer to Hanida, Tokyo's domestic airport, a two-hour flight to Nagasaki airport, followed by an 1.5-hour bus ride from Nagasaki to

Figure 6.4   Huis ten Bosch theme resort, Japan.

Table 6.1 Business volumes for HTB (1996–2003)

	1996	2000	2003
All visitors	3.8 million	2.93 million	2.15 million
International visitors	331 000	221 000	199 000
Internationals' ratio	8.7%	7.5%	9.3%
Source of internationals			
Taiwan	248 000	124 000	67 000
Hong Kong	40 000	57 000	15 000
Korea	33 400	30 300	109 300
China	0	980	4950
Occupancy rates	70.9%	63.6%	48.0%
International ratio	14.4%	19%	17.0%

Source: Takeuchi (2004).

the resort; resulting in a seven-hour journey across Japan when transfers and waits are included.
- HTB was envisaged as a long-stay resort, which is not a familiar concept to the Japanese market.
- The development costs were excessive, as were the depreciation rates.

The challenge is to turn around what had become a deteriorating situation for the resort. The evidence of the decline and possible clues to its resurrection can be seen in Table 6.1.

The future?

Mr Takeuchi is optimistic about the future because 'now the figures make sense', but HTB is planning to make adjustments beyond price considerations.

- The large devaluation of the resort assets after it went into receivership makes the finance company believe it now can offer admission and room rates at competitive prices.
- HTB is adding entertainment aspects to the resort, to complement existing attractions like strolling, museums, shopping and international dining. It feels evening entertainment like shows and fireworks will bolster overnight stays.
- It is concentrating on developing overseas markets, by encouraging direct flights into Nagasaki airport. It hopes to take advantage of

Japan's current 'Asia Inbound Strategy', which hopes to raise international visits from 5.5 million to 10 million within a few years.

■ China is to be the main target, but there may be problems with visas.
■ HTB is developing new attraction packages. It is promoting golf and honeymoon packages and hopes to add a true casino, one without the handicap of current government limits on wagering and prizes.
■ It wishes to work with local and regional tourism organizations to enhance Kyushu's regional appeal and promotion to the Asian market. In this way it hopes to develop into a regional tour base as well as being a destination in its own right.

When Mr Takeuchi's presentation was received HTB was in the early stages of recovery, with considerable enthusiasm for the future, based on the hard lessons from the past. HTB continues to face the regional destination difficulties of access and differentiation, as discussed in the Australian Ernst and Young report. Its Japanese/Asian uniqueness in portraying a seventeenth century Dutch city landscape is a clear differentiator, but whether it is what the market wants and whether they will they be able to access it without too much difficulty or too great a cost remains to be seen. These are still the unknowns and part of the adrenalin excitement of being in the resort business.

Grand Hotels Bad Ragaz Health, Spa and Golf Resort, Switzerland

Grand Hotels at Bad Ragaz in the beautiful 'Heidiland' area of East Switzerland is a resort company that provides a positive example of resort financial management. The resort is near the Glarner Alps and is located in the upper Rhine valley. It focusses on health and tranquility within this beautiful setting (Figure 6.5). Its public financial report (Table 6.2) shows that in 2004 its net gross revenue was 87.5 million CHF (Swiss Francs) which was a small 2 per cent increase over its 2003 total of 85.6 CHF. Its earnings and profits declined to 8.5 million CHF and 2.8 million CHF respectively in 2004 – still satisfactory results in such a competitive business.

The resort contains adjacent five star and four star hotels 'to enchant the guests with "old fashioned" values that have rarity value in our hectic lives; extensive parklands with mature trees, and attentive staff and a pace of life that leaves time for inner peace and tranquility' (Grand Hotels, Bad Ragaz, 11 March 2005 press release). To fulfil these promises the resort offers a combination of 237 elegant rooms and suites in its two hotels,

Figure 6.5 Grand Hotels Bad Ragaz, Switzerland.

Table 6.2   Financial statement for Grand Hotels Bad Ragaz, Switzerland 2003 and 2004

	2003 (in million)	2004 (in million)
Revenue	CHF 85.6	CHF 87.5
Income	CHF 34.7	CHF 34.1
Earnings before taxes	CHF 9.2	CHF 8.5
Cash flow	CHF 14.8	CHF 14.9
Annual profit	CHF 3.5	CHF 2.8
Balance	CHF 225.7	CHF 2001.3
Equity	CHF 76.7	CHF 78.1

thermal baths, a health club, sport training facilities, the Swiss Olympic Medical Centre, a golf course and a small casino. The resort has developed its reputation throughout Europe for its sport training and fitness facilities and has hosted several national and professional club teams as part of their pre-season or tournament preparation. Among its successful associations in this regard have been Greece and its successful 2004 European Soccer championship, Werder Bremen and its German Soccer championship and Liverpool with its European soccer Champions League title in 2005.

To provide a business structure that can deliver on the customer promises the resort has organized its offerings and organization along the lines of independent divisions, each with its own head. These divisions are interlinked and report to the company CEO (Figure 6.6).

It is notable that the organizational structure of the resort follows Porter's Value Chain very closely, as outlined on p.32. The business has been divided into functional areas for its financial reporting, consisting of the Grand Hotels, Medical Centre, Golf Course and Club, Thermal Spa and Casino; plus into the administrative areas of Finance and Control, Marketing, Human Resources and Buildings and Grounds. This level of reporting clearly distinguishes the potential profit centres, the functional areas, from the support areas of administration and maintenance. As a result management and shareholders have a clear picture of how much each section is contributing to the overall financial picture of the resort.

To help track its financial return from each division and venture the resort has set up a detailed financial audit for each major division within the resort's offerings. The Grand Hotels division reported an increase in arrivals but a drop in overnight stays and occupancy rates between 2003 and 2004 (Table 6.3). Its source of visitors reflected more customers

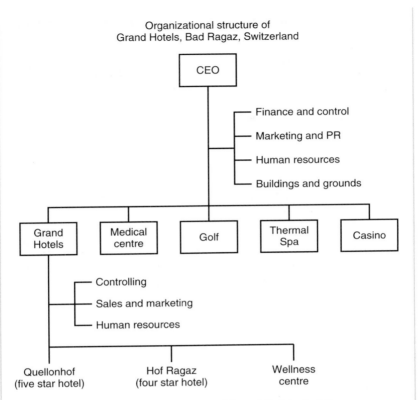

Figure 6.6 Organizational structure of Grand Hotels Bad Ragaz, Switzerland (based on Grand Hotels Bad Ragaz, Annual Report, 2004: 7).

from Europe beyond Switzerland and Germany, with fewer activities in 2004.

On the other hand the Wellness Centre experienced a substantial growth in visits, from hotel guests and day visitors, raising its business volume 5.5 per cent to 10 063 visits. Yet, Table 6.4 reveals within this general increase in activity there were growth areas like 'full massage' and declines in others like 'shiatsu' massage.

With the detailed auditing of each division within the overall business of Grand Hotels Bad Ragaz management is able to detect problems, such as changing public tastes early on and is able to make responsible adjustments to the product mix or the marketing strategy. This level of detail provides shareholders, and members of the public like this author, with a clear picture of the resort's financial health and a guide to its

Table 6.3 Activity profile for Grand Hotels Bad Ragaz, Switzerland 2003 and 2004

	2003	2004
Arrivals (day visits)	20 954	21 726
Overnight stays	96 892	95 046
Occupancy rates	79.7	78.1
Number of rooms	237	237
Number of employees	1023	1020

Table 6.4 Wellness centre activity profile at Grand Hotels Bad Ragaz, Switzerland 2003 and 2004 visits

Activity	2003	2004
Full massage	3780	4255
Partial massage	865	830
Foot massage	516	545
Shiatsu massage	378	87
Lymph node drainage	324	363
Spa special	3672	3423
Personal trainer	0	460
Pilates instructor	0	44
Diet consultant	0	57
Total visits	9535	10 063

prospects. It comes as no surprise, therefore, that the resort has won a transparency award for its financial reporting or to find that the synergistic relationship of business structure and auditing has provided a clear picture via which management has been able to change its balance over time in order to maximize value.

Questions

1 How well have you used the suggested planning stages for a major decision in your life – such as a university degree or the purchase of a car? Try it, you might find it illuminating and you will certainly find it helpful.

2 Why would you want to initiate the *Management and Operation Phase* of the resort planning process prior to opening the resort? What are the advantages and disadvantages to such a timetable?

3 Gunn proposes developing resort destinations as interlinked systems of component parts. Assess how well this concept will work with either a single resort hotel *or* an urban resort destination, providing real examples to support your conclusions.

4 Ernst and Young's review of Australia's investment cycles between 1980 and 2002 revealed some major changes of fortune, with significant impacts on resort ownership. Take a nation of your choice and review its investment history over a 30–50-year period, and determine if similar relationships can be uncovered.

5 Quiggin proposes the risk factor in PPPs should be allocated according to demand volatility, how would this apply to the resort sector? Consider the various types of resort in constructing your response.

6 HTB management considers the new financial figures now make this resort a viable business operation. Examine its product and location to assess how likely they are to succeed in terms of its anticipated international market demand.

References

Arlidge, J. (2006). Dubai's building frenzy lays foundation for global power. *The Sunday Times*, May 21, Business 10–11.

Australian Procurement and Construction Council (2002). *Discussion Paper: Key Issues on Procurement through Public Private Partnerships (PPPs)*. Deakin, ACT: Australian Procurement and Construction Council.

Christaller, W. (1964). Some considerations of tourism location in Europe. *Papers and Proceedings of Regional Science Association*, **12**, 95–105.

Clifford, H. (2003). *Downhill Slide*. San Francisco: Sierra Chub Books.

Dredge, D. (1999). Destination place planning and design. *Annals of Tourism Research*, **26(4)**, 772–791.

Ernst and Young (2003). *Resorting to Profitability*. Sydney: TTF Australia.

Fitzgerald, P. (2006). PPPs – the next big thing or big mistake? *Australian Fabians*. www.fabian.org.au/1053.asp. Accessed on 11 August 2006.

Gee, C.Y. (1996). *Resort Development and Management*, 2nd edn. East Lansing, Michigan: Educational Institute of the American Hotel and Motel Association.

Grand Hotels, Bad Ragaz (2004). *Geschäftsbericht 2004*. Bad Ragaz, Switzerland: Grand Hotels, Bad Ragaz.

Gunn, C.A. (1997). *Vacationscape: Developing Tourist Areas*, 3rd edn. Washington, DC: Taylor and Francis.

Huffadine, M. (1999). *Resort Design*. New York: McGraw-Hill.

Inskeep, E. (1991). *Tourism Planning: An Integrated and Sustainable Development Approach*. New York: Van Nostrand Reinhold.

Jenkins, C.L. (2004). Overcoming the problems relating to seasonality: the case of Dubai. *Proceedings of Tourism: State of the Art II Conference*. Glasgow: Strathclyde University, CD Rom.

King, B.E.M. (1997). *Creating Island Resorts*. London: Routledge.

Laws, E. (1995). Tourism in Dubai. *Tourist Destination Management*, pp. 166–194. London: Routledge.

Lundgren, J.O.J. (1983). Development patterns and lessons in the Montreal Laurentians. In *Tourism in Canada: Selected Issues and Options* (P.E. Murphy, ed.), Western Geographical Series Vol. 21, pp. 95–126. Canada: University of Victoria, BC.

Montgomery, G. and Murphy, P.E. (1983). Government involvement in tourism development: a case study of TIDSA implementation in British Columbia. In *Tourism in Canada: Selected Issues and Options* (P.E. Murphy, ed.), Western Geographical Series Vol. 21, pp. 183–209. Canada: University of Victoria, BC.

Murphy, P.E. (1985). *Tourism: A Community Approach*. London: Methuen.

Pearce, D. (1989). *Tourism Development*, 2nd edn. New York: Longman.

Murphy, P.E. (1997). Attraction land use management in Disney theme parks: balancing business and environment. In *Quality Management in Urban Tourism* (P. Murphy, ed.), pp. 221–233. Chichester: John Wiley and Sons.

Quiggin, J. (2004). Risk, PPPs and the public sector comparator. *Australian Accounting Review*, **14(2)**, 51–61.

Sharpley, R. and Sharpley, J. (1997). *Rural Tourism*. London: International Thomson Business Press.

Sheil, C. (2002). The trouble with PPPs: an unholy alliance. *Evatt Foundation*. http://evatt.labour.net.au/publications/papers/51.html. Accessed on 11 August 2006.

Smith, R.P. (1992). Beach resort evolution: implications for planning. *Annals of Tourism Research*, **19(2)**, 304–322.

Stanton, J. and Aislabie, C. (1992). Up-market integrated resorts in Australia. *Annals of Tourism Research*, **19(3)**, 435–449.

Turner, B. (1994). The valuation of resort condominium projects and individual units. *Journal of Property Valuation and Investment*, **12(4)**, 9–36.

Victoria (2002). *Victoria's Tourism Industry Strategy Plan, 2002–2006*. Melbourne: Tourism Victoria.

Walker, N.T. (1983). Partnership perspectives in tourism and recreational property development. *Tourism Management*, **4(1)**, 25–34.

Zehnder, L. (1975). *Florida's Disney World: Promises and Problems*. Tallahasee, Florida: Peninsular Publishing.

7

Marketing issues for resorts

Introduction

This chapter highlights certain aspects of general tourism marketing which take on a special emphasis with respect to resort marketing because of its special features and problems. It starts with place marketing, since resorts are attempting to sell themselves as complete destinations and special places. Then it moves to how resorts can market their changing product emphasis over time, with a current focus on lifestyle. This is followed by examining how resorts attempt to market themselves as different types of product and place as the seasons change.

Since many resorts are small in scale they have to pay particular attention to finding effective and efficient ways to market their products. Increasingly this requires close attention to the distribution channels of the tourism industry and a keen eye for unexpected opportunities and innovative approaches. It also requires regular monitoring of performance to judge local trends and how well they fit with general sector trends or signify new opportunities.

Many of these factors can be brought together through branding, which has evolved from a marketing tool into a more generic management strategy. Branding is no longer concerned just with the business' projected image it is also about what the customer wishes to achieve through the purchase, especially with experiential products like resort vacations. Furthermore, to obtain the most from customer-centric branding requires the collaboration of all business enterprises within a resort and the appropriate preparation of staff, to ensure all are promoting and presenting the promised brand message.

Place marketing

As mentioned earlier resorts need to attract and hold guests, so the total resort package must be appealing. Resorts are generally selling a place–bound product such as a beach–mountain– or heritage experience. Even when the principal attraction is limited or focussed in scale it needs the associated development of its local setting to make it a complete destination package. An early reference to the importance of place as a marketable product was Ashworth and Goodall's (1990) book on *Marketing Tourism Places*. In that book Ashworth and Voogd (1990: 6) maintain:

> Tourism destinations can undoubtedly be treated as products. They are logically the point of consumption of the complex of activities that comprises the tourism experience and are ultimately what is sold by place promotion agencies on the tourism market.

They go on to note that the selling of tourism places will only be effective if tourist destinations and tourists are treated differently to the marketing of manufactured products.

When discussing resorts as places Goodall (1990: 66–68) places them within the wider destination domain of global regions or national markets. Within these tourist 'destination area opportunity sets' as Goodall calls them, he feels potential visitors will group resorts into subsets according to their:

1. accessibility via different forms of transport.
2. different types of accommodation, such as full service or self-catering.

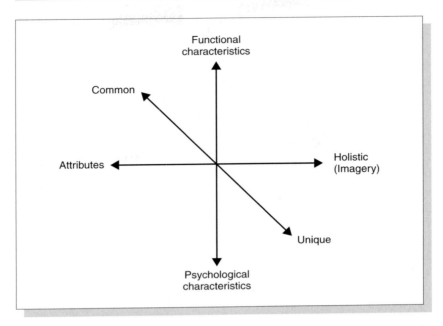

Figure 7.1 Components of the destination image (Echtner and Ritchie, 1991: 6).

3. target markets, such as mass (tour groups) or select (FIT) markets.
4. detailed segmentation of visitor characteristics and motivations.

In this sense Ashworth's and Goodall's observations are confirmed by Echtner and Ritchie's (1991: 6) later summary of destination image formation. They see destination (place) image as a combination of that place's functional and psychological characteristics, which along with the visitor's perceptual search for the place's individual attributes leads to its overall holistic image (Figure 7.1). In terms of these two characteristics, a matrix can be created onto which a destination can be located along a commonality continuum. This continuum will range from being 'commonplace' and therefore open to intense competition, to 'unique', with the distinct differentiation advantages that situation offers.

Place marketing is a good way of describing destination and resort marketing. It is distinctively different from simple product marketing because in addition to the regular product marketing, it involves consideration of the external task environment and the multitude of stakeholders who make up the place. This becomes very evident in Kotler et al.'s book *Marketing Places* (1993: 18–19), which while oriented to the manufacturing sector still has much relevance to resort place marketing. Kotler et al.

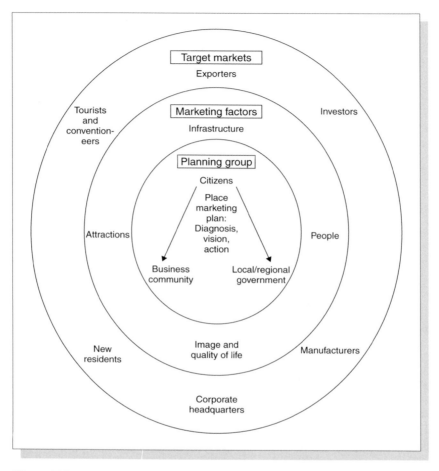

Figure 7.2   Levels of place marketing (Kolter et al., 1993: 19).

maintain that place marketing embraces four activities:

1. designing the right mix of community features and services.
2. setting attractive incentives for the current and potential buyers of its goods and services.
3. delivering a place's products and services in an efficient, accessible way.
4. promoting the place's values and images so that potential users are fully aware of the place's distinctive advantages.

To achieve these four activities requires three levels of place marketing, which have a close similarity to the earlier environmental scanning concept, as shown in Figure 7.2.

1. The *Local Planning Group* represents the business community, local citizens and government officials who plan, develop and market the local place. While in Kotler et al.'s mind such a place is primarily a city or state, there is no reason why their triumvirate of stakeholders cannot involve a resort hotel, integrated resort complex or wider resort destination.

2. To market the place will require the *marketing factors* not only of the place under consideration but also of the immediate wider community. Their infrastructure, like roads and airports, will be needed to bring guests to the place/resort; their image and attractions should be in harmony with the brand image of the place/resort; and the residents and government of this wider area should be supportive of the way the place/resort is marketed.

3. At the macro scale are the *target markets* that the place/resort is attempting to draw from the global market. Resorts would be most interested in tourists and new residents, if they have a real estate component in their product mix. Like manufacturing, resorts are export earners. While industry creates exports and 'basic income' (new income for the city) which raise local earnings and living standards, tourism and the resort business act as export industries by bringing in basic income via visitor/guest spending.

Place marketing not only highlights the necessity to market the total destination, including its local and regional characteristics, but raises the need to foster greater collaboration between the various stakeholder groups. Buhalis and Cooper (1998) have raised the issue of 'competition versus collaboration' in destination marketing and make a strong case for including all tourism businesses, large and small, into strategies that concentrate on attracting customers, improving profit margins, and presenting a more unified and competitive product to the distribution channels. They emphasize the importance of considering SMEs in this process, which means in a resort situation the dominant companies and departments must create meaningful partnerships with the smaller players, to create bigger total profits for all from harmonious marketing programmes and amalgamated product development. A good example of this at work in the general business environment is Porter's cluster theory.

Cluster theory marketing

Porter notes that many world famous industrial centres have long lost their initial comparative advantages over time, be they 'first-mover' advantages or natural resource endowments, but they have maintained their global dominance because those early advantages have been replaced by certain management advantages. These new advantages have been fostered by clustering, or coming together in a common cause. Porter (1998: 199) describes clusters as 'A geographically proximate group of interconnected companies and associated institutions in a particular field, linked by commonalities and complementarities'. Can you think of a better description of a resort? Especially when Porter (1998: 205) goes on to say that 'viewing a group of companies and institutions as a cluster highlights opportunities for coordination and mutual improvement in areas of common concern (such as marketing) without threatening or distorting competition or limiting the intensity of rivalry'.

Clusters involve the business units of a geographic area that work collaboratively to draw customers to their common location, where as individual rivals they then compete to draw said customers into their own specific business. This describes the ideal of resorts and other tourism destinations, where the marketing mantra should be 'sell your destination first and your own business second' if businesses want to maximize the exposure of their destination cluster and their individual businesses within that cluster. But to be effective clusters need to go beyond the collaborative marketing strategies of destination marketing organizations.

Clusters need to enhance the individual business' competitive capacities by creating a lasting competitive advantage for the area. This can be done in three ways according to Porter (1998: 213):

1. *Increase the productivity of constituent businesses.*
   This can be encouraged by common market and operational research that is either undertaken by an industry-related research centre or a local educational institution.
2. *Increase constituent businesses' capacity for innovation.*
   This can be aided by government support, either through grants or a tax structure that encourages the creation of Research and Development Units.
3. *Stimulate new business formation that supports innovation and thereby expand the cluster.*
   Local government and industry can encourage new and complementary businesses by providing an entrepreneurial environment and a clear image of what the cluster represents.

It should be noted that these three cluster contributions to a more competitive position will involve an effective partnership between the constituent businesses, support institutions, local and central governments – all working towards a common objective of increasing the appeal and responsiveness of a cluster to changing market conditions. While cluster theory holds much promise for marketing and development strategies, most of the conceptualization and research has involved manufacturing rather than service industry situations. This is beginning to change as illustrated in Chapter 2, but more needs to be done to promote the competitive advantages in developing a cluster oriented marketing approach and its links to the newer concepts of branding.

Changing product emphasis

Resorts have survived and prospered by changing with the times, adopting new consumer tastes and technologies and integrating them into their product and marketing mix. In Roman and medieval times the emphasis was on physical and spiritual health, later when resorts catered primarily to the wealthy elite the common strategy was to create oases of luxury tranquility or socializing. North America witnessed the creation of Arcadian palaces in the wilderness (Stern, 1986) and England extensions of the royal court in Bath and Brighton. In more recent times as the resort concept was adopted by the masses, the product emphasis changed to greater personal activity and entertainment (Butlin and Dacre, 2002; Rothman, 1998). The emphasis swung to sport, adventure and seeing the stars of music hall, radio and television. Now, as has been discussed earlier, a highly varied resort market is pursuing their personal lifestyle choices and an aging population is shifting its emphasis back to health and wellness.

As the product and audience changed so did the promotional emphasis. In the early days it was word of mouth and the influence of opinion leaders like royalty or the new industrial barons. To reach the masses resorts turned to the influential publicity and media outlets of their day. For the nineteenth century wilderness resorts of North America this was largely through the posters and speakers supplied by the railways serving the western states and provinces, supplemented by the growing power of the press. In the twentieth century first the popular press became a major source of information, supplemented later by magazines, radio and television. Being a highly visual experience resorts have favoured pictorial means of marketing, presenting the grandeur and excitement of their offerings through professionally created images and increasingly in association with well-known personalities. These modern celebrities act like the opinion leaders of the past, and link their celebrity status and experiences to their product endorsements. For many this is more believable than a direct advertisement outlining the benefits of a resort experience. Now the pictur-esque and latest conditions of a resort can be brought into potential cus-tomer's homes via the Internet and webcams. Virtual tours of the resort's principal attractions and facilities are possible over the Internet and for surfers and skiers the latest conditions can become the final convincer.

The continual evolution of the resort product and its associated promo-tion can be seen in the current emphasis on lifestyle experiences. Pine and Gilmore (1999) introduced the concept of the 'experience economy' and claim 'experiences are events that engage individuals in a personal way' (Pine and Gilmore, 1999: 12). As such they offer more than the standard product and service, they offer a personalized experience that cannot be duplicated. 'While the experience itself lacks tangibility, people greatly value the offering because its value lies within them (as happy memories), where it remains long afterward' (Pine and Gilmore, 1999: 13). The key example of this provided by the authors is a family visit to Walt Disney World resort, where the shared experience is a joint happy memory for all concerned.

These experiences are increasingly related to lifestyle pursuits, the self-actualizing peak of Maslow's (1970) needs hierarchy and the holy grail of successive 'me' generations. An example of this is provided by Kurosawa's newspaper article on what makes a good resort hotel. She feels in this 'world of terrorism and uncertainty' we have turned to cocooning, both at home and on our vacations.

> The latest trend in travel is not high-altitude trekking or exploring remote and difficult reaches – it is the emergence of hotels as com-plete travel destinations . . . In a nut shell, sightseeing is out and beau-tiful 'residential hotels' are in.
>
> (Kurosawa, 2006: Travel-11)

She goes on to describe a series of resort hotels around the world, noting rooms have become 'sanctuaries'; celebrity chefs are turning meals into culinary experiences; hotel bars and clubs are 'part of the cocooning experience, becoming style destinations in their (own) right'; the boudoir offers a range of luxuries and the bathrooms a range of bathing options with a selection of 'the world's most desirable soaps and lotions'. In other words, many customers are seeking a lifestyle of creature comforts and security, and they want to be pampered.

Lifestyle segmentation is being examined and used more to link resorts to specific guest groups and to improve their levels of satisfaction. More resorts are attempting to identify and serve specific lifestyle vacation interests. At present the 'lifestyle' offerings range from the exotic and erotic (Desire Resorts in Mexico) to interests like gastronomy (Raffles Hotels and Resorts' Doc Cheng and Jaan operations), often with an emphasis on luxury (Luxury Lifestyle Hotels and Resorts).

Marketing changing seasons

A key challenge for seasonal resorts is to revise their image in accordance with the changing seasons. With each seasonal change they must convince the public they now offer a different and appealing new set of characteristics and opportunities, compared to the season just past. This need for re-imaging is faced by manufacturing companies only when they make major changes to their product line, such as the introduction of a new car model; but even then it often involves a variation on the theme rather than a dramatically different product. In contrast, for seasonal resorts the changes occur at least once a year and these changes usually involve a dramatic change of emphasis that requires a different promotional message. This can best be illustrated by examining seaside resorts in the northern and southern latitudes and ski resorts.

Seaside resorts outside of the tropics have major seasonal variations in temperature, with warm summer seasons emphasizing the beach, sea and outdoor activities; while the colder winter season emphasize indoor activities, opportunities for quiet reflection and 'bracing' winds. Such is the marketing dilemma facing many European and North American seaside resorts, which have to promote two distinctly different products to two very different markets. In the summer the emphasis is on young families and outdoor activities. In the winter the marketing focus changes to a seniors and the conference/convention market with its emphasis on indoor activities and socializing.

Blackpool in England is a traditional seaside resort that emphasises the beach and outdoor activities during the summer, complemented by beach-related entertainment. Outside of the summer months it attempts to extend its summer season into the autumn with a different marketing emphasis – its famous 'Blackpool Illuminations' over September and October. These six miles of lights and laser displays along the front attract thousands of visitors. In addition Blackpool emphasizes its indoor facilities over the low season, as potential conference and trade show venues can bring additional business to the under-performing accommodation, restaurant and retail sectors during the slow months. Blackpool, like other mature seaside destinations, is also hoping to change its image and marketing emphasis with the development of a super casino. The town has entered the national competition to host a super casino, along the lines of Las Vegas operations, which if successful will require yet another image make-over (Blackpool Citizen, 2006).

The situation for ski resorts is similar, with an image emphasis on the excitement of winter sports for a few months followed by a more extensive period emphasizing activities and charms that have very different attributes. In contrast to the youth emphasis and adrenalin rush of the ski season, mountain resorts need to promote entirely different sport activities or re-invent themselves as scenic and peaceful natural environments in the other months. It is a difficult market challenge to convince people that it is worthwhile to visit a ski resort outside of the ski season. It requires a careful market analysis of the local situation, including a competitive analysis of traditional summer activities like a beach holiday, and the development of appropriate attractions and image for a non-snow season in the mountains. It can be done, as is apparent in the busy resort township of Banff, where golf and wildlife viewing along with the arts and cultural activities of the Banff Centre have provided strong summer interest.

The seasonal nature of many resort destinations requires seasonal marketing campaigns to emphasize the different product focus associated with each season. Shaw and Williams (1997) in discussing the post-1970 decline of many British coastal resorts examined a variety of factors that contributed to this decline. They note it is not simply external factors, such as cultural change and ease of access to the Mediterranean sunshine that are to blame for the decline, for they feel more could have been done with strategic product development and marketing. In this regard they quote Gordon and Goodall's observations about using a resort's tourism product as a logical starting point in any discussion of resort marketing:

> Tourism industry products are rather more elusive than those of many other sectors, being the joint products of many agents in different activities. In essence, they involve an experience produced from a combination of activities, resort and accommodation characteristics, together with some resources supplied by the tourists themselves. Resorts may produce a number of distinguishable products, with each being to some degree differentiated from those offered by rival resorts.
>
> (Gordon and Goodall as quoted by Shaw and Williams, 1997: 9)

For seasonal resorts, as most of Britain's coastal resorts are, a more prominent seasonal product offering and associated promotional effort, could have identified differentiated product seasons and stimulated more year-round business.

To ensure their products are distinctive and directed to the appropriate market segments, as outlined by Gordon and Goodall's above comments and with respect to competitive advantage, more resorts are turning to branding.

Branding

Branding is an identification process, used to distinguish the products and services on offer from a seller that helps to differentiate their particular business from its competitors in a crowded marketplace. There are several distinct components to the branding process. Each has its own role to play in helping to make a business' products an instant reference point or benchmark when a consumer is considering the purchase of such a product. Sometimes a product and business has such a dominant position that its brand name becomes synonymous with the product itself, such as Scotch Tape or Cellotape for adhesive tape depending on which part of the world you inhabit.

The *brand name* is the part of the branding process that has become vocalized and converted into a major marketing campaign, so it becomes the reference point in consumers' minds. In terms of resorts there are several well-established brand names such as *Shangri-la Resorts*, *Club Med* and *Butlins*, each of which should convey its own particular type of resort experience. The brand or part of the brand, such as its name or logo, can be converted into a trademark which provides legal protection to maintain the seller's exclusive right to use the brand name, logo or principal features. If a business does not actively support and protect its trademark it is likely to loose them to general usage and common currency, which explains in part why companies like Disney spend so much effort on protecting their trademark and brand image. Disney's past investment and development of a family focussed business, that now includes resorts promoting the same values, can so easily be copied and transformed by other enterprises for their own purposes without such legal protection.

The work of de Chernatony and McWilliam (1990) show many products have two dimensions to their *brand image* – 'functionality' and 'representationality'. The functionality of a brand refers to the functional benefits it delivers to the consumer. The representationality is what the brand says about the user. In the context of selecting a resort vacation it is likely that both dimensions come into play, but will vary according to the consumers' personality and interpretation of external cues. De Chernatony and McWilliam recommend a different management emphasis for the two dimensions. If a business' customers emphasize the functionality dimension, as they are likely to do with local or regional resorts, it should focus on product research and development. If, on the other hand, customers have a high representationality dimension it should focus more on consumer lifestyles and the communication of its brand's symbolic meaning to consumers, to ensure it receives the relevant reference group endorsement. Thus, international resorts that depend on distant markets are well advised to appeal to customers' sense of living out their dreams. They should emphasize the exotic (tropical islands), challenges (championship courses), family togetherness and fun (theme park and beach resorts) or spectacular natural beauty (national and wildlife parks).

There are several advantages to branding for resorts which help them to face some of the issues raised earlier in this chapter. This is because branding is no longer looked upon as only a marketing tool to help differentiate one product or resort from another. It should be viewed also as a management tool to help create genuine competitive advantage (Middleton and Clarke, 2001). By encouraging a business to focus on what products and service levels to offer the customer and to gear the whole experience to fulfilling those objectives, a business will create added value for the customer and a superior position with respect to its competitors.

One of the advantages offered by branding as a management tool is *image clarification*. Every resort needs to establish a clear and attractive image in the minds of consumers so that its offerings stand out in the cluttered marketplace. In addition to selecting attributes that appeal to desirable market segments the resort needs to leverage its brand image with respect to internal operators, to develop core values throughout its product offerings, staff skills and organizational structure. In this way the product experience should support the advertised image with everyone working to supplement the selected image.

Closely associated with the selected image is the *positioning* of a business in the minds of consumers. Brands encourage people to select those products and experience images which provide the benefits they seek. By defining the business in terms of its important attributes a resort will enable guests to compare it and differentiate it from competing products

---

Table 7.1 Development of a positioning plan

---

1. Define and measure market segments of relevance to the business.
2. Select which segments to target.
3. Determine what targeted segments expect and prioritize when making their purchase.
4. Develop products which cater specifically to those needs and expectations.
5. Evaluate positioning and images of competing products and businesses as perceived by the targeted segments.
6. Select an image which sets the *product(s)* apart from competing products, thus ensuring that the chosen image matches the aspirations of the target segments.
7. Tell target segments about the product (*promotion*) as well as making it available at the right *price*. This is the development of the marketing mix, and for resorts will need to make good use of the distribution channels and the uniqueness of sense of *place*.

Source: (after Dibb et al., 1994, cited in Horner and Swarbrooke, 1996: 153).

---

in their minds. 'Effective positioning therefore, involves the organisation differentiating its products and services in the eyes of the target customers' (Horner and Swarbrooke, 1996: 153). They go on to recommend Dibb et al.'s (1994) step approach to developing a positioning plan (Table 7.1), where step six involves selecting 'an image which sets the product (or products) apart from competing products, thus ensuring that the chosen image matches the aspirations of the target customers'. It does this by utilizing the four Ps of the traditional marketing mix.

To bring image building and positioning to a successful commercial conclusion requires the development of *packaging*, particularly in the case of resorts where the experiential product is so varied and made up of several component parts. Each business entity within a resort should be supporting the resort's brand image and positioning through its individual contribution to the guest experience, whether that be in a core or peripheral performance area. This is easier to achieve in a single facility like a resort hotel, but even here management has to work to ensure each function and department is supporting the promoted brand image and objectives. The task becomes more complex as the scale of resort operation increases to integrated resort complex or to a resort destination, where in addition to internal management coordination there is the growing need for inter-organizational collaboration.

Horner and Swarbrooke (1996) have noted the link between branding and packaging, and recommend several specific ways to improve their synergy. Among these are constant referrals to the brand name and logo throughout the business environment, something which Disney does to perfection in its resorts. Another suggestion is to provide attractive and welcoming entrances, such brand entrances will clearly demarcate when the guests is leaving the regular working world and entering the promised land of rest and recreation, as noted in Chapter 6. Yet another is to develop other organizations and businesses as collaborators or partners, in either selling the resort or bringing guests to the door. Developing joint operations to promote and sell the resort brand will bring benefits to both the resort and surrounding communities.

The advantages of branding extend beyond the primary objective of more focussed and effective marketing, by influencing other areas of management. Successful branding helps to create guest loyalty, attracting the targeted market segment(s) back for repeat visits or to resorts in the same chain. This not only reduces the marketing costs per visit but helps to attract favourable financing, joint ventures and other financial advantages due to the recognition and success of the brand name (Seaton and Bennett, 1996: 343). In addition Seaton and Bennett consider a clear and successful brand helps management identify their goals and purpose more clearly to staff, creating standardized operating systems and staff training. Finally, some suggest a fully integrated branding policy can assist with risk management. Middleton and Clarke (2001: 133) consider 'Branding helps reduce medium and long-term vulnerability to unforeseen external events . . . Recovery time after a crisis may be shorter, whilst resilience to price wars or occasional hiccups may be improved', because of a brand's clear positioning in the public mind and its association with specific qualities.

One important word of caution has been expressed with regard to the rise of branding – brands should exist to serve the customers and not the other way around. Rust et al. (2004) point out that brand management must always be customer centred if it is to be effective; for them that means emphasizing its customer equity rather than the brand's equity. 'Most companies today are geared towards aggrandizing their brands (focussing on things like their position in the global brand recognition charts), on the assumption that sales will follow. But for firms to be successful over time, their focus must switch to maximizing customer life value – that is, the net profit a company accrues from transactions with a given customer (over their lifetime)' (Rust et al., 2004: 112). This net profit is the customer equity a business holds in a customer, and as customers' life cycle and lifestyle change the brand must be prepared to adjust to their changing needs, even to the extent of creating new brands for them. This is what Honda did in creating the Acura line of cars for those early Honda customers who had become successful over their lifetime and wanted luxury to go along with the reliability and efficiency that was the hallmark of the Honda brand. In effect the true value of a brand is what it means to the customer, not what the company believes to be its differentiating strengths. For resorts intent on building guest loyalty and long-term relationships over their entire lifetime this means they must listen to their different customers and be prepared to offer different packages and brand images within their total product offerings.

Services marketing and management

Branding will only work well when a resort delivers on the brand promise. While some of the product promise will be based on elements beyond the control of management, such as the weather, a significant aspect of the vacation experience product will depend on the quality of the service delivered by all staff, ranging from instructors to waiters and from water engineers to dishwashers. A business promoting a brand name has to develop standards, systems of delivery and quality assurance programmes to get the most out of its investment. To do this the entire operation must support the brand name and ideals, ensuring that core and peripheral areas of the business are in synchronization to produce the type of product and vacation experience customers have come to expect through the brand promotion. This will require extensive service development and coordination if the resort is to satisfy the expectations of its targeted guests.

Pioneers in the area of service marketing research, Berry and Parasuraman (1991: 5) consider 'service quality is the foundation for services marketing because the core product being marketed is a performance'. As with all performances, some of the cast are on stage (the instructors and waiters) and others are back stage (the engineer and dishwasher); but all need to know how to contribute to the performance's success and should be ready to respond to situations like absent staff, late arrivals and particular guest needs. To deliver on the brand promise will require internal marketing of the brand to all staff and a demonstration of their important contribution and role in the business. This will require a commitment to leadership and empowerment as exemplified in Berry's (1995) book '*On Great Service*', where he recommends businesses:

- Stress personal involvement in the product delivery (vacation experience).
- Emphasize the trust factor, (empowering people to handle the 'moments of truth' when they come face to face with customers).
- Encourage service leadership learning (emphasize the fun in handling different people and situations on a daily basis, and learning how to get the best out of each situation for both parties).
- Promote the right people (so you have a core of motivated and experienced staff to train future staff and casuals).

Therefore, resorts will need to support their external brand marketing with intense internal marketing and staff preparation if they are to deliver the special attention to detail and guests that help to differentiate them in the competitive tourism market. The Ritz Carlton Hotel Company exemplifies this approach and is a case study in the Human Relations chapter.

The growing relevance of service marketing to resorts can be illustrated in two research papers reporting on the delivery of resort service in two different parts of the world. The first relates to Korea's Cheju Island which 'is known for its natural environment, pristine beaches and unique cultural/historical sights' (Khan and Su, 2003: 118) and is also a favourite honeymoon destination for many Asian couples. Khan and Su conducted an analysis of Korean visitors expectations regarding their Cheju visit using a derivative of the famous SERVQUAL scales (Parasuraman et al., 1988, 1991) to take into account the island's ecotourism emphasis. Their ECOSERV scale confirmed the relevance of the original SERVQUAL scales, with 'assurance' being the most important service dimension for Korean visitors, followed in descending order by 'tangibles', 'reliability', 'responsiveness', 'eco-tangibles' and 'empathy'. The new factor of 'eco-tangibles', which referred to 'the presence of facilities and equipment that was environmentally appropriate and safe', was not as dominant as some would have expected given the resort location emphasized ecotourism. This result does confirm, however, the continual importance of the original five dimensions described by Parasuraman et al.

The second case relates to the resort community of Estes Park in the Rocky Mountains of Colorado. The critical summer business of this resort had been in decline for several years and an 'action research' study conducted by the local community revealed that 'problems and barriers in delivering quality customer service' was a major problem (Thomas, 2002: 380). A key feature of action research is to not only identify a problem but to suggest a solution. The Estes Park study confirmed that inconsistent service was a direct result of the lack of any customer service training programme, little effort among the providers of tourism services, and low awareness of the importance of customer service as a key marketing and management tool to attract new and repeat visitors. The suggested solution was to develop a tourist-centred customer service campaign, that was designed and executed by the community and branded as 'Smiles Above'. Thomas (2002: 389) considers this research and action approach rallied the 'community around a common theme that engages its stakeholders in adapting business and customer service behaviours which can generate the needed revenues and gains in market position'.

Summary

This chapter has demonstrated how the differentiating characteristics of resorts should lead to distinctive types and styles of marketing. If resorts are to attract and hold guests they need to emphasize their 'sense of place' qualities through place marketing, focussing not just on the core products but on the ambience and image of the total resort community. An important way to encourage greater collaboration and unity of purpose within the resort community is to adopt key features of the cluster theory, which goes beyond industry collaboration to embrace synergistic relations with government, community leaders and even tertiary education institutes.

It is apparent that resorts face major marketing challenges when their product appeal changes with the seasons. In many cases marketing has been dominated by high season concerns, to the detriment of developing secondary and innovative markets for the low season. One way to encourage a more balanced seasonal focus to marketing is to use branding as both a marketing and management strategy.

This chapter ends with two very different aspects of resort marketing. The first refers to the successful branding of a resort destination – Las Vegas, Nevada. Las Vegas conjures up a brand image of entertainment and gambling in a desert oasis town and using the work of local historian Hal Rothman we can see how this branding process was developed both as a marketing and management device. The second relates to an integrated resort complex – Whistler, BC. It focusses on resort marketing's need for accurate data in order to pursue a meaningful and successful promotional campaign. In Whistler, like more ski resorts, the emphasis has been to develop into a four-season resort, and its regular surveys reveal it has been successful in this regard. An important component of this success has been its monitoring of visitors and businesses, which allows it to measure trends and visitor patterns as well as overall visitor numbers.

Case studies

Las Vegas, Nevada, USA

The historian Hal Rothman, in his book entitled the *Neon Metropolis* demonstrates that a key to Las Vegas' international stature was finding innovative ways to fund the then new concept of building a desert city based on the hedonistic principles of entertainment and tourism. The '"miserable dinky little oasis town" as the mobster Meyer Lansky supposedly called it, and without transportation that made it easy to reach or air conditioning to make the stay bearable' (Rothman, 2002: 3) needed to find external supporters with money to create a modern city through tourism. In short, it had to sell itself as a tourism destination (place) to both business investors and tourists. In Rothman's view Las Vegas is a true twentieth century city, 'whose attractiveness was lost on Americans until after World War II and to the mainstream (global market) until well after 1975' (Rothman, 2002: 3), and whose success can be attributed to the use of branding as both a marketing and management tool.

It was not until 1945 that the early and small-scale development associated with the railways and military bases was overshadowed by the arrival of Benjamin 'Bugsy' Siegel and the introduction of organized gambling. Although Lansky and his associates had been considering Las Vegas as a gambling venue for several years, 'in most accounts Siegel receives (the) credit for envisioning the complicated relationship between gambling and status that turned the Flamingo Hotel into Las Vegas's first national destination' (Rothman, 2002: 10). While Siegel can be viewed as the champion of this new economic activity it would have gone nowhere without the financial backing of criminal syndicates. In the national competition for development capital after World War II a small and insignificant city like Las Vegas was never going to compete successfully for the peacetime recovery dollars with the major industrial cities by using the standard sources and channels of capital – the banks, bond and stock markets. It needed to find alternative sources to fund alternative economic development models. 'In southern Nevada the need for capital was so great that almost everyone looked the other way when it came to mob dollars . . . Anyone with money to invest was welcome, even Benny (Bugsy) Siegel' (Rothman, 2002: 12).

Mobster-connected financing could only take the development of a gambling– entertainment city so far, so the next growth spurt for the destination came in the late sixties with the arrival of Howard Hughes (subject of *The Aviator* movie) and a significant change in the state gaming laws. Hughes' entry into the casino industry brought a corporate profile and respectability that had previously been lacking. 'A man of his stature and wealth had little problem manipulating regulatory bodies in a state with weak government' (Rothman, 2002: 21), so he bought the Desert Inn which was the site of his penthouse hide-away, along with several other casinos, a television station, residential developments and thousands of acres of undeveloped land. By the time he had finished 'the tycoon controlled about one seventh of the state's gaming revenue, one-quarter of that in Las Vegas, and more than one-third of the revenue generated on the Strip' (Rothman, 2002: 20). Hughes was aided in this process by a significant change to the state's gaming laws when it introduced the Corporate Gaming Act of 1967. This act 'eliminated the requirement that each stockholder had to pass a Gaming Control Board background check . . . . Passage of the law opened the door for an infusion of corporate capital and raised the stakes in gaming. Corporations could now invest, inaugurating a new capital regime that brought Las Vegas closer to the primary avenues of capital formation' (Rothman, 2002: 21).

The Corporate Gaming Act came about in part because of the lobbying by Corporate and Financial America to have access to this new lucrative service sector business called gaming and tourism. By the late sixties Las Vegas had become an acceptable and popular diversion for much of the public and with the completion of the post-war economic recovery in industry, highways and housing Corporate America was looking for new areas and activities in which to invest. By having the investigation roadblock removed it meant that corporations were now free to invest their shareholders' assets in the gambling business without having to check their shareholders' individual backgrounds for criminal records.

In 1970 the Hilton Corporation purchased the Flamingo and International Casino resorts. 'With the arrival of Hilton and its enormous success in Las Vegas – by 1976, 43 percent of the gross revenues of the 163-hotel chain came from its Las Vegas operations – legitimate capital became available' (Rothman, 2002: 22). With evidence such as this and the new freedoms presented by the revised Corporate Gaming Act the pendulum of capital provision switched from the mob and the Teamsters Union to the much deeper pockets of conventional financing institutions. This not only created more casinos and their associated resort development, it also helped to bring about a change in the style of that development.

As Rothman (2002: 24) observes 'Once its capital came from the main-stream, its attractions could be shaped to the tastes of the mainstream audience. Las Vegas promised a luxury experience at a middle class price; now it could offer that price to the entire middle class. The gradual easing of the stigma of gaming and the willingness to merge gaming with conventional postwar attractions on the scale of Disneyland increased Las Vegas's reach ... Sin City became more palatable and maybe even marginally less sinful'.

The widely reported Disneyfication of Las Vegas occurred with this increased corporate investment as companies and individuals tried to appeal to a wider family market and in the process sanitized much of the actual and perceived seediness of past gambling establishments. One sign of this was the growing use of the term gaming, which does not have the same negative connotations for some. Another is the embracement of the 'experience economy'; or as Rothman (2002: xiii) describes it: 'In an age when goods no longer offer true distinction, we use experience to prove that we're special, to set ourselves apart from others, to win the ultimate battle of the cocktail party by having the most interesting story to tell'. The experience sold in Las Vegas today is the spectacular – spectacular resort casinos that often bring elements of past civilizations to the Strip, spectacular shows that are usually built around established stars, a base from which to visit the desert landscape with its spectacular Hoover Dam and Grand Canyon, and even its own light rail system to keep the destination in the forefront of urban transport planning (Figure 7.3). Little of what is on offer within Las Vegas is authentic in the academic sense, but 'in an age when faux beaches and resorts captivate tourists, Las Vegas appears no more inauthentic than any place else' (Rothman, 2002: 34).

According to Rothman (2002: 38) 'The malleability of the city makes it (all) possible. Las Vegas has yet to develop a fixed (static) identity ... In Las Vegas nothing is real and you know that . . . Las Vegas is (a) script. You write it, you pay to produce it, and it's yours to do with as you please'. This historian's empathetic view of his home town captures the essence of customer-centred branding. Las Vegas has established a global brand image of being a gambling–entertainment destination, but that is just its basic framework because it encourages visitors to build their own fantasies onto this image and structure. This enables Las Vegas to become what the guest wants, to become a customized and very personal experience. Evidence of this success can be seen in its excellent tourism numbers and the fact that 'by 1997 non-gaming expenditures made up 52 per cent of the total revenue in Las Vegas, and the percentage is rising' (Rothman, 2002: 39).

Figure 7.3 Spectacular Las Vegas.

Whistler, BC, Canada

Whistler has emphasized the attractions of its destination outside of the ski season to good effect, and one could say it is approaching the ideal 'Four-Season' situation. By marketing its golf courses, hiking trails and lakes it has become an outdoor recreation – nature tourism centre in the summer months (Figure 7.4). Also it has built on its overall reputation to attract conferences and seminars in the shoulder seasons. Its visitor numbers in the six months of summer have exceeded its winter six months for the past five years, but the room nights sold and revenue generated are still more concentrated in the winter season (Table 7.2).

Figure 7.4 Summertime in Whistler, British Columbia, Canada.

Table 7.2   Seasonal visitation at Whistler, BC, Canada

	Visitor estimates			Room night share	
	Summer (May–October)	Winter (November–April)	Total (May–April)	Summer (%)	Winter (%)
2000/2001	1 158 029	907 650	2 065 679	40	60
2001/2002	1 224 437	849 540	2 073 977	39	61
2002/2003	1 075 087	872 671	1 947 758	42	58
2003/2004	957 270	862 764	1 820 034	39	61
2004/2005	1 169 448	837 054	2 006 502	43	57

Source: Tourism Whistler.

Normally, when one sees a table representing visitor numbers in tourism it is usually good practice to be cautious, if not skeptical, because in open societies and markets it is not possible to count every visitor. In the case of the Whistler numbers, however, considerable effort has been made to create a reliable 'destination visitor attendance estimation model' (Kelly et al., 2006). Kelly et al. (2006: 8) report on how 'Tourism Whistler has made a conscious investment in acquiring visitor survey information in a systematic and comprehensive fashion', to understand the number and characteristics of this resort's visitors. It does this by taking data from a variety of sources:

- Aggregate monthly hotel figures on room nights sold, average length of stay and average number of people per room.
- Daily intercept surveys of visitors to determine their type of accommodation or whether they are day visitors, party size and length of visit.

From these data a simple programme can calculate the number of visitors and the average number of visitors per day. It is from this model that the figures in Table 7.2 have been derived. To check the validity of their model (Tourism Whistler) has compared the trends over the past nine years with other business indicators such as ski ticket sales (correlation of 0.93), total rounds of golf (0.93) and road traffic counts (0.87). Given these good correlations the authors conclude they have developed a robust system of visitor number estimation, and a system that deserves to be copied more widely.

Such figures and the quality of information they contain is an invaluable marketing aid, because they provide hard data on the success of promotional campaigns and can provide pointers to changing customer patterns and emerging market trends.

Questions

1 Why is place marketing even more important to a resort destination than to other tourism businesses and destinations? Explain how use of Porter's cluster theory can facilitate the development of strong place marketing.

2 Pine and Gilmore's 'experience economy' should remind resorts they are selling vacation experiences. How can resorts take advantage of the experience economy and build meaningful experiences for their guests?

3 Imagine you are the Destination Marketing Organization CEO for one of your country's coastal resorts, which consists of a highly variable seasonal tourism business. Explain the steps you would take to market this real resort destination on a year-round basis, and compare your proposals with its actual policy.

4 Discuss the various elements of branding and demonstrate how they can be integrated into a management strategy for a resort of your choice.

5 Compare and contrast de Chernatony and McWilliam's two dimensional description of brand imaging with Echtner and Ritchie's destination image dimensions in Figure 7.1.

6 More destinations are planning to introduce gambling in one form or other as a resort attraction. What marketing lessons can they apply from the Las Vegas experience and would an element or suggestion of mobsterism be helpful or a hindrance?

References

Ashworth, G. and Voogd, H. (1990). Can places be sold for tourism? In *Marketing Tourism Places* (G. Ashworth and B. Goodall, eds), pp. 1–16 . London: Routledge.

Berry, L.L. (1995). *On Great Service: A Framework for Action*. New York: Free Press.

Berry, L.L. and Parasuraman, A. (1991). *Marketing Services: Competing Through Quality*. New York: Free Press.

Blackpool Citizen (2006). Resort on list of 27 for super casino. www.blackpool/citizen.co.uk/display.var 725867.0. Accessed on 14 April 2006.

Buhalis, D. and Cooper, C. (1998). Competition or co-operation? In *Embracing and Managing Change in Tourism* (E. Laws, B. Falkner and G. Moscardo, eds), pp. 324–346. London: Routledge.

Butlin, Sir B. and Dacre, P. (2002). *The Billy Butlin Story 'A Showman to the End*. London: Robson Books.

de Chernatony, L. and McWilliam, G. (1990). Appreciating brands as assets through using a two-dimensional model. *International Journal of Advertising*, **9**, 111–119.

Dibb, S., Simkin, L., Pride, W.M. and Ferrell, O.C. (1994). *Marketing Concepts and Strategies*, Second European Edition. London: Houghton-Mifflin.

Echtner, C.M. and Ritchie, J.R.B. (1991). The meaning and management of destination image. *Journal of Tourism Studies*, **2(2)**, 2–12.

Goodall, B. (1990). Opportunity sets as analytical marketing instruments: a destination area view. In *Marketing Tourism Places* (G. Ashworth and B. Goodall, eds), 63–84. London: Routledge.

Horner, S. and Swarbrooke, J. (1996). *Marketing Tourism, Hospitality and Leisure in Europe*. London: International Thomson Business Press.

Kelly, J., Williams, P.W., Schieven, A. and Dunn, I. (2006). Toward a destination visitor attendance estimation model: Whistler, British Columbia, Canada. *Journal of Travel Research*, **44(1)**, 1–8.

Khan, M.M. and Su, K.D. (2003). Service quality expectations of travelers visiting Cheju Island in Korea. *Journal of Ecotourism*, **2(2)**, 114–125.

Kotler, P., Haider, D.H. and Rein, I. (1993). *Marketing Places*. New York: The Free Press.

Kurosawa, S. (2006). Please do not disturb. *The Weekend Australian*. March 6–7, Travel-11.

Maslow, A.H. (1970). *Motivation and Personality*, 2nd edn. New York: Harper and Row.

Middleton, V.T.C. and Clarke, J. (2001). *Marketing in Travel and Tourism*, 3rd edn. Oxford: Butterworth-Heinemann.

Pine II, B.J. and Gilmore, J.H. (1999). *The Experience Economy*. Boston: Harvard Business School Press.

Parasuraman, A., Zeithaml, V.A. and Berry, L.L. (1988). SERVQUAL: a multiple item scale for measuring consumer perceptions of service quality. *Journal of Retailing*, **64(1)**, 12–40.

Parasuraman, A., Zeithaml, V.A. and Berry, L.L. (1991). Refinement and reassessment of the SERVQUAL scale. *Journal of Retailing*, **67(4)**, 420–450.

Rothman, H.K. (1998). *Devil's Bargains: Tourism in the Twentieth-Century American West*. Lawrence, Kansas: Kansas University Press.

Rothman, H.K. (2002). *Neon Metropolis*. New York and London: Routledge

Rust, R.T., Zeithaml, V.A. and Lemon, K.N. (2004). Customer-centered brand management. *Harvard Business Review*, **82(September)**, 110–118.

Seaton, A.V. and Bennett, M.M. (1996). *The Marketing of Tourism Products: Concepts, Issues and Cases*. London: International Thomson Business Press.

Shaw, G.T. and Williams, A. (eds) (1997). *The Rise and Fall and British Coastal Resorts*. London: Mansell.

Stern, R.A.M. (1986). *Pride of Place – Building the American Dream*. Boston: Houghton-Mifflin.

Thomas, D.F. (2002). The impact of customer service on a resort community. *Journal of Vacation Marketing*, **8(4)**, 380–390.

8

Environment and site management

Introduction

Resorts and the environment are linked inextricably, both in the minds of the guest and management. This strong association between resorts and their environments has been recognized by Shaw and Williams (2002) in their typology of tourist resort developments, in which they identify 'coastal', 'alpine' and 'mixed' environments. To these we could add several other environmental categories. A distinctive 'desert' category has arisen given the development of resorts such as Palm Springs, Arizona and Las Vegas, Nevada in the US, Ayres Rock which is now called Uluru in central Australia, and the phenomenal rise of Dubai in the UAE. Likewise, we could identify rural resorts that focus on the natural delights of country living and its heritage, like the wine districts around the world and the stately homes of Europe, some of which now form the basis for a resort business. Possibly in the near future we may be able to add a 'space' category, if the orbiting space station takes on a tourism element. To develop the resort – environment link to its fullest potential will require careful stewardship and management, for many of the environments that attract resorts are sensitive and fragile, and some are dangerous.

In all resort-environment situations resorts have the opportunity to differentiate themselves through features of their environmental setting. Sometimes the environment is the main attraction and careful access needs to be provided to bring guests into contact with it, along with education to maximize the enjoyment and appreciation, as happens with national park oriented resorts. At other times the environment provides an opportunity to participate in a sport or recreational activity such as skiing, golf or white water rafting; where the environment needs to be adjusted and maintained for such activities if they are to be sustainable over the long run. In many cases, however, the environment simply forms the backdrop to other major resort activities such as rest and relaxation, the swimming pool or even the casino. While it is not being used physically it is still an important visual and psychological contributor to the resort image and requires careful maintenance. Hence, in all situations resort management needs to consider their environmental setting and to manage it with respect to a variety of different interests and users.

An important component of the environmental settings is how the resort designs its own structures and integrates them into the landscape and how it manages this community it has created. The buildings and other structures will need to be both distinctive and able to blend in with the existing landscape. They need to be appealing to guests and efficient to operate, and in some cases they should be whimsical if the resort is emphasizing fun. Increasingly, there is a call to respect and integrate with the local landscape and traditions, by building with local materials and blending with traditional architectural styles.

To provide an appealing environmental setting and structure for a resort along with the capacity to maintain these components while guests enjoy their vacation experience requires the development of a sustainable resource strategy. Sustainable not just in terms of the environment but also in terms of guest appeal and appreciation, so that it can provide a sound financial basis for the resort's long-term development and continuity. This will involve a clear vision that appeals to a variety of relevant stakeholders, especially the targeted customers; the careful integration of the resort's structure and activities with the environment; the monitoring of its impacts on the surrounding and regional environments, because its development will inevitably modify these environments; and the will to control negative impacts in light of its vision statement and sustainable future.

Sustainability for resorts

The Brundtland Report on *Our Common Future* brought the possibility of sustainable development to public attention with its description of that management goal.

Since that work was published there have been numerous conferences on how to bring about this management goal, most notably the 1992 United Nations Conference on the Environment and Development (UNCED Earth Summit) in Rio de Janeiro. This conference led to the creation of *Agenda 21*, which is an ambitious undertaking given that 'its goal was nothing less than to make a safe and just world in which all life has dignity and is celebrated' (United Nations, 2002). Not surprisingly such an ambitious and challenging goal has experienced both success and failure since its introduction. The biggest success has been to raise the world's awareness of the environment and to encourage large corporations to adopt, to varying degrees, more environmentally constructive policies. This is exemplified by the Green Globe Awards programme promoted by the World Travel and Tourism Council (Green Globe, 2006) and numerous voluntary codes of conduct adopted by various tourism businesses (Murphy and Murphy, 2004: 170–172). One of the more significant failures in terms of tourism, which is dominated by small- and medium enterprises, has been the difficulty in translating the academic papers and government reports into manageable operational processes for these small businesses (Murphy and Price, 2005).

Duality of sustainable development for resorts

Since resorts need to be developed as a business, the entire integrated resort complex or resort part of an urban conglomeration must learn how to combine business development needs with conservation and other aspects of sustainable development. Lewis and Green have observed that strategic planning, including that for sustainable development, involves a

Table 8.1   Comparison of planning and entrepreneurial approaches

	Planning approach: rational management	*Entrepreneurial approach: phase-shift management*
Management vision	Based on an 'objective' view	Based on a 'subjective' view
Time horizon	Long-term goals and strategic vision	Short-term gains with long-term personal vision
Locus of control in the development process	Monitoring and regulation of development resources	Monitoring and influence of development process
	Stakeholding of interest groups	Personal stakeholding
Decision-making	Consensual	Individualistic
Resource management	Known resource allocation	Unknown resource accumulation
Business/resort progression	Iterative	Discontinuous

Source: Lewis and Green (1998: 144).

continuous balancing act between the long-term objectives of the resort planner and the entrepreneurial nature of the resort businesses. To them there is a fundamental difference between the two parties, with the planner striving 'to control, integrate and allocate resources in order to achieve pre-determined objectives' while the entrepreneur/business person is 'constantly in search of opportunities, which are frequently found through innovation, intuition and a willingness to embrace unforeseen dynamic changes' (Lewis and Green, 1998: 141, 142). The contrast in these two approaches can be seen in Table 8.1 and its relevance to a sustainable development policy for resorts is undeniable.

One of the more obvious differences between the planning and entrepreneurial approaches is their respective time horizons. For the resort business, while it may have a long-term vision and goals that match sustainable development objectives in general, it has to consider the short-term record of its season or annual performance and its return to shareholders. If the revenue and profit generation is on target then the vision and goals remain in play, but if they fall short the business must consider alternative revenue generating options, just to survive.

The different decision-making approach is another factor that distinguishes the two components of resort planning. The planner increasingly seeks consensus from the various stakeholders in and outside of the resort to develop a sustainable development plan that is likely to receive sufficient support to succeed. The business operator may take advice from experience or colleagues but in the end the success or failure of their business rests with their personal decisions. This is why senior managers receive a substantial part of their income through bonuses, representing 'pay for performance'.

Finally, the whole business resort development process is seen differently by the two groups. The planner looking at the macro level and over a long time period sees a continuous trend line, much like Butler's Tourism Area Life Cycle (TALC) theory. But the businessperson with their annual reporting to their shareholders and bankers see development as a series of discontinuous steps. Some years will be good, but other years may be poor due to no fault of the entrepreneur, thereby requiring a delay to the vision's progress or maybe a complete reassessment. Lewis and Green provide a good example of this with respect to the external impact of declining snowfall during the 1980s in European ski areas. They note the planners attempted to tackle this problem with a long-term and reactive solution by steadily increasing the variety of winter tourism activities, so as to reduce the dependence on snow. In contrast, the skiing operators whose business was inextricably linked to snow attempted to tackle the problem head on, with a short-term and pro-active approach to provided artificial snow and to use previously out-of-bounds areas.

Pro-active planning

Although the entrepreneur-business approach will always differ from the formal planning approach, there is still more room for collaboration than is commonly realized. If the entrepreneur is shown the positive long-term benefits of a strategic planning concept, like the sustainable development of their business, it can be integrated into their individual planning and operational procedure. This is how many corporations and businesses have approached conservation and sustainability – as a long-term cost control and marketing measure, which can build the value of their business assets.

Howatson (1990) in a report for the Conference Board of Canada revealed many Canadian companies were adopting progressive environmental management practices and adjusting their corporate priorities and policies to maintain their profitability in the global marketplace. His report emphasized the importance of being pro-active in terms of environmental management, for such an approach provides the type of customized operational procedures that will work best for the company, in addition to meeting their corporate social responsibilities to local communities and the environment. Howatson, quoting from an Arthur D. Little Inc. survey of US corporate environmental management practices, identifies three positions a company can adopt regarding the environment and sustainable development:

Position 1: A *reactive* approach to environmental problems, tackling problems as and when they arise.
Position 2: *Conforming* to legislation by establishing systems and programmes to comply with regulations.
Position 3: A *progressive* approach, by moving beyond compliance to foresee hazards and regulations before they occur or are imposed.

Howatson notes most Canadian corporations had moved into position 2, as concern for the environment and a push toward greater sustainability occurred. But he feels corporations are missing an opportunity to better control and guide this aspect of their business if they do not become pro-active and move into position 3 by making the environment part of their corporate culture.

Some resort companies have taken such a pro-active approach and are benefiting in a variety of ways from this longer-term sustainable development approach. In a book prepared in conjunction with the Globe '92 conference in Vancouver on sustainable development, Hawkes and Williams (1992) provide a series of positive case studies on 'best environmental practice in tourism' that includes some resort examples.

One on the 'greening' of Canadian Pacific (now Fairmont) Hotels and Resorts emphasizes the benefit of working closely with the company's employees to bring about a comprehensive and successful environmental programme. It points out that use of the 3 Rs for *r*educing waste, *r*ecycling and *r*e-using materials has produced potential and actual long-term cost savings, substantial staff support and an improved corporate image (Hawkes, 1992: 13). An examination of the Great Barrier Reef Marine Park in Australia reveals how resorts have worked with park officials to provide sustainable development for both parties. 'The Great Barrier Reef Marine Park Authority is charged with a difficult task: that of taking a balance between development and protection of the fragile Great

Barrier Reef' (Kelleher, 1992: 54). The park achieves these two contra-dictory goals through a zoning process using four zonal categories:

1. *Preservation Zones*, in which virtually all human uses are prohibited.
2. *Scientific Research Zones*, which permit only strictly controlled scien-tific research.
3. *Marine National Park Zones*, which permit scientific, educational and recreational uses;
4. *General Use Zones*, which permit some commercial and recreational Fishing.

and by requiring recreation and tourism activities to seek operating per-mits that effectively allows regular inspection and impact assessment. In these ways the collaboration of park planners and tourism operators pro-vides 'an example of the practical application of the principles defined in the World Conservation Strategy' (Kelleher, 1992: 58).

Many of these efforts would go under-appreciated if it were not for marketing, which brings these policies and achievements to the attention of the public. More and more resort businesses and the tourism oper-ations within them, are selling themselves as environmentally friendly undertakings. Those that are serious about this often join accreditation systems which assess the environmental quality and practices of the operation before giving it their seal of approval. However, in the minds of some the processes of accreditation are still in their infancy and remain inadequate, while some marketing claims beggar belief and require stricter monitoring and control.

Applying sustainable development principles

Although there is some discussion concerning the divergent directions of sustainability and development, many consider them to be linked, like two sides of a coin, which with the appropriate management can harmon-ize the two forces into one combined and unified whole. A major chal-lenge is to move its development from the pages of academic papers and government reports to the strategic management of real tourism resources and communities, as we find in resort situations. It is here that the difficulties of measurement, organizational behaviour and assessment have come to the fore and have led some management people and aca-demics to question the utility of the concept. Among the techniques that have been suggested and tried with respect to sustainable development are carrying capacity (CC), Limits to Acceptable Change (LAC), Visitor Impact Management (VIM) and Ecological Footprint (EF) approaches.

Carrying capacity

CC has been rightfully described as 'a phrase delightful in its simplicity, complex in its meaning and difficult to define (or measure)' by Barkham (1973: 218).

The concept is *simple*. Each area of a resort environment can handle a certain number of visitors before the increasing number of visitors starts to destroy the area through over use. The point at which an area starts to deteriorate is its CC threshold, and increased use beyond that point will cause environmental stress and eventual degradation.

Closer examination of the concept reveals it is actually very *complex*. There is not necessarily a direct relationship between level of use and impact, and there are at least two dimensions in play. On the physical side, there is the impact on the local natural environment, but in terms of tourism one also needs to consider the guests and their human response to the changing situation. Some guests may be very sensitive to the changing conditions in the environment, especially those who have come to participate directly with that environment; others, who see and use the environment as a backdrop to their primary functions may be less aware and concerned about environmental changes. Thus management needs to consider tourist perceptions as well as the physical conditions of the environment in resort settings.

Finally, there is the issue of *definition and measurement*. Neither the physical – nor the behavioural scientists can provide a specific definition or measure of CC for each and every situation. For the biologist the natural CC will vary from site to site, depending on physical features like aspect and soil structure, types of users like native animals or tourists, and upon the season with its different climatic conditions. For those seeking to understand the attitudes and opinions of visitors, the variability will occur across visitor types, age groups and societal norms, and their measures will be influenced by the techniques used to understand the guests' mental processes.

The multi-dimensional nature of CC has been clearly described by Williams and Gill (2004) and developed by Glasson et al. (1995). Glasson and his associates have described CC as a capacity network, or capacity web, that involves three hard, objective and quantifiable dimensions

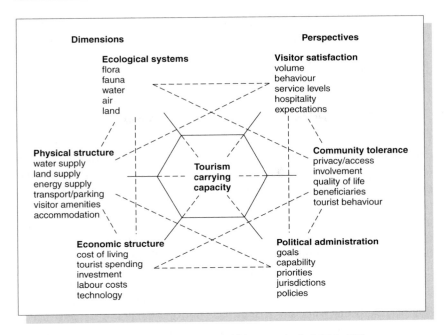

Figure 8.1 The carrying capacity web (Glasson et al., 1995: 52).

linked with three soft, more subjective and qualitative perspectives (Figure 8.1). The more objective dimensions include the area's economic-, physical- and ecological structure. The more subjective perspectives include visitor satisfaction, community tolerance and political administration. Each needs to be considered in the management of a specific site and applied in conjunction, where relevant, to the long-term goal of establishing and nurturing the area's sustainable development.

This multi-dimensional interpretation of CC further complicates its definition and measurement. First, we have to decide whose CC we are considering before attempting to measure it. Is it the state of the physical environment, the views of the planners and entrepreneurial business people or those of the guest? Furthermore, none of those categories is constant. Each of the variables under consideration will live up to the name 'variable' and change over different sites, purposes and vacation priorities. To illustrate how challenging this apparently simple building block to sustainable development can be, the following attempts by the World Tourism Organisation (WTO) and United Nations (UN) to provide practical guidelines is offered.

In a guide entitled *What Tourism Managers Need to Know* for the WTO, Consulting and Audit Canada (1995) recommends using CC as a core indicator of sustainable tourism, along with social impact, waste management and other indicators. But when it comes to recommending measures the advice is restricted to developing a 'composite measurement of the quality, quantity and sensitivity of the (resort) site's environmental assets and capacity of built structures' (Consulting and Audit Canada, 1995: 15). The UN's *Guidelines on Integrated Planning for Sustainable Tourism Development* defines CC as 'the maximum number of tourists that can be catered to while making full use of the tourism facility and amenity without causing undue damage to the environment' (United Nations, 1999: 113). It recommends creating a continuum (scale) showing the intensity of use suited to a particular environment or site, with no direct tourism use at one pole and unfettered tourism use at the other. But once again details regarding description (classification of variables) and measurement are missing, so it is left to management to create such a scale.

Inskeep (1991: 352–354), a leading tourism planner, has attempted to fill this gap with his work on measuring environmental impact. His 'basic model for environmental impact' reveals the difficulties managers of resort environments will face trying to implement a CC approach to sustainable development. He suggests the preparation of a checklist for likely negative environmental impacts to a site. This could include features such as:

- air pollution;
- surface water pollution;
- ground water pollution;
- noise pollution;
- solid waste disposal problems;
- damage or destruction of flora and fauna;
- land use and circulation problems;
- pedestrian and vehicle congestion in general and at peak times;
- landscape aesthetic problems such as building design, landscaping and signage;
- damage to historic, archaeological and other cultural sites;
- generation of erosion and landslides;
- damage from natural environmental hazards such as earthquakes or hurricanes.

Inskeep recommends each relevant feature from the above list, which should be generated according to each site and type of resort being envisaged for that site, be assessed along a scale in terms of its possible impact on the local and regional environment. Inskeep provides an example of this approach, which shows that in some cases such as air quality, ground water quality and road traffic it may be possible to develop quantitative data using existing sources like government reports. But in most cases this information will need to be gathered by the resort developers and operators themselves since local situations are unlikely to be part of regular government statistical reports. For other features, such as landscape aesthetics and potential damage to natural or cultural resources, qualitative judgments will be needed. Here the objectivity may falter because of different stakeholder priorities and the genuine difficulty of assigning a value to such factors. A value of some sort is needed to operate Inskeep's evaluation matrix because an assessment has to be made concerning whether to expect a 'no impact' to 'serious impact' environmental consequence. There are no set standards for these scalar classifications and in fact they can be expected to vary from site to site and resort development situation to situation. Hence, all attempts to conduct a scientific and objective CC analysis will be fraught with measurement and interpretation difficulties.

A direct application of CC within a tourism context has been undertaken by the Queensland Parks and Wildlife Service (personal communication, 2007). They note that acceptable standards of park conditions and use are determined either through specified legislation and management planning or more commonly through operational planning, and acknowledge that 'the definition of acceptable future conditions and the assessment of sites against those conditions is an imprecise science' (Queensland Parks and Wildlife Service, 2007: 3). They have, however, attempted to create an 'informed judgement' system to determine whether existing recreation use levels can be sustained given the impacts that are being experienced within the parks. They have created a 'Sustainable Visitor Capacity' measurement process for key visitor sites within their parks that follows earlier work on recreational CC and Inskeep's (1991) planning approach.

Queensland Parks and Wildlife Service utilizes a scoring system on the site's physical criteria, social criteria and management criteria, using a scale ranging from 1 (very low) to 10 (very high) on a variety of indicators. An overall average score is calculated from these scales and used to assess whether the existing use situation is sustainable; with average scores of six or above on the 10 point scale indicating management actions are required to bring the visitor activity back to a more sustainable level. Along with the overall scores their assessment exercise provides pointers as to what types of management action is likely to be most useful. It could suggest that the site can accommodate increased visitor use or needs to reduce impacts through actions such as hardening sites to make them more resilient to visitor use. Another option may be the use of management strategies to reduce the volume of visitor use by changing access to the site, issuing permits or even closing the site to allow for regeneration.

Limits to acceptable change

The realization that the scientific rigour associated with the CC concept is hard to achieve in real world situations has caused some to seek alternative management frameworks. Stankey et al. (1985) developed their ideas while seeking multiple uses for US National Forests, where they recognized the relevance of stakeholder perceptions to the calculation and applicability of a CC framework. Instead of trying to establish finite and predictable links between use level and impact, which is the basis of CC, Stankey et al. suggested a more practical approach involving:

- assess the likely impact of an activity on the destination,
- agree in advance what degree of change will be tolerated,
- monitor the industry (resort) on a regular and systematic basis,
- decide what actions will be taken if toleration standards are exceeded.

This is the basis of LAC which was set out in the nine sequential steps shown in Table 8.2.

Three important management improvements come with the LAC method. First, it recognizes that any human interference with a natural system will change it forever and that is certainly true of tourism, which has been described as an 'agent of change'. So the emphasis becomes what level of change is acceptable; and for resort management what level and type of change to the local environment will support the resort vision. Second, is the recognition that the environment is not simply a resource base or physical setting; it includes economic and social conditions plus political and managerial inputs. The political factors undoubtedly reflected the periodic forestry policy changes from Washington DC faced by the US National Forests authority, but as has been noted earlier government policy and its changing directions has a major impact on tourism and the resort investment climate. The acknowledgement of managerial influence is germane because few if any management decisions result in a neutral or benign impact. Once a management direction has been determined and acted upon it will have repercussions throughout the resort system, so management should be viewed as an active ingredient of the total resort environment. Third, this framework encapsulates the four

Table 8.2   LAC planning process with the four functions of effective management

1. *Define issues and concerns – leadership*
   economic
   social
   environmental
   political/institutional constraints
2. *Define and describe opportunity classes – leadership*
   resource
   social
   managerial
3. *Select indicators of resource and social conditions – planning*
   economic
   social
   environmental
   political
4. *Identify existing resource and social conditions – planning*
   current status of indicators
   standards database
5. *Specify opportunity class standards – planning*
   acceptable, observable, measure limits
6. *Identify alternative opportunity class allocations – organization*
   type of use
   location
   timing
7. *Identify management actions – organization*
   direct
   indirect
8. *Evaluate and select alternative management actions – controlling*
   costs versus benefits
   consensus building
   management capability
9. *Implement and monitor – controlling*
   compare against standards
   adjust management strategies accordingly

Source: after Stankey et al. (1985).

functions of management. It seeks input and *leadership* from a variety of relevant stakeholder groups. It brings them into the *planning* process, producing a vision for the area from these stakeholders. It provides guidelines for the *organization* of different land use and activity options. It brings the monitoring and responsive policy changes of the *controlling* function into the process. In total it represents a comprehensive management process that can operate effectively with a sustainable development goal.

Unfortunately, the LAC approach is restricted in its usefulness by two constraints. The first is the same weakness as the CC techniques that are imbedded within it – it is difficult to collect detailed information on all aspects of the 'capacity web'. As a result there is the real threat of general 'quality standards' being adopted arbitrarily, or at such a low level they may not be able to identify long-term and cumulative impacts. The second is that while the inclusion of various stakeholder groups in community significant decisions is valid and desirable, it can lead to delays and higher costs for the developer and businesses involved. Various strategies and processes are being developed within the planning field to develop collaborative rather than conflict situations (Murphy and Murphy, 2004), but the time and cost of such an approach needs to be appreciated and accepted as a necessary step on the path to a more communal assessment of what constitutes acceptable change and sustainable development.

A study by Needham and Rollins (2005) illustrates the difficulties and costs incurred in seeking the perceived acceptable standards of different stakeholder groups. In their study of summer use of the Whistler Mountain ski area they found significant differences in group perceptions regarding a 'minimum acceptable condition'. This indicates there is a need for negotiated common ground, and further consideration of collaborative planning techniques.

Visitor impact management

VIM takes the focus away from the physical environment and places it on the major agent of change in many settings – the tourist. It represents a more focussed management tool for resort management, in that its primary concern is the interactional experience between guests and the environments they have come to enjoy; subsumed within the need to keep those environments healthy and attractive to produce a sustainable development future. VIM shows we need to better understand the nature of tourist–environment encounters and impacts, and the factors behind their occurrence. This process reveals the fluid nature of tourist–environment relationships, that all tourists are not alike or looking for the same experiences. That all environments are not alike and will vary in their resistance and stress levels according to season and tourist priorities, as well as volume.

Since the relationship between use and impact is expected to be neither linear nor uniform five key interrelationship principles have been identified for examination (Glasson et al., 1995: 59–61):

- There is no single predictable response between the use of a setting and the visitor/host experience.
- Most impacts do not exhibit a direct linear relationship to user density.
- There is an inherent variation in the levels of tolerance between different groups in different settings.
- Some types of activity cause different impacts due to varying intensities of use and visitor characteristics.
- Tourist impacts are influenced by any number of site-specific and seasonal variables.

To examine these variable relationships requires on-site surveys of the landscape and the visitor, looking beyond simple descriptive factors such as volume of visitors, visitor to host ratios, length of stay, visitor activities and flora and fauna stress conditions; to search for reasons for the choices taken and their resulting impacts. This level of data and analysis takes time, resources and skill, but a lot can be accomplished by management through using its eyes and ears. Guests' body language and off-the-cuff comments to each other reveal much about how well a resort is meeting their expectations.

VIM surveys and management tools can be applied in a large variety of locations. Most have been applied in national park settings where the authorities are trying to find the right long-term balance between allowing recreation activities and the conservation of local flora and fauna. But they can also be used in high-density urban settings. Glasson et al. (1995) have used VIM techniques to study the type and distribution of visitor activity in Oxford, England, producing a series of management strategies designed to support Oxford's goal of enhancing visitor and host experiences of the city. Canestrelli and Costa (1991) have used a 'fuzzy linear programming model' to calculate Venice's socio-economic CC for its historic centre of St. Mark's Square. Their calculated CC of about 25 000 visitors per day is regularly exceeded, with peak day numbers reaching up to 200 000. So Venice needs to consider its visitors' experience and satisfaction levels in addition to the wear and tear on its heritage fabric and the danger of rising floodwaters. In fact it has now introduced a 'Venice card' as one way to control excessive demand, through pre-booking and more flexible charging systems.

Overall the VIM techniques offer two types of sustainable development strategy – 'hard' line and a 'soft' line (Glasson et al., 1995: 152–154). 'Hard' line approaches involve physical and/or financial restrictions on the access to sites and cities. The closure of a site or an attraction that is suffering from the excess pressure of visitors is one of the most extreme measures that can be taken and is a disaster from a management perspective because of lost revenue and reputation. Since accessibility is a key factor contributing to excessive use, its control is often the most visible form of hard line action, as in the case of entry fees and restricted viewing times for the most desirable attractions. 'Soft' measures include planning and marketing designed to modify behaviour and choice. In terms of planning, lesser known activities and attractions can be developed and promoted to spread the visitor load. This often involves a marketing component to convince visitors to try these 'new' options in high season or to visit the whole site out of high season. The author's personal experience of such attempts has not been particularly positive because the resort, national park or city often has forgotten to use both planning and marketing; thus leaving the guest or tourist to seek out these new delights on their own. However, as Glasson et al. (1995: 154) note, '"soft" and "hard" measures are not mutually exclusive'. It is often best to use a combination of the two to achieve sustainable development, and the proportions should change as conditions merit it.

Ecological footprint

A new indicator of sustainable tourism has been suggested to overcome some of the weaknesses in past measures, namely their localness and the exclusion of the travel component. The EF has been proposed as an 'accounting tool that enables us to estimate the resource consumption and waste assimilation requirements of a defined human population (resort) in terms of a corresponding productive land area' (Wackernagel and Rees, 1996: 9); and Hunter and Shaw (2007) argue it should become a key environmental indicator of sustainable tourism. The EF accounts for a person's use of energy, foodstuffs, raw materials and water along with the associated costs of transport-related impacts such as the carbon dioxide from burning fossil fuels, the costs of waste and pollution, and loss of productive land to the construction of roads and buildings in any activity. In terms of tourism Hunter and Shaw (2007: 55) feel that the local perspective of past sustainability measures 'underplays the recognition of tourism activity as a user of natural resources at the global scale', particularly as the measures we have looked at above take no account of the resource consumption and pollution involved in getting guests to the resort. Hunter and Shaw note that the transit zone (the distance and modal choices between home and the destination) can reach up to 50 per cent of the total EF for international trips involving air travel.

Hunter and Shaw (2007: 49) propose a 'gross tourism EF' should consist of two components, those that are generated in the transit zone and at the destination area. Calculations of the per capita environmental costs in these two components will need to be adjusted by subtracting the normal environmental costs incurred at the tourist's point of origin while s(he) is away from home, to provide a net assessment of the vacation's environmental costs.

Obviously such calculations will be complex and beyond the means of most resort management, but this big picture of the true environmental cost of a resort visit cannot be ignored. As the world becomes more conscious of global warming, water shortages, pollution and disappearing resources there will be greater pressure on all types of business to demonstrate their individual contributions to the world's physical health. Among these tourism and resorts will be of special interest, given their dependency on air travel in many cases and that they are viewed as a luxury and discretionary activity by many. Following the advice of Howatson (1990) it may be time to become more pro-active and to develop sustainability indicators that will enable resorts to lead future environmental policy rather than follow it. However, these indicators should be part of overall management schemes, and certain changes are being proposed in that regard.

Alternative management options

Given the difficulty in developing operational management techniques to assist with the goal of sustainable development, the search for alternative methods continues. *Growth Management* has been proposed as an alternative and more practical development management tool for resorts by Gill and Williams (1994). They claim 'the essence of growth management is how best to capture the benefits of growth while mitigating the consequences – in essence then, growth management is a systematic impact management strategy' (Gill and Williams, 1994: 213).

Gill and Williams view growth management plans as a way to guide a resort community's vision of its desired growth and development path. In most cases resorts depend on land use planning controls to provide the framework for their vision, embedding the principles of the vision into these comprehensive plans via zoning and density controls. In a growing number of cases these plans are supplemented by public investment strategies, such as affordable housing and community facilities, and the application of fiscal incentives or disincentives to provide such facilities and amenities as underground parking and landscaping.

Gill and Williams (1994: 214) consider 'there are two important features which distinguish growth management from more established planning approaches'. First, it is a *dynamic* approach that facilitates consensus building among stakeholders. Second, it incorporates the *implementation mechanisms* needed to achieve its objectives. They illustrate these two points with respect to the mountain resort communities of Aspen, USA and Whistler, Canada.

In Aspen local authorities have 'moved away from rigid master plan maps to a situation where the plans (are) developed through public communication and community consensus' (Gill and Williams, 1994: 215). This has resulted in a confirmation of some of the original concepts and changes to others. For example, the focus on community development continues to emphasize a balance between the needs of residents and visitors, but the resort's new growth centres policy channels development into areas where it can be served efficiently by public facilities and services. Employee housing has been excluded from the development competition system, whereby development proposals are ranked on the number of points they accumulate. These points are now oriented to meeting community needs such as an employee housing provision, a public facility provision or transport link, as well as design and energy efficiency qualities. In Whistler much effort has been put into providing affordable employee housing (see case study at end of Chapter 9), certain 'ice times' have been scheduled for residents only at the local ice arena, and less formal information/consultation meetings have been attempted in the form of 'living room' meetings, to bring the views of stakeholders out into the open and to start the search for workable consensus building.

Overall, Gill and Williams consider that a growth management approach provides a less restrictive and more human approach, which allows communities to plan and control their own futures collaboratively and comprehensively along the lines expressed in Figure 8.2. This figure reveals the importance of including several components of a successful resort development that are mentioned elsewhere in this book, along with a commitment to managing growth so it does not destroy the

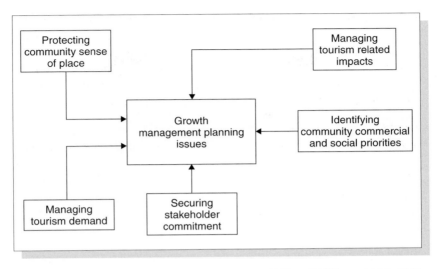

Figure 8.2 Growth management planning issues (Gill and Williams, 1994: 219).

environmental, economic and social functions of sustainable development. In the first instance it re-affirms the importance of protecting the resort's 'sense of place'; it promotes the management of demand through developing a resort that appeals particularly to the targeted market; it emphasizes the importance of identifying environmental impacts along with commercial interests and community priorities. All of these pragmatic dimensions are brought to bear on guiding the planning and management of growth, and will sometimes indicate a 'no growth' option is the best option.

While the Gill and Williams suggestions emphasize a communal approach to achieving sustainability through growth management, Flagestad and Hope (2001) emphasize the development of *Sustained Value Creation*. They argue there are close similarities between running a business and operating a tourist destination, which allows for the application of strategic management theories developed for the firm to be applied to a tourist destination. One of the more obvious overlaps in their mind is Porter's competitive advantage theory, as advocated in Chapter 2 of this book. They do note, however, that the overlap is not perfect, for differences between a firm and destination can exist in terms of boundary issues and the interpretation of efficiency. So they propose the term 'sustained value creation' rather than 'sustainable competitive advantage' to reflect 'the combined community, stakeholder and business goals of 'strategic success' in a destination' (Flagestad and Hope, 2001: 450).

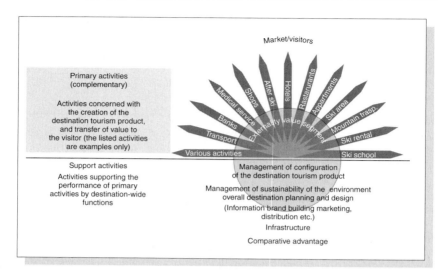

Figure 8.3 Value fan for winter sports destinations (Flagestad and Hope, 2001: 455).

In their assessment of the literature and tourism operations relating to snow resorts, Flagestad and Hope feel that European resorts have tended to emphasize a 'community model' of development, whereas North American resorts are viewed as emphasizing a 'corporate model' of development. The resorts on both continents are attempting to create a sustainable competitive position, but through these different approaches. Flagestad and Hope consider these two approaches can both benefit from the development of an alternative approach that builds on the work of Porter.

They start by asserting Porter's value chain configuration is not well suited to a resort's 'value creation' because of the non-sequential production process in a resort destination (Flagestad and Hope, 2001). Therefore, they propose a variant called a 'value fan' that emphasizes a site and individual focus for the resort destination activities, supported by a block of administrative functions that are designed to assist the whole destination (Figure 8.3).

To integrate the value fan into a strategic management approach requires two tasks according to Flagestad and Hope. Task 1 is management of the destination's *tourism product mix configuration*, developing the right blend of products to meet customer expectations and create the best value prospects for guests and local businesses. Task 2 is management of *sustainable development* through the stewardship of natural, cultural and social components. In this way task 1 can be viewed as representing the corporate interests of resort development, while task 2 takes on a community approach, and in the process becomes a more balanced management strategy.

Conflicting demands and land uses

Within the operation of a sustainable development management strategy it is inevitable that resorts will face the challenge of managing conflicting guest demands and activities. Planning to avoid or minimize conflict between activities begins with an analysis of guest preferences and behaviour patterns, first in general terms and then how they would relate to a specific site. Sweeting et al. (1999) place this stage as step 2 in their three-step tourism land use planning process where:

Step 1: sets the objectives and assign roles (core and support).
Step 2: determines the tourism, environmental and socio-economic priority areas.
Step 3: synthesize these priorities to form a zoning plan.

To guide resort development concerning general preferences there are academic studies, past plans and actual experience with various users. A more careful match between guest wishes and the final product can result in a higher quality tourism product, long-term sustainability, market differentiation and reduced costs and conflicts (Sweeting et al., 1999: 48).

A practical way to minimize conflict and maximize satisfaction is through the utilization of zoning and social engineering. 'Zoning regulations demarcate specific areas (within the resort) for different types of land uses and the development standards to be applied within each land use zone as a means of controlling land uses according to the plan and ensuring that standards are followed' (Inskeep, 1991: 432). In resorts these zones frequently include the careful placement of low-, medium- and high-density accommodation areas in quiet but accessible locations. Public areas like commercial complexes for retail-, transport- and entertainment- purposes need to be central and easily accessed, but sufficiently separated from the accommodation areas by distance or screening.

Mill (2001) has demonstrated how resorts can benefit from using design principles and practices taken from park planning experience. He quotes from Rutledge (1971) that the design of natural areas should address eight major principles:

1. Be sure that everything has a purpose.
2. Design for people.
3. Satisfy both function and aesthetics.
4. Establish a substantial experience
5. Establish an appropriate experience.
6. Satisfy technical requirements.
7. Meet needs for the lowest possible cost.
8. Provide for supervision ease.

(Rutledge, 1971: 79)

These principles represent the objectives of resort zoning in that they promote a principal purpose for each area of land; relate it to the recreational/tourist experience of the guest; and to the natural capacity of the land for sustainable development.

To support the physical arrangement of its zones a resort will need to encourage guests to adopt and adapt to this spatial planning of their vacation visit. The term 'social engineering' was discussed by King (1997) in his detailed comparative examination of resorts in Fiji and the Whitsunday Islands of Australia. While he came to no decision on the appropriateness of this label, the business focus of this book finds it highly relevant in the context of working with the customer to ensure physical plans like zoning work best for them and the operators.

The starting point for social engineering occurs with the promotion of a resort. 'The language of advertising is used to convey messages that receivers and potential consumers use to make judgements about what can be expected at the resort. Since island resorts are artificial creations, a social atmosphere or ambience must be engineered' (King, 1997: 188). Thus, the physically planned and developed resort must relay its intentions (products and image) accurately to potential visitors, to ensure they are willing collaborators in the resort image and experience upon arrival.

Two areas where zoning and social engineering will find clear synergies are in the development of ambience and convenience. To develop the right appeal for certain market segments requires the creation of 'an agreeable ambience in which guests will feel relaxed and at ease' (King, 1997: 188). Zoning can assist with this by providing the appropriate combination of land uses and where necessary separating discordant activities by screening or distance. The social and activity relations within resorts need to be 'played out in "convenience" as opposed to "obligation" based encounters' (King, 1997: 175). This means zones should be laid out to maximize the natural convenience of guests and there are classic examples of this in resort situations. One is to have a bar/restaurant facility close to both the 18th hole and swimming facilities, so it is possible to relax and reminisce after the physical activity. Another is to construct walking trails that not only exhibit and conserve the natural beauty of the area but are graded in terms of difficulty and effort.

To this point we have been discussing primarily the management of a sustainable environment within resort areas, but in the world of commerce we need to draw customers and guests to these environmental oases. This is not simply a matter of marketing, for as the Disney Corporation has demonstrated so clearly with its theme park development, it is also about creating a clear distinction between the outside real world and the inside resort world. As guests approach the resort they need to be placed in the right frame of mind, the entrance(s) to the resort should be welcoming and offer a foretaste of what is to come, and the access routes within the resort should be convenient and appealing.

Product design

Sense of place

'One of the primary objectives of resort planning and design is to create a sense of place' (Urban Land Institute, 1997: 111). Most guests are coming to a resort to experience something special and something different from home. An important part of this difference is the resort destination's distinctive character, a character derived from its geographical location, its climate, history and people – the unique qualities of that place which over time has differentiated it from other locations and societies on this earth. It is imperative, therefore, that when introducing a commercial resort enterprise into those local unique environments the developers do everything in their power to retain and enhance the local sense of place as a primary differentiator.

Since in many cases it is a resort's physical setting that draws guests the physical environment's protection becomes of paramount importance. A common starting point is the creation of the land use zones discussed previously, but within these zones it becomes necessary to determine areas of development concentration or banishment. Larry Helber, a noted resort planner, has been quoted with regard to development zones in noting 'concentration is important in site planning to produce social nodes or "positive congestion", along with placement of activities/attractions that enhance user convenience' (Urban Land Institute, 1997: 114). But certain areas should be avoided in terms of physical development. These include such obvious locations as steep slopes that are subject to landslides or avalanches, and the habitats of endangered flora or fauna. Others are less obvious because the impacts of development take time to emerge or are less visible.

In the first category of 'impacts taking time to emerge' are beaches. These may at first seem like a developer's dream – resilient and cleared by nature with its daily tidal surges. But beaches are living geological features, much like volcanoes, and are part of the ongoing long-term coastal erosion process. As the local wave action attempts to straighten out the coastline, beaches grow when they are fed by the erosion of local headlands, they are destroyed by severe storms like cyclones, or slowly starved and shrunk by the loss of headland mineral sources due to the interception role of groynes. Any development that interferes with this littoral process is doomed to eventual failure and high maintenance costs, as Miami Beach has found in maintaining its famous 'raison d'être' (Time Magazine, 1979).

In the second category of 'invisible impacts' are the coastal mangrove wetlands. These straggling swamp-like environments, located between the dry mainland and tantalizing beaches and bays, have appeared to many developers as natural reclamation projects. But we have discovered these untidy buffers between the fresh and salt water realms are some of nature's most important breeding and nursery grounds for fish and birds. To introduce seawalls, land fill and controlled lagoons or canals that maximize waterfront real estate means the death of significant wildlife numbers, with impacts felt locally and elsewhere as the food chain contracts.

The challenge becomes one of finding a balance with nature, that produces sustainable development and a product which is convenient and appealing to prospective guests.

Multiple use

Many resorts have developed a multiple use product design in order to cater for a range of guests and to seasonal variations in demand. To operate successfully multiple usage requires the development of synergistic relationships and the separation of conflicting relationships.

The development of synergistic relationships within a resort destination provides many opportunities to create attractive product packages. The Urban Land Institute (1997: 2–7) identifies several synergies in terms of accommodation, advocating a 'combination of hotels, time-shares and second homes increases the number of potential amenity users over a more substantial portion of the year', a prospect that is dealt with in more detail in Chapter 9. Given the expense of land and equipment it is also desirable to create multiple usage out of outdoor recreation investment. Many ski resorts have introduced summer activities to their ski-slopes, where the land has already been cleared and serviced by lifts. Now over the summer chair lifts take guests up the slopes for a variety of activities that can include hiking, mountain bike riding, mechanical luge runs, links golf or grass skiing.

A growing multi-functional use for those resorts with good access to major urban centres, either directly through proximity and a good road system or indirectly through access to a major international or national airport, is to offer their product and profile as a conference and meeting venue. This becomes the emphasis in the slow seasons and takes advantage of the resort's reputation for excellence in terms of its core activities and service quality. Even though the ski or beach season may be over and the key event long passed, the resort profile in these areas will provide a useful and different perspective for the conference and meeting market – a market that is always looking for something fresh for its clients.

Building design

To help make resorts more appealing and efficient a great deal of attention needs to be placed on the actual building design of a resort. The resort needs to take maximum advantage of its site location in terms of views and access to its principal attractions, to utilize the most convenient layout so staff and modern equipment can be used with the maximum efficiency, but within the constraints of aesthetics and sustainable development.

The first crucial step is to prepare an adequate infrastructure that will not only support the anticipated volumes of visitation in the short term, but will provide the ability to add-on elements as and when the resort expands its business. In addition the provision of infrastructure and associated utility services need to be invisible. Few guests wish to see the water storage and treatment facilities; but as we will see in the case of Kingfisher Bay Resort there is an opportunity at times to place such elements in the table of attractions. Furthermore, no guests would appreciate their views of the environment being spoiled by overhead wires or other utilitarian obstructions. In short, a well designed resort should avoid all the infrastructure shortcomings experienced at home, and this is an area in which Walt Disney World excels.

The buildings that stand on the infrastructure should be supportive of the sense of place concept in terms of style and building materials. In mountain locations this generally means extensive use of timber and stone, with steep roofs to encourage snow slippage and thus reduce the weight stress on roof trusses. In tropical beach resorts, some buildings need to reflect traditional designs, using thatch, wattle and daub, with open areas to allow the evening sea breezes to cool down the warm interiors. Where more modern creature comforts (air conditioning) or health regulations (food storage and preparation) need to be addressed, modern building designs can still include features and materials representing the local sense of place.

Education

All of this emphasis on sustainable development and sense of place will raise the price of resort building and development, so how are resorts to recoup these extra costs and remain competitive? One obvious answer is to educate the potential guest regarding the care and attention that has been spent on developing a sensitive and attractive environment for their visit. Another is to use the opportunity to educate and entertain (edutain) guests about their environment and their role in maintaining it.

Much of this education goes out in the form of promotional material for the resort. The marketing of a resort, which emphasizes its vision and features is an attempt to educate the public about what it has to offer. In a growing number of cases these advertisements emphasize the environmental sensitivity of resort destinations, to the extent that more are committing to environmental accreditation schemes.

Once on-site there are a growing number of educational programmes about the local environment and community. In many cases these take the form of in-room pamphlets explaining the local environment and the resort's attempts to act as a responsible member of the global community. In other cases there are seminars for those who would like to learn more about the local environment and culture. There can be tours to take guests to see the local physical and cultural environments and encourage them to develop an appreciation for the local sense of place within and around the resort. Although the most effort and appreciation for environmental education occurs within ecotourism resorts, there is some degree of environmental education in all resorts, even if it is restricted to the now ubiquitous requests to conserve water and protect the local environment, by setting aside only soiled towels for the laundry.

An important feature of 'edutainment' regarding the environment is that it needs to compete with an increasingly sophisticated world of television documentaries. These documentaries bring dramatic wildlife and heritage stories into the home via large screens and computer graphics that will be difficult to emulate in the field. As a result resorts will need to raise their levels of presentation and edutainment if they wish to attract and satisfy guests interested in local environment and culture.

Waste management

An important element of this education process is the growing interest in waste reduction and resorts are certainly excellent locations in which to promote the three Rs of the waste management hierarchy, because resorts can easily become scenes of excessive consumption. When guests are on holiday, especially in up-market luxury resorts they do not generally think about conservation. Tuttle (1994) in her study of water use in a variety of holiday venues on Orcas Island in the Puget Sound of Washington State, USA found a rising consumption level associated with grander accommodation choices. The up-market resort also had the most unfavourable comparative statistics when vacation usage rates were compared with home consumption (Table 8.3). Tuttle does not provide average household size figures for Orcas Island and Seattle, but if one took a conservative figure of 2 people per household then the home consumption would be halved and produces the estimated per head consumption figures in the brackets. If the average household size was any larger, the differential between vacation and home would be even larger.

The reason for the different vacation consumption rates is the varied facilities and practices within each type of accommodation. The B & B hotel had no swimming pool, shipped its laundry off-island and watered its garden with unmetered and untreated water. The condominium hotel had a pool and jacuzzi, linens were washed on-site, and each condo-unit had a washer–dryer and a kitchen and bathroom, plus it had larger

Table 8.3   Varying levels of water usage between vacation and home sites

Accommodation types	Average water consumption (litres/person/day)
Vacation B & B Hotel	225
Condominium Hotel	299
Upmarket Resort	649
Home	
Orcas Island (per household)	455–569* (228–285)
Seattle (per household)	758 (379)

*The range is dependent on whether the household has access to a well or other water system.
Source: Tuttle (1994).

grounds to water in the summer. The resort had four swimming pools and a jacuzzi in the summer, and one pool and a hot tub operating in the winter. Every guestroom had a full bathroom and some had two. Linens were laundered on-site, and water was used at the marina to fill boat storage tanks and to wash boats. The extensive grounds and landscaping were not drought tolerant in design, but were watered with untreated and unmetered water.

With usage figures like those described by Tuttle, along with substantial solid waste output, resorts have been eager to adopt waste management strategies. The cost of supplying fresh water, treating waste water and disposing of solid waste has grown with rising affluence, declining resources, and a lack of acceptable disposal sites, but as the world's resources have declined and become more expensive there has been an economic as well as environmental rationale for recycling. This had led to the development of a more comprehensive waste management hierarchy of strategies.

The *waste management hierarchy* is a set of management priorities in the following order:

1. *waste avoidance*: practices which prevent the generation of waste altogether;
2. *waste reduction*: practices which reduce waste;

3. *waste reuse*: direct reuse of waste materials for the same grade of use;
4. *waste recycling or reclamation*: using valuable components of waste in other processes;
5. *waste treatment*: to reduce hazard or nuisance, preferably at the site of generation; and
6. waste disposal.
(Australian Commonwealth Environment Protection Agency, 1992: 11)

In the above hierarchy, the first four stages should be the preferred approach, being selected over waste treatment or disposal options wherever possible. The ideal situation would be to have closed loops in overall material flows, with no usable materials lost as waste.

To make such a management strategy work all stakeholders need to be educated and brought on board. The incentive is there for management in the form of additional differentiation and long-term cost savings, but needs to have the support of regular staff to move from theory to practice. Hawkes (1992: 13) reports that the Chateau Whistler's successful 'greening' was due in large part to staff members who 'prove(d) to be invaluable as a resource for ideas, information, enthusiasm and action'. Finally, and most significantly the guest must be educated that this is the way to go forward; especially if we are to convince guests to take shorter showers, accept unpackaged communal jams and condiments, walk to nearby activities or wait for a bus, and not to treat the toilet as a general waste system. All of our ambitions for sustainable development within resorts will come to naught if we cannot educate and convince the consumer, and there is room for improvement in this area.

Summary

This chapter has demonstrated the importance of caring for the physical environment of a resort site, and has illustrated the need to adopt a sustainable development approach to the management of this resource. The underlying concern with sustainable practice is not to exceed the CC of the land, but for resorts this is a challenging concept to implement due to the human perceptions and physical conditions associated with leisure activities in the natural environment. However, the chapter presents a series of alternative techniques to implement sustainable development, that as refinements of the CC concept can offer management a combination of resource management strategies.

An important aspect of the resort experience is how well the site design links together the natural features of the resort with guest interests. In conjunction with a sustainable development approach should be an emphasis on retaining the area's sense of place. This is an increasingly recognized destination differentiator, and resort management needs to design the resort layout in a way that achieves sustainability with local materials and culture.

The two case studies that conclude this chapter are examples of how resorts can achieve sustainable development objectives through careful management of their environment. The first case refers to Walt Disney World's massive investment that turned marginal farmland into a most desirable location, by working with nature on a large scale. It has resulted in a benchmark operation in terms of environmental planning and management. The second involves a much smaller scale operation, but the Kingfisher Bay ecotourism resort has not only developed an harmonious facility within the sand dunes of Fraser Island, it has demonstrated how ecotourism education can be extended to explaining and minimizing human impact on the environment. It has taken the daring step of placing its wastewater management plant on the list of local attractions, bringing to the notice of its ecotourist guests the relevance of a well managed system to the future of our environment.

Case studies

Walt Disney World, Florida, USA

The Disney company assembled some 43 square miles of marginal farmland and swamp, located 16 miles southwest of Orlando, at an average price of $200 per acre. The area was not developed until a new political jurisdiction (the Reedy Creek Improvement District) was created, as discussed in the Governance chapter, because of the need for comprehensive planning and development control to transform this marginally productive land into a major resort. By the end of the millennium, according to Capodagli and Jackson (1999: 41) less than half of the acreage had been used and the undeveloped land value had risen to 'more than $1 million per acre'. As such Walt Disney World's environmental development provides a benchmark case of how to develop land in a sustainable and productive manner.

The basis of Disney World's environmental achievement is water management, for this marginal land was subject to flooding in the summer months and drying out over the rest of the year, except for the swamp-land depressions. The water levels are now maintained at normal seasonal levels by a series of 17 self-regulating dams and several natural and artificial storage lakes throughout the property. The quality of water passing through the 40 miles of irrigation canals is monitored constantly. The natural drainage is from the north and water enters the district at 11 different points. Each entry point is monitored daily and the water can be refused and diverted if its quality falls below acceptable standards.

These procedures enable the Reedy Creek Improvement District to provide the quality and appropriate seasonal flow of water necessary to maintain the natural vegetation and wildlife of the central Florida wetlands. Within the developed resort area to the north of Interstate 4 this means extensive open space between the tourist attractions, including rough pasture, woodlands, streams or dry river beds depending on the season. To the south of the freeway buffer is a preserved and wild wetlands conservation area, which generally goes unnoticed because public admission is prohibited. The result is a secure conservation area that operates adjacent to an international tourism magnet which draws millions of visitors a year.

In order not to contaminate the fragile wetlands and surrounding buffer zone, the prime tourist attractions have been designed to have minimal environmental impact on their surroundings. A tertiary sewage treatment plant removes 97 per cent of suspended solids and much of its waste water is returned to the ecosystem via irrigation of the local golf courses and an ornamental tree farm. In this way the sewage treatment plant and the irrigation canals maintain the flushing and filtering system of the local vegetation's kidney function and replenishes the Reedy Creek Improvement District's water table. This contrasts to the less controlled development experience of surrounding regions, where a dropping water table has led to the creation of well named 'sinkholes' and the subsidence of land and buildings into the ground at some locations.

Within the developed area the various theme parks, residential, retail and recreation areas have been located in respect to the overall water management plan. The major theme parks have been built on natural or artificial islands to protect them and their considerable investment against periodic floods. Each park has been constructed over an infrastructure system of 'utilidors' (utility corridors), where the electricity, water and sewage systems are located above the heads of staff, as they go about preparing for their duties before appearing on stage via secluded side entrances. Hence, if there is a need to repair or upgrade a service the theme park streets remain untouched and unimpeded as the work is carried out from below. Many of the storage lakes have been converted into prime accommodation and recreation sites, and some canals form a pleasant water transport link between different facilities. Golf courses have become a major feature of Walt Disney World's appeal and they are situated within the floodplain areas because their occasional flooding would not be disastrous, but merely add to their natural green lustre. Even the secluded accommodation units associated with these areas have been built on pedestals that will keep the expensive equipment and furnishings above the 25 year flood level (Figure 8.4).

In addition to preparing for future flooding the Reedy Creek Improvement District prepared for the environmental impact of millions of visitors. The majority of visitors are directed to the 'hardened' sites of the Magic Kingdom, EPCOT and Disney-MGM Studios, along with their accommodation complexes and Downtown Disney; where visitor activities are directed by various pathways and buildings. People are moved between these points with dispatch and minimal impact on the environment by providing monorail and bus systems of public transport that encourage many to leave their cars behind. The tons of litter generated by the visitors are not only swept up with alacrity but are speedily removed from the major tourist centres via an underground vacuum system that leads to a compaction plant and incinerator. The incinerator is one which cleans its own stack emissions so that air pollution is minimized and its heat is used to create hot water for the resort.

This high level of forethought has enabled Walt Disney World to develop both a sustainable environment and a profitable business. Disney World has been developed into 'a vacation resort at which the visitor is expected to spend a large amount of time (and money); the idea has been turned into a total holiday destination' (Bryman, 1995: 67) and as such it needed to provide a variety of experiences within a pleasant environment. The environmental planning based on the water management framework has delivered such an environment in central Florida, where previously the land was considered and valued as marginal. In 1999 Michael Eisner, the then CEO of Disney stated that 'Even after setting aside land for three new theme parks and 60 000 hotel rooms, and 9 000 acres for a permanent nature preserve and wildlife conservancy, there remained some 9 000 available acres south of US 192'

Figure 8.4 Walt Disney World Resort (USA), beyond the theme parks.

(Eisner with Schwartz, 1999: 407). It is that area where Disney World has completed Walt Disney's 'unrealized dream for a city of the future' and constructed the town of Celebration. One focus of Celebration is on health, with the goal of emphasizing 'prevention, diagnosis, health and wellness' (Eisner with Schwartz, 1999: 408). In this way Disney World has become the complete resort, complementing its original short stay and entertainment functions with permanent residency and a human health emphasis to imitate what it has achieved with the natural environment.

Kingfisher Bay Resort, Queensland, Australia

In contrast to the grand scale of Walt Disney World, Kingfisher Bay Resort on Fraser Island offers an ecotourism experience that not only presents the wonders of nature but also shows human's role within it. Fraser Island is the world's largest vegetated sand bar island and is on the World Heritage List, it measures 120 by 14 kilometers and is protected as the Great Sandy National Park. One place to stay on this large island is the 160-acre (64 hectares) Kingfisher Bay Resort, which has combined luxury accommodation with an ecotourism theme. It provides an education centre and a variety of tours with respect to the island's unique environment; but in following the tenet of the quote on its lodge wall:

We only preserve what we love,
we only love what we understand,
we only understand what we study.

The resort has also demonstrated how we can live more harmoniously within such an environment by including its waste water treatment plant as part of that learning process.

The resort has a tertiary treatment plant that is close to the main facilities, but in a secluded area. It has a capacity to handle 1500 people which the resort comes close to achieving at its regular peak seasons of Christmas, Easter and Whale Watching. As with all tertiary treatment plants this well run plant produces no unpleasant aromas and most of the waste is water, which after cleansing is fed back into the local ecosystem. The remaining sludge is placed into large scale worm farms where they mix with vegetable matter and recycled paper to create a rich compost. The compost is used on the plant's herb farm which supplies the resort kitchens (Figure 8.5).

Figure 8.5 Kingfisher Bay Resort's (Australia) ecotourism message and attractions.

The novel aspect of the Kingfisher Bay Resort waste water treatment facility is that it is not closed to the public, but quite the reverse – it is open to public scrutiny and education. This is done through a series of information boards that guide the visitor through the three treatment phases, ending with the worm farm and highly productive herb gardens. What was our human waste has been treated before being safely returned to the island ecosystem and what is regularly characterized as an infrastructure cost has been converted into an attraction component and revenue earner for this ecotourism business.

Questions

1 Critically analyse the Brundtland Report's definition of 'sustainable development' from a resort management point of view, along the same lines the book examined Barkham's description of 'CC'.

2 Explain what is meant by 'hard' and 'soft' controls within VIM systems, and illustrate their effectiveness or otherwise at a resort of your choice.

3 Discuss which level of management would be most appropriate for the implementation of the 'EF' indicator and how resorts should be assessed within such a technique.

4 Compare and contrast the merits of using Porter's 'value chain' to Flagestad and Hope's 'value fan' for a beach resort management structure.

5 Examine the entrances to three resorts, that cater to a local-, regional- and national/international market respectively and analyse how well they are catering to the needs of their prime clientele.

6 'Walt Disney World has demonstrated you can have a protected conservation area right next to a major tourist attraction'. How has Disney's environmental planning enabled this, and are there any lessons that could be transported to national park resorts?

References

Australian Commonwealth Environment Protection Agency (1992). *National Waste Minimization and Recycling Strategy*. Canberra: Department of Arts, Sport, Environment and Territories.

Barkham, J.P. (1973). Recreational carrying capacity: a problem of perception. *Area*, **5**, 218–222.

Bryman, A. (1995). *Disney and His Worlds*. London: Routledge.

Canestrelli, E. and Costa, P. (1991). Tourist carrying capacity: a fuzzy approach. *Annals of Tourism Research*, **18(2)**, 295–311.

Capodagli, B. and Jackson, L. (1999). *The Disney Way: Harnessing the Management Secrets of Disney in Your Company*. New York: McGraw-Hill.

Consulting and Audit Canada (1995). *What Tourism Managers Need to Know*. Madrid: World Tourism Organisation.

Eisner, M.D. with Schwartz, T. (1999). *Work in Progress*. London: Penguin Books.

Flagestad, A. and Hope, C.A. (2001). Strategic success in winter sports destinations: a sustainable value creation perspective. *Tourism Management*, **22(X)**, 445–461.

Gill, A. and Williams, P. (1994). Managing growth in mountain communities. *Tourism Management*, **15(3)**, 212–220.

Glasson, J., Godfrey, K. and Goodey, B. (1995). *Towards Visitor Impact Management*. Aldershot: Avebury.

Green Globe (2006). The Green Globe Program. www.greenglobe.org. Accessed on 21 May 2006.

Hawkes, S. (1992). The 'greening' of Canadian Pacific Hotels and Resorts: The Chateau Whistler case. In *The Greening of Tourism: From Principles to Practice* (S. Hawkes and P. Williams, eds), pp. 9–13. Burnaby, BC: Centre for Tourism Policy and Research, Simon Fraser University.

Hawkes, S. and Williams, P. (1992). *The Greening of Tourism, from Principles to Practice*. Burnaby, BC: Centre for Tourism Policy and Research, Simon Fraser University.

Howatson, A.C. (1990). *Toward Proactive Environmental Management*. Ottawa: Conference Board of Canada.

Hunter, C. and Shaw, J. (2007). The ecological footprint as a key indicator of sustainable tourism. *Tourism Management*, **28(1)**, 46–57.

Inskeep, E. (1991). *Tourism Planning: An Integrated and Sustainable Development Approach*. New York: Van Nostrand Reinhold.

Kelleher, G. (1992). Sustainable development of the Great Barrier Reef Marine Park. In *The Greening of Tourism: From Principles to Practice* (S. Hawkes and P. Williams, eds), pp. 53–58. Vancouver, BC: Centre for Tourism Policy and Research, Simon Fraser University.

King, B.E.M. (1997). *Creating Island Resorts*. London: Routledge.

Lewis, R.D. and Green, S. (1998). Planning for stability and managing chaos. In *Embracing and Managing Change in Tourism* (E. Laws, B. Faulkner and G. Moscardo, eds), pp. 138–160. London: Routledge.

Mill, R.C. (2001). *Resorts: Management and Operation*. New York: John Wiley and Sons.

Murphy, P.E. and Murphy, A.E. (2004). *Strategic Management for Tourism Communities: Bridging the Gaps*. Clevedon: Channel View Publications.

Murphy, P.E. and Price, G.G. (2005). Tourism and sustainable development. In *Global Tourism* (W.F. Theobald, ed.), 3rd edn, pp. 167–193. Amsterdam: Elsevier–Butterworth Heinemann.

Needham, M.D. and Rollins, R.B. (2005). Interest group standards for recreation and tourism impacts at ski areas in the summer. *Tourism Management*, **26(1)**, 1–13.

Queensland Parks and Wildlife Service (2007) *Tourism in Protected Areas*, Appendix 1: Sustainable Visitor Capacity and Field Assessment Sheets; and personal communication, March.

Rutledge, A.J. (1971). *Anatomy of a Park: The Essentials of Recreation Area Planning and Design*. New York: McGraw-Hill.

Shaw, E. and Williams, A.M. (2002). *Critical Issues in Tourism: A Geographical Perspective*, 2nd edn. Oxford: Blackwell Publishers.

Stankey, G.H., Cole, D.N., Lucas, R.C., Peterson, M.E. and Frissell, S.S. (1985). *The Limits of Acceptable Change (LAC) System for Wilderness Planning*. Washington D.C.: US Department of Agriculture and Forestry.

Sweeting, J.E.N., Bruner, A.G. and Rosenfeld, A.B. (1999). *The Green Host Effect: An Integrated Approach to Sustainable Tourism and Resort Development*. Washington D.C.: Conservation International.

Time Magazine (1979). Costly facelift for an old resort. *Time*, August 13, 29.

Tuttle, C. (1994). Sustainable water supply for future Orcas Island tourism development. *Proceedings of Quality Management in Urban Tourism: Balancing Business and Environment*. Faculty of Business, University of Victoria, Victoria, BC, pp. 89–98.

United Nations (1999). *Guidelines on Integrated Planning for Sustainable Tourism Development*. New York: United Nations Economic and Social Commission for Asia and the Pacific.

United Nations (2002). *Johannesburg Summit 2002 – agenda 21*. www.johannesburgsummit.org/html/basic-info/agenda21.html. Accessed on 21 May 2006.

Urban Land Institute (1997). *Resort Development Handbook*. Washington D.C.: Urban Land Institute.

Wackernagel, M. and Rees, W.E. (1996). *Our Ecological Footprints: Reducing Human Impact on the Earth*. Gabriola Island: New Society Press.

Williams, P.W. and Gill, A. (2004). Addressing carrying capacity issues in tourism destinations through growth management. In *Global Tourism* (W.F. Theobald, ed.), 3rd edn, pp. 194–212. Amsterdam: Elsevier–Butterworth Heinemann.

World Commission on Environment and Development, Chair – Gro Harlem Brundtland (1987). *Our Common Future*. Oxford: Oxford University Press.

9

Community and housing relationships

Introduction

This chapter examines the relevance of community to resort decision-making and focusses on one important business and community factor for resort management, the provision of housing options for guests and staff. Every level of resort development has elements of community within its structure, especially if we take the following two descriptions of community as our guide:

> Community comes from the word communion, to share a common task together. And it's in the sharing of that task that people do bigger things than they knew they were capable of. Then there really is something to celebrate.
>
> (Roddick, 2000: 55) (Internal community)

> Community is a self-defining term 'based on a sense of shared purpose and common goals.'
>
> (Joppe, 1996: 475) (External community)

The community that Anita Roddick refers to is the company staff or internal community, which in a resort situation will be a varied assembly of people and talents. However, for resorts there is also the external community that includes the neighbouring communities or surrounding metropolis, plus regional or national relationships. The external communities supply its labour force, provisions, complementary attractions and activities and the essential goodwill. The emphasis of this chapter will be on developing the community links between individual businesses (resort hotel, ski-lift company or restaurant) within a resort community and between the resort and its surrounding communities, to draw targeted market segments to the destination area.

Community relations are taking on a larger role for resorts as the investment process becomes more complex, the sustainable development objectives more political and the competition more fierce. Huffadine (2000: 41) observes 'the construction project, financing of infrastructure, and later the supply and staffing of the resort will depend on local goodwill and labour'. If the resort and local community are to survive in the competitive global tourism market, Rogers (2001: 136) feels the 'Triple Bottom Line audit concept (needs to be) recast for application to community development'. In Rogers' view, to produce a competitive resort within a sustainable community framework would call for a business partnership between the two that:

- utilises nature's ability to provide for human needs, without undermining its ability to function over time;
- ensures the well-being of its members: offering and encouraging tolerance, creativity, participation and safety;
- empowers people with shared responsibility, equal opportunity, access to expertise and knowledge and the capacity to affect decisions which affect them;
- consists of businesses, industries and institutions which collaborate as well as compete, are environmentally sound, financially viable and socially responsible, and which invest in the local community in a variety of ways.

(Rogers, 2001: 137)

This is the type of community relationships that this chapter addresses, and a prime concern should be that tourism is an agent of change for a community. Change occurs in the community power base by creating new 'winners' and 'losers', by bringing it into contact with new ideas and priorities, it can restructure local society and by developing new market conditions it will place new demands on the local resource base.

Tourism as an agent of change

When resorts bring large numbers of guests to a destination they become inverse factories, bringing customers to their product which has been pre-assembled and resourced for their enjoyment rather than shipping the product out to customers around the world. Said customers were at one time visualized as being benign, taking photographs and leaving only footprints; but as the reality of mass tourism has revealed even tourists with the finest of intentions create significant local impacts. The reality has often been different from earlier naive expectations. The physical impacts have included stress and erosion of the environment; social impacts have included a westernization of local cultures; economically certain sectors have benefited such as entrepreneurs and the young and female workforce, while others have lost labour to the bright lights of resorts or lost access to their traditional resource base; and all have suffered from a dramatic rise in local housing costs if the resort destination becomes a popular second home or retirement community.

Many of the above issues have been linked to successful resort development and the general growth in tourism because of their visibility and apparent direct correlations. Saveriades (2000: 154) notes in his survey of residents in Cypriot seaside resorts:

> It is widely accepted that there have been changes in the lifestyle, traditions, social behaviour and moral standards, especially of the younger generation. In many cases young Cypriots have adopted values about sex, dress and morality quite different from traditional ones.

But one of the reasons residents make such correlations is that tourism is highly visible and as a result receives the blame for change by association, without sufficient acknowledgement that the world itself is changing. To use the example cited by Saveriades, the youth of Cyprus would also be influenced in their attitudes to sex, dress and morality by the general media revolution (television, music and tabloid press), the freer global exchange of information (Internet) and worldwide decline in traditional values and morals, regardless of whether they had resorts and tourists in their home regions or not.

Someone who has thought about the changes brought about by tourism and how we respond to them is Brown, in her book *Tourism*

Reassessed: Blight or Blessing?. Brown (1998: 115) acknowledges that 'the impacts of tourism cannot be divorced from the wider context in which it occurs' and notes it has been conditioned not just by major features of the post-industrial era and the dominance of western capitalism, but by the discrete responses of host environments. Within those receiving areas there are conflicts of values and priorities, and different levels of influence.

> It depends on how the (tourism) industry responds to structural changes in the world economy and, above all it depends not only on who is affected, but also on who is in charge of who gets affected. In other words, we are back to power and politics.
>
> (Brown, 1998: 78)

Brown, like others before her, observes that the boundaries between social, economic and environmental impacts become increasingly blurred the more they are examined; tourism can have negative impacts along one dimension while creating positive impacts elsewhere, and such assessments are not the same for different groups of people. All these situations suggest the need for consultation and trade-off. Brown (1998: 125) suggests one way to achieve this is to recognize 'the individualism that has reached its apotheosis under late capitalism is now being attacked through the advocacy of movements such as communitarianism, an attempt to blend socialist ideas of the common good with individual responsibility'. If one treats Brown's 'communitarianism' as a movement that is concerned with a common good rather than individual success, then this becomes a community approach.

Community approach

A community approach to tourism development was advocated by Murphy (1985) in his model of ecological tourism planning (Figure 9.1). This recommended treating the development of any tourist destination as a living ecosystem, combining the consideration of business concerns along with those of economic, environmental and social impacts. In this way, all the principal dimensions of tourism development could be assessed at once and the search for an acceptable balance between the positive and negative impacts along all four dimensions can be undertaken in a comprehensive manner. In addition the model stresses that all destinations operate within an open system whereby the development and planning priorities of different scales and government levels need to be considered.

Since the introduction of this concept there have been many studies and papers that have supported the validity of this approach to tourism planning, including the important point that communities are not necessarily

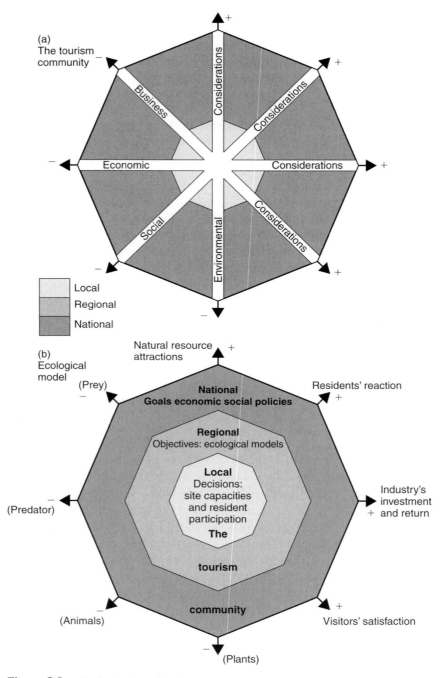

(a)
The tourism
community

Considerations

Considerations

Business

Economic

Considerations

Considerations

Social

Environmental

Considerations

Local

Regional

National

(b)
Ecological
model

Natural resource
attractions

(Prey)

National
Goals economic social policies

Residents' reaction

Regional
Objectives: ecological models

Local
Decisions:
site capacities
and resident
participation
The

Industry's
investment
and return

(Predator)

tourism

(Animals)

community

Visitors' satisfaction

(Plants)

Figure 9.1 Ecological model of community tourism planning.

homogeneous . . . each of the various sectors within the host society – the entrepreneurs, public planning authorities, general public and conservation groups – will have their own paradigms of behaviour and attitude (Ryan, 2003: 282–283). This confirms the presence of different priorities within the groups along each dimension and emphasizes the importance of working together to obtain the 'best' and most sustainable community outcome of any tourism development, including resorts.

More recent work on community tourism has stressed the importance of considering various stakeholder groups, examining the power structure in host communities and working towards the development of more collaborative processes. Murphy and Murphy (2004), utilizing their varied experiences with community tourism planning and the literature on its pros and cons, have suggested the new thrust needs to 'bridge the gaps' between stakeholder groups. To transfer a host destination's tourism potential into a sustainable and community supported reality will require collaboration between groups.

Collaboration

Murphy and Murphy (2004) emphasize the healthy aspects involved with conflict of opinion and explore ways in which it can be managed to produce more robust and successful tourism outcomes. In their chapter 'Working Together' they report how conflict can have positive outcomes like throwing up new ideas, fostering better understanding and raising general interest and creativity. They review the evidence of past planning and consultation processes and the pervading influence of power imbalance in most decision-making processes. To break the top–down approach to planning and to reduce the negative impact of the power imbalance they report on the success of a variety of participation techniques in their application to tourism issues.

An important start to collaboration is to develop integrity in any planning negotiations and in this regard Fisher et al. (1991) suggest four steps toward *Principled Negotiations*. These are:

1. *Separate the people from the problem.*
   Forbid personal attacks and concentrate on the objective assessment of the issue.
2. *Focus on interests not positions.*
   Adopted stances on issues limits the objectivity of assessment, so encourage participants to broaden their perspective or to view the issue from a different angle.

3. *Invent options for mutual gain.*
   Encourage participants to generate a variety of ideas and options and look for common threads and win–win situations.
4. *Insist on using objective criteria.*
   Use pre-established and objective criteria that have been accepted by all parties to evaluate ideas and suggestions.

Susskind et al.'s (1999) conflict assessment technique is another useful approach, especially when the planning issue is particularly complex and involves many stakeholders. This technique involves third party input to identify the relevant stakeholders and primary issues that underlie a conflict. It can be viewed as a preliminary step to the actual negotiation process, one that identifies the likelihood of establishing a workable consensus.

Collaborative decision-making and the development of consensus should be viewed as a search for mutual gains or a win-win solution. Under these circumstances an essential part of the negotiation process is to pre-determine what level of consensus will be acceptable to all parties. Susskind et al. (1999) have identified three levels of consensus, which in declining order of satisfaction are:

1. Participants strongly support the solution.
2. Participants can 'live with' the solution.
3. Some participants do not support the solution, but agree not to veto it – in other words they are prepared to give it a chance.

It is advisable to strive for solutions that stakeholder groups can 'live with' rather than hold onto an idealized outcome.

Resort experiences

Huffadine (2000: 47–48) observes 'approvals to develop and operate a resort generally depend everywhere on political viewpoints . . . Local government, business, and community leaders need to know how the proposal will fit in and benefit the community before any decisions about the project are made'. This requires working together and the careful and caring use of power.

Such processes are already underway. Inskeep (1991) has shown the importance of resort development and community consensus by placing them together in his influential text on tourism planning and by citing numerous examples in his cases of resort development. But one of the clearest examples of the benefit of community consultation and collaboration is provided in a comparative study of two resort developments in North Sulawesi, Indonesia by Simpson and Wall (1999).

Simpson and Wall compare and contrast the development experiences of the Paradise Beach Hotel and Resort, hereafter referred to as Paradise, and the Hotel Santika Manado, hereafter referred to as Santika. 'Paradise and Santika are both coastal resorts in the same province . . . both developments required the displacement of small agricultural communities; and both are the first major tourism developments in their immediate vicinities' (Simpson and Wall, 1999: 287). After assessing each resort's impact on their local environment, economy and social structure Simpson and Wall note there have been notable differences, many of which relate to their community relations.

Paradise, as a luxury resort established primarily for the international market, was committed to the protection of the environment and scored well in that regard. But its emphasis on a highly professional staff resulted in few positions for local workers and its desire to create a self-contained resort minimized contact between visitors and local people. Simpson and Wall (1999: 293–294) make the following specific comments:

A legally binding management plan exists for Paradise, in which the hotel owner agrees to provide residents (of both local villages) with training in the hospitality industry. However, in 1997, hotel staff and local residents agreed that no local people had been trained to work in hospitality positions at the hotel and experienced people from other parts of the country staff the skilled positions . . . The management plan also required the owner to provide local residents with courses in cottage industries (with the intention of producing local crafts for sale in the hotel gift shop), and seminars on entrepreneurship. The courses and seminars have not been offered . . . Local people also had no choice in the requirement to move and give up their farmland, no influence on the terms of their compensation.

Santika, in contrast, was developed as a luxury resort hotel for a 'mix of national and international guests' and since it is less isolated 'guests frequently leave the grounds and walk through the village, and it is also easy for visitors to go into the city or tour the local countryside' (Simpson and Wall, 1999: 287). However, since it is more integrated into local society and development Santika has placed less emphasis on environmental protection. It has continued the local building policy, placing its hotel and marina on a 'protected' mangrove shoreline. 'Some treated wastewater from (its) sewage treatment plant is recycled in watering the hotel grounds, while the rest is emptied into the ocean' (Simpson and Wall, 1999: 290).

However, with respect to its economic and social impacts Santika has developed a positive and mutually beneficial relationship with the local community since the early stages of its development. Simpson and Wall (1999: 295) note some specific advantages arising out of this relationship:

> As well as receiving fair compensation (for their land), the local community was also included in the process of choosing the site for their new homes . . . . the local people appreciated that they were involved in the decision-making process . . . . and were properly represented in the negotiations for compensation.

> Current employment of locals at the hotel is another extremely important element of the community's support for the hotel, including the fact that young people are being trained for skilled positions in the hospitality industry.

> Since the hotel is actually in the village . . . . the people of Tonkaina are able to provide goods and services to the hotel.

Simpson and Wall (1999: 295) conclude from their comparison of these two recently constructed coastal resorts that 'although the physical settings are slightly different, resulting in different environmental impacts, major differences in consequences for residents appear to be associated with differing developmental and management styles'. They feel the more collaborative approach of Santika has paid dividends for the resort (more supportive local community, good supply of local labour, complementary attraction of a healthy cultural destination) and for the residents (more diversified economy, more work for young and female workforce, social contact with outsiders). They note that similar relationships were promised at Paradise, but at the time of writing had failed to emerge. While, they fail to analyse the significance of the different markets the two resorts appear to be pursuing, they do make a case that resorts can benefit from cultivating their community relationships. To facilitate such synergies between resorts and their surrounding communities will require education on both sides, and information for that process exists.

Mutual education

If communities and resorts are to work together to create the synergies that can bring mutual benefit and sustainable long-term development they need to be educated on how to bring these promises to fruition. Nelson (1995: 311) feels 'the time has come for the tourism industry to reach out to community groups and government to make sure that the tourism products that they are developing serve the community at large, as well as tourists and investors'. He considers the three key stakeholder groups of tourism industry, government and community should come together and learn what is good for them individually and as a shared community of interests. He proposes that marketing can take on an educational role in this process by 'developing tourism products that are both socially responsible and profitable' by:

1. steering travellers toward more constructive forms of tourism;
2. accessing the needs of host communities; and
3. monitoring residents' perceptions of how tourism impacts quality of life issues in their communities over time.

(Nelson, 1995: 308)

Since this book is examining resorts as sustainable businesses it will examine these three suggestions in terms of Nelson's remarks and the work of others.

Steering travellers toward constructive forms of tourism

Nelson advocates the selective use of marketing to encourage the type of visitor and guest that a destination wants, and a shift from short-term goals of growth to a longer-term marketing policy that sustains the quality of life for the host community. Go (1992: 103) supports such an approach, noting:

> resident responsive tourism is the watch word for tomorrow. Community demands for active participation in the setting of the tourism agenda and priorities for tourism development and management can no longer be ignored.

This is certainly the case for an increasing number of destinations, where citizen input to the marketing image and message, either directly or indirectly, is becoming the norm because it is the resident who has to live with and support the marketing theme.

Destination marketing organizations (DMOs) no longer feel beholden to attract and welcome all visitors. Instead DMOs pursue preselected targeted segments by educating these target markets about the product they offer and the types of interest for which they are designed to cater. Marketing in this respect should be viewed as an education tool for the visitor and host alike. An attempt to attract the type of visitor the host destination and resort is best able to satisfy on a sustainable basis, and therefore leading to the most constructive forms of local tourism.

Assessing the needs of host community

Nelson maintains that market research can be used to determine the needs of the host community. He notes that determining what the public wants can be difficult because there is a variety of opinion, and that opinion changes over time in response to changing circumstances. But he feels the widespread experience gained via past market research, including segmenting markets and changing market demands, is well suited as a framework to detect community priorities and to point the way to achieving these.

Various studies have demonstrated ways to assess community attitudes and use them to encourage consensus building in a broader approach to tourism development. Lankford and Howard (1994) have developed a tourism impact attitude scale (TIAS) to provide a reliable measurement of how residents viewed local tourism development. An early finding of their work was 'if people feel they have access to the planning/public review *and* that their concerns are being considered, they will support tourism' (Lankford and Howard, 1994: 135). To determine what form that support will take requires someone to educate the residents about the various options and to encourage development of a public consensus regarding the direction to take. Murphy (1988) has used the Delbecq technique for group problem solving with good effect in Victoria, BC, Canada. Haywood (1988) recommends the use of scenario projections, Ritchie (1985) has recommended the nominal group technique to encourage consensus building. So there are plenty of tested methods to uncover what community attitudes are, what they are attached to and how to bring this information into a consensual decision-making arena. The public, industry and government stakeholders can be educated using such processes and techniques, but what is needed is the will to apply them and commit to a community focus.

Monitoring perceptions over time

Nelson makes the point that quality of life issues, including tourism, will change over time and that market research techniques can be used to poll residents and monitor these changes. Simpson and Wall (1999) make the point that their analysis of the two resorts in Indonesia is a snapshot, that as the resort destinations mature the relationships will change and the resulting impacts in the community could swing from good to bad, or vice versa.

The long-term development process of a typical resort is linked to the product life cycle and with that comes a change in the type of visitor (alocentric to psychocentric), a change in product emphasis (from basic to more luxurious accommodation) and a rise in community action (as residents note the increased commercialization of their community). Butler's Tourism Area Life Cycle (TALC) theory reveals these changes but it requires regular monitoring to identify the stage changes and to trigger the necessary changes in planning and marketing.

It is worth noting the parallels between Nelson's three marketing/education approaches to develop and maintain a sustainable quality of life in a tourist destination and the major functions of business management. His first step – steering travellers toward a constructive form of tourism, is another way to describe resort *planning* and the development of a vision for the resort. His second step – accessing the needs of the host community is a call for more comprehensive *organization* and practice. It recognizes that the host community is an important player in the success of any resort and needs to be integrated into the resource allocation process. The final step – monitoring perceptions as they change over time, is the *control* function. This involves the regular monitoring of the resort business to ensure it is meeting its vision objectives, and if not to provide data that can guide remedial policies. Behind all this is the need for *leadership*, to be innovative in terms of both business and community in order that the benefits may be long term and widely appreciated.

Local entrepreneurship

One way the benefits of resort development may be converted into long term and appreciated advances is if the local population has the opportunity to become involved as business partners in the venture. This mainly occurs as entrepreneurial opportunities which allow local people to serve some aspect of the guests' needs. The opportunity to develop supplies for the major businesses within a resort or to provide secondary services such as local transport or gifts and souvenirs has been a major source of local business since resorts first developed. Simpson and Wall (1999) mention the presence of local entrepreneurship as being a positive feature of Santika and its absence at Paradise as a cause for concern among the local population.

In another study of resort development in Bali, Long and Wall (1995) examined the consequences of community-based, small-scale tourism development by local entrepreneurs. They found that while there were general economic benefits for those local residents engaging in various support activities, there were major social and cultural costs. Long and Wall (1995: 254) found 'small-scale tourism development was occurring through a process of informal diffusion, but without regard for long-term implications and possibly at a rate which was too fast'. The development of homestay accommodation, in particular, impinged on family life and threatened the 'cultural integrity' of village *banjars* – local organizations that provide support and social cohesion in traditional Balinese society. They equated this rapid growth of local entrepreneurship and the development of capitalist ways with the 'tragedy of the commons', where what is unique and special about the local culture becomes overwhelmed by western customs and priorities. In such situations they claim there is little opportunity for local residents to 'actually learn how to enter the tourism industry' or to appreciate what they must sacrifice in order to enter this business, even on the fringes.

Once again we see the need for those who are considering tourism as a livelihood to be educated and prepared for all its manifestations. Large corporations can create separate front – and back – stages, small family businesses the world over do not have the capacity for such luxuries. Large businesses have sufficient staff to guarantee holiday and rest breaks for everyone, small businesses do not. Large businesses have reserves and financial backers, small businesses have limited resources and the biggest frustration is seeing an opportunity but not having the capital to pursue it. These differences between the large and the small, the powerful and the exposed within a resort community become very apparent over the issue of housing.

A community, however it is defined, refers to someone's home – the place where they live and wish to bring up their families. The neighbourhoods they wish to protect and the real estate values they like to see maintained. It is for these reasons that the remainder of this chapter focusses on the issue of housing within resort communities.

Housing types

Housing in resort communities should be designed to accommodate the variety of needs and tastes for both guests and staff. For guests there must be the type and amount of accommodation that suits the targeted market(s). This will need to provide a range of qualities to suit the varying income and interest levels within these target markets. Staff housing issues are particularly important for isolated resorts, where resort companies may be the prime or only source of housing for staff. Even if a resort is located within an urban area the issue of housing is still an important one, although the focus is more on cost than availability. Most front-line tourism positions, as with other industries, receive low to modest salaries which makes the need for low-cost housing imperative to this industry. Unfortunately from this point of view, many resort destinations are located in beautiful and expensive real estate markets where the cost of housing would challenge a physician let alone a ski instructor or a pastry chef. So a major challenge for resorts and their surrounding communities is to find innovative ways to modify local housing markets to ensure there is room and opportunity to secure decent housing for all income groups.

Guest housing

The ideal accommodation for guests is a range of options and prices. Not everyone needs or can afford deluxe full-service accommodation, so unless a resort is willing to see the development of ancillary lower price accommodation in adjacent areas, it needs to include a range of accommodation styles within the resort. The different types and styles of accommodation can be separated by zoning and hidden from the view of non-users by careful landscape planning.

The majority of rooms are generally provided in the major hotel(s), where room sizes, location and standards can offer an internal variety of accommodation and prices. In integrated resort complexes these core guest accommodations are often combined with apartment and townhouse style housing. These are used either independently by their owners or are offered to the major hotel(s) as a supplementary pool of accommodation under their management. In an urban setting resort accommodation will be in competition with other users, some of whom may be helpful to have and others less so. In the first capacity is the presence of nearby complementary accommodation offerings, which can either supplement the resort complex's room numbers or offer alternative style accommodation for those wishing to attend the resort for a special function, such as a conference or awards banquet. In the second capacity are those alternative accommodation offerings that house the resort's potential full-time guests and permit them to treat the resort complex as a short-term day user or just as an observer.

The rise of second home and timeshare housing markets over the past 30 years has changed the accommodation pool of many resorts dramatically. Nowhere is this more apparent and argumentative than in the ski resorts of North America, where for some the big three resort corporations of Vail Resorts Development Company, Intra-West Corporation and American Skiing Company have changed the lifestyle of traditional skiing for the worse. 'Their search (for profit) has led them to move aggressively into real estate development and the conversion of ski areas into high-volume, industrial-scale, four-season resorts' (Clifford, 2003: 44).

Clifford (2003) is a vocal opponent of how the modern business approach to providing more varied accommodation options, along with the reasons for a more year-round utilization of corporate and personal investment, is being used to create four-season mountain communities. The basis of his argument appears to be a desire to retain the intimate skiing communities and camaraderie of the past:

> What is almost universally left unsaid by resort executives (when promoting their new four-season concepts) is that there is a real cost to converting a ski town into a year-round, full-to-the-gills resort. The town's atmosphere and fabric are transformed. Life in the ski town starts to look a lot more like the daily rat race anywhere else.

> What those who promote development fail to understand, or willfully ignore is that it was precisely that act – keeping others out, by choice, by geography, or by the nature of the local economy – that made so many ski towns special.

> (Clifford, 2003: 59)

This hankering for the past amidst the democratization of yet another elitist form of recreation and tourism echoes the anguish of certain board members of all-male clubs and schools. They bemoan the loss of their 'golden days' while economic realities force them to include more members of the world market.

Interestingly enough, Clifford's response to the four-season real estate resorts lies in developing a more community-oriented approach to development, as advocated in this chapter. Instead of continuing with what he describes as the corporate model, Clifford (2003: 235–238) advocates a community approach to future ski resort development. 'The idea of a community taking control of a ski resort is not anti-capitalist; it is the best realization of capitalism ... what local ownership really accomplishes is to put a community more directly in charge of its fate' (Clifford, 2003: 236).

It should not be forgotten that in these communities there will always be an unequal balance of power among stakeholders, with those who generate income for the community possessing an influence disproportionate to their number. In addition there is the power and authority of senior levels of government, which have wider responsibilities to their diverse constituents. Therefore, the type of solution advocated by Clifford is not anti-capitalist, it is a call for a more locally sensitive development. In some ways it is a combination of the growth management and 'triple bottom line' perspectives, in that it wishes to see commercial success operate in a sustainable manner, such that local environmental, economic and social priorities are considered.

That the current corporate model requires some adjustment in the housing area is supported by two other papers that have examined the ski resort areas of Colorado. Venturoni et al. (2005) have examined the economic and social impacts of second homes in the four mountain resort counties of Colorado, they found:

> Second homes are different in that they are not just residences, but an industry creating a demand for workers. Second homes drive up property values, including residential housing for workers. Because of this, it becomes especially important for elected officials and community planners to understand and estimate the secondary (community) effects of second homes in tourist-based economies.
>
> (Venturoni et al., 2005: 11)

The evidence they present to support the above assessment is that second home development in these counties has led to:

- By 2001 60 per cent of homes in the four county study area were second homes.
- Much of the increase has occurred over the past few years, as part of the rising global house market. Between 1998 and 2004 Summit County and Pitkin County 'home market values' increased by over 40 per cent, Grand County by over 60 per cent and Eagle County by over 75 per cent. This compared with an 18 per cent rise in the home market value in a 'standard city' over the same time period (Long et al., 2005: 10).
- Second home property values in the four counties were very high. In Eagle County they were on average $785 000 for a single family dwelling and $443 000 for a multi-family unit in 2003. In Summit County the average for a single family dwelling was $486 000 and for a multi-family dwelling was $255 000. In contrast 'the standard US home market value in 2004 was roughly $100 000' (Long et al., 2005: 10).

- The fastest growing population within Colorado from 1990–2000, with an overall population growth of 73 per cent, was in the four ski resort counties.
- During the same time period the Hispanic population experienced a 268 per cent growth. (This group started from a smaller base population, but they are primarily service workers.)
- There has been a general labour shortage since around 2000. For example, Eagle County which is home to Vail and Aspen resorts among others, had a 'labour force shortage of 9797 workers in 1997, a shortage that is expected to grow substantially (estimated to be 20 000 or more) by 2020' (Venturoni et al., 2005: 5).
- Second homes were occupied for limited periods, with the 'full-time household equivalence' usage being 29 per cent a year for single family dwellings and 23 per cent in condominiums – approximately 90 days per year.
- 'Across the region, second home construction and spending was estimated to be the largest driver, supporting about 31 600 jobs or 38 per cent of all jobs' (Venturoni et al., 2005: 9).
- Second home development creates jobs in construction, followed by their maintenance, operation and use.
- 'Second homes have generated the need for more workers, but the rise in property values and subsequent housing costs have made it difficult for the workers to live within a reasonable distance of their place of work' (Venturoni et al., 2005: 11).
- Local residents (not second home owners, whose primary residence is elsewhere) have moderate to modest median household incomes, recording $62 682 for Eagle County, $59 375 for Pitkin County, $56 587 for Summit County and $47 756 for Grand County.

As the authors conclude, such evidence should be taken into account by community planners and policy makers 'for its effective use in growth management and community planning' (Venturoni et al., 2005: 12).

Timeshare

Second homes are not the only form of housing for guests that has been growing in popularity over the past years, another is timeshare accommodation in its various forms. Timeshare is the system whereby a guest purchases an accommodation unit, generally an apartment style unit, for a set period (usually in weekly increments) each year in a resort or resort destination. The advantage to the guest is a guaranteed time and price each year at that resort, and if they join an exchange company, like

Resort Condominiums International (RCI) based in Indianapolis or Interval International (II) based in Miami, they can exchange their personal timeshare for others located in resorts and tourist destinations around the world. However, timeshare 'should be considered and positioned as a vacation/leisure concept, not as a real estate product' (WTO, 1996: 2) in that, unlike second homes, there is generally no chance for asset appreciation since most agreements have a set time period, after which ownership of the building reverts back to the resort or developer.

There are advantages for both the guest and resort in the development of quality timeshare accommodation. For the guest the prime advantage over second homes or regular hotel accommodation is affordability. Let us say that the guest bought a timeshare of a furnished multi-bedroom condominium apartment within a resort that has a 'market value' of $800 000. A week's purchase of that condominium apartment would be $15 385 ($800 000 ÷ 52 weeks). If the length of agreement ran for 20 years, then the week would cost $769 each year; which given the expected inflation over 20 years would be 'next to nothing' for the final few years. In addition to the initial purchase price there will be legal fees, management fees for maintenance and exchanges and certain weeks of the year will be more expensive than others, but it still presents an attractive way for guests to enter luxury resort living. For the resort it is an attractive way to boost cash flow, especially in the development phase, and since a regular turnover of timeshare guests can be expected it will likely increase spending in other areas of the resort business.

It is not surprising that the timeshare concept has proved to be very popular, particularly in the US, and after a rocky start in some places it has developed into a substantial market segment of the resort business. It has also evolved as this segment has adjusted to consumer demands. Some guests have found the idea of a set period too constraining, so to provide them with more flexibility they purchase points. This is the approach of Disney's 'Vacation Club' (n.d.). By purchasing points for $98.00 per point (in 2005) you could purchase the minimum allowance of 150 vacation points for $14 700 (plus dues of $574 per year) or the maximum allowance of 2000 vacation points for $196 000 and annual dues of $7652. This entitles you to choose when and where you stayed with Disney resorts or associated quality resorts around the world. These associated resorts include world famous hotels and resorts, plus cruises, safaris and adventure tourism tours. It enables the guest to determine how long they would like to stay, and what size and style of accommodation they wish on a particular trip. It also allows guests to bank their points for up to a year, if they want to rise to a higher level or are forced to miss out one year due to ill health. In other words, it offers maximum flexibility and customization.

Over time the timeshare name has undergone modification in some parts of the world. The Urban Land Institute (1997) refers to a move toward 'vacation ownership' over 'timesharing', but one that has really sprung to the fore over recent years is 'fractional ownership'. This is a composite of timeshare and second home ownership, which allows the possibility of asset appreciation. 'The term fractional development refers to shared ownership of real property ... (customers) view their purchase as a long-term investment that will appreciate over the years, protected by a strong management team that strives to maintain the high quality integrity and feel of the resort' (Sanderson, 2005: 1). Key features to success for such developments according to the international accounting firm of Grant Thornton (Sanderson, 2005: 2) include:

- Fractional developments tend to be larger homes.
- Fractionals work best in markets where the cost of a wholly owned second home is out of reach for most households.
- Most successful high-end fractionals offer extensive and luxurious amenities on the level of a five star hotel.
- Resorts accessible from a large market by both automobile and airplane may have a competitive advantage over more isolated resorts.

According to Ragatz and Associates (a US second home consulting specialist) there were 170 fractional ownership resorts in North America as of March 2005. High-end fractional ownership properties are called 'private residence clubs' in Canada, and are emerging in popular ski resort areas and major holiday destinations such as the Okanagan Valley and Victoria, BC. One such club, the Royal Private Residence Club located on Kelowna's Lake Okanagan waterfront 'offers buyers the opportunity to purchase a third, sixth, twelfth, or whole villa for prices ranging from C$63 900 over C$1 million' (Sanderson, 2005: 2).

Staff housing

One of the key staffing issues for resort developments is to find or provide adequate accommodation for staff, so staff can provide the round-the-clock levels of service and maintenance required in a resort. This is always an issue because of the high staff–guest ratio within most resorts, the shift work and the seasonality, but it becomes critical if the resort is isolated and cannot find sufficient help and accommodation within local communities.

In order to operate at their best, workers at all levels require accommodation that offers a chance to sleep, unwind and socialize with family and friends. To achieve such a situation a resort requires a local source of mixed housing, some for families and others for single adults; a range of well maintained housing with prices that allow for purchase or rent; the provision of local services such as shops, schools and recreation; and easy access to work. In many resort destinations, where the resort businesses are either within or near to an existing urban area most of these criteria can be met, but there is often a 'catch 22' situation, when these resort destinations become popular second home and retirement communities they face rising house prices.

The growing popularity of second homes in the Colorado ski resorts has led to an increasing exclusion of service workers from those areas, as their salaries do not allow them to compete in the local housing market. 'Up until 1987, over 50% of the workforce for Pitkin County was housed locally; it has since dropped to less than 40%. This drop corresponded to the general time frame when real estate costs began to rise dramatically in the county, particularly in the resort town of Aspen' (Venturoni et al., 2005: 5). The result is that an increasing number of workers, especially those in front-line positions, are forced out of the resort area and into a commute situation. So in rural and regional areas regular commuter 'rush hours' are created when shifts change, which emulate those major urban rush hours many people hoped to avoid. This adds increased stress and cost to all concerned, the staff, the management and the environment.

The beauty and amenities of resorts have encouraged many previous guests to return as retirees. This has also changed the local housing markets as retirees have different priorities to most families and have the money from the sale of their old home in distant metropolitan areas to buy their way into a resort community and change its housing balance. According to Rothman (2002), this is what has happened to Las Vegas since the arrival of air conditioning. It has gained momentum over the past 10 years as baby boomers start to retire and more are converting their metropolitan house dollars into a cheaper retirement home along with a retirement nest egg. Clark County in Nevada, the home of Las Vegas, recorded a 122 per cent increase in its over 65 population between 1990 and 2004 compared with the average US increase of 16.8 per cent (*The Economist*, 2006). This level of growth not only raises local house prices it changes the spirit of the community. Martin et al. (1996: 301) have noted there is 'an inherent problem with locating retirement communities within growing resort communities. It may be unrealistic to expect retirees who cannot see the benefits from further (tourism) growth of the community to support expansion'.

Rothman notes Las Vegas initially welcomed the new retirees with planned retirement communities in the 1970s and 1980s, but now 'the retirement of baby boomers spells a transformation as great as any in American demographic history' (Rothman, 2002: 150). Part of that transformation has been in the type and cost of housing, which is reducing the traditional housing market supply used by the resort service workers. Another is that while retirement creates its own service economy it is inherently different from that of the standard resort type. 'Many of the occupations that retirees depend on require higher levels of skill than making beds or cleaning rooms, and such jobs – nursing, physical therapy rehabilitation, and running medical imaging equipment – pay well' (Rothman, 2002: 151); which adds yet more competition for the housing of resort employees.

All of the above housing issues for resort staff become magnified for those resorts which are truly isolated from the urban network and force the resort developer to provide some form of staff housing on-site. The need to provide on-site housing creates higher costs for the resort, because even where employees are required to pay for their accommodation it is generally provided at a subsidized rate, compared to local prices. For the staff, under such circumstances, the type and style of accommodation is strictly limited. It often consists of dormitory or multi-unit accommodation, and such facilities are often insufficient in the most popular resorts so families or groups of individuals need to scour the local rental market for a home or face a commute.

Another issue for worker and management is where to place staff housing within the resort. The form of staff housing is primarily utilitarian, so should be situated away from the major guest areas. This separation will provide staff with some degree of privacy, but what of their need to have a true separation from their work environment? In isolated resorts it is often difficult or impossible to achieve such a separation, so workers are often obliged to use the same facilities as guests, be it the general store, a pub or the major attraction of a ski hill. Regardless of the planning and management strategies adopted to provide staff housing on-site, such housing is often a major issue for human relations and a happy and effective service environment. This issue is explored in more detail in the following Human Relations chapter.

Summary

This chapter has demonstrated the need for resorts to work with local communities, to develop sustainable returns from the area's sense of place by creating meaningful partnerships that permit both the resort and community to guide development and derive mutual benefit from the business. It recognizes that tourism will always be an agent of change and that if resort and community work in harmony they are more likely to reduce the negative impacts on local society and culture. An important part of such a process is the mutual education that should develop between the resort and host community, and the search for mutual win-win situations.

One key function in community relations is the role of housing. Guest housing will remain one of resorts' key revenue streams, but there will be times when resorts will be glad to have assistance from surrounding communities, such as with peak period overflows or the provision of alternative accommodation options. Staff housing is an area where resorts depend extensively on surrounding communities to provide a range of options for their workers. However, if a resort is truly isolated it will need to incur the added expense and responsibility of providing its own staff accommodation; and the more money and attention resorts put into this facet of the operation the more likely they are to have a happy and productive staff.

The difficulty associated with resorts and staff housing is the focus of this chapter's two case studies. The first is extracted from the work of William Hettinger, who has studied this problem throughout North America. The second focusses on the efforts of Whistler ski resort in British Columbia to overcome some of the difficulties in providing staff housing that Hettinger and this chapter have described.

Case studies
Housing market failure responses

A regular problem in successful resort destinations is the rising price of housing that makes it difficult or impossible for low and middle income households to find decent affordable housing in the community in which they work. Reference to this worldwide problem has been made by

Hettinger (2005), who's book *Living and Working in Paradise* has explored the problem in great detail. His experience shows a housing market failure in tourism destinations occurs 'when externalities exist in the housing market, supply and demand become unbalanced, leading to market failure in the form of unaffordable housing costs and displaced local residents' (Hettinger, 2005: 23).

Hettinger identifies three principal externalities that distort the local housing market in popular tourist destinations. They are:

1. Topographical constraints – where the resort destination clinging to a mountainside or sandy beach is restricted in its outward growth by difficult terrain.
2. Growth management, land use and zoning regulations that alter the supply side of the housing equation. In many cases the topographical constraints can be exacerbated by the presence of development restrictions due to the presence of conservation orders on surrounding national forests or parks. In some cases housing is treated as an afterthought coming second in priority to the revenue generating features of a resort design.
3. Second home demand alters the demand side of the housing equation, bringing in cashed up buyers from higher priced markets to compete for the finite number of houses or lots within the resort destination.

All of the above features are in place in this author's former home in Victoria, BC, Canada. Victoria is a popular tourist destination on the southern tip of Vancouver Island which has a house price average way beyond its size and importance as an urban centre. This is because being on an island there are definite physical boundaries to its expansion and these natural constraints have been exacerbated by the encircling of the central area by a green belt, designed to save what little agricultural production remains in the area. To compound the situation further, the city is located in the 'banana belt' of Canada, which makes it a prime destination for a growing number of retirees from the big and wealthier cities elsewhere in the country. The result is a very tight market for first home buyers, many of whom now have to live considerable distances from work in Victoria and commute to work on increasingly crowded roads.

Hettinger's solution to this problem is for tourist destinations to intervene and attempt to redress the imbalanced housing market. This can be done either through the direct public provision of affordable housing units or via regulations requiring the private sector to assist in this regard. Publicly provided affordable housing does not have a very good record or helpful image in tourist destinations. Its utilitarian style and bulk is often too visible and obvious, and such facilities can present the lack of maintenance and care commonly associated with rental properties. The presence of regulations and incentives to have the private sector provide affordable housing generally results in smaller projects that are more scattered throughout the community, so they do not become so obvious and disparaged. But in either case Hettinger (2005: 27) points out that 'second home conversions have mitigated some of the success of affordable housing programs' because it is impossible for local governments to control general market pressures and tendencies; so the success of affordable housing programmes should be seen in relative not static terms.

Hettinger provides four tourist destination case studies to illustrate his points, one of which is Whistler in British Columbia, Canada. This four-season mountain resort will be examined in more detail below.

Whistler, Canada

Whistler is a resort municipality designed to support and complement the twin ski-mountains of Whistler and Blackcomb in British Columbia. It has grown into a major international four-season resort and will, with Vancouver, be the site of the 2010 Winter Olympic Games. The community and housing challenge for Whistler is to provide a broad range of housing for an entire community within the constraints of scarce building land and rising real estate prices. To tackle this challenge Whistler has attempted to supplement the private and commercial housing market with lower-cost non-market alternatives.

Hettinger (2005: 133–138) demonstrates conclusively that Whistler is suffering from the type of housing market failure outlined above. The tourism orientation of the town is confirmed by the 2001 census that shows 45.3 per cent of the workforce was in tourism related occupations, most of whom needed to live close to work given its shift nature and concentration in Whistler. Seasonal workers represented 28 per cent of Whistler's 13 543 peak winter workforce, indicating the need for considerable short-term accommodation. Housing data showed that housing costs in Whistler were 64 per cent higher than in the rest of British Columbia and 166 per cent higher than in Canada, in 2003 the average price of a free-market single family house was C$950 000 and the average price of a free-market condominium apartment was C$460 000. It is not surprising therefore, that 'the average family in Whistler cannot afford to purchase the average-priced house in the community' (Hettinger, 2005: 134).

In 1997 the local authorities created the Whistler Housing Authority (WHA) 'to oversee the creation, administration and management of resident restricted housing in Whistler' (WHA, 2002: 4). Resident restricted housing is 'housing for rent or for purchase that is restricted through a ground lease or housing covenant, which limits the occupancy to those who qualify as an employee or retiree, (where) resale price and rental restrictions may also apply' (WHA, 2002: 12). As such it is affordable housing offered to workers in the resort industry and related areas as a rental or ownership proposition. Since 1990, partly through the initial efforts of its predecessor the Whistler Valley Housing Society, the WHA has facilitated the creation of more than 4000 beds, exclusively for the local workforce in a variety of housing forms. Most of the housing is in apartment or townhouse style, and there is a hope that the WHA can move from its current even split between rental and ownership tenure to more of an emphasis on ownership, as the resort area reaches its planned expansion limits and product maturity.

The initial funding for these initiatives came from an 'Employee Works and Service Reserve, popularly referred to as the Housing Fund' (WHA, 2002: 5). The money came from developers of commercial and tourism accommodation properties, who were required to either build housing for their future employees or to contribute to this fund so that the WHA could do so on their behalf. This fund was levered two to one with financing and used to create 160 rental units (about 500 rental beds) which are owned by the WHA. The larger portion of beds were created through working with developers at the rezoning stage.

An important feature of the WHA's policy is 'to provide a nest and not a nest egg' (Wake, 2005). The WHA can provide houses at lower prices than the open market, thanks to minimal land costs, lower construction costs and a not-for-profit policy; so when owners come to sell they would make a substantial windfall profit in the open market. Therefore, restricted housing ownership comes with covenants that limit resale through the WHA and allow only a modest capital gain.

While the WHA has performed an essential service and contributed to the community spirit of Whistler, where now '32 per cent of residents live in affordable housing' (Hettinger, 2005: 26), it is experiencing some frustrations from its own success. Its goal has been to provide sufficient low-cost housing for the resort workforce, but with the resort's success and continued growth it has faced a moving target and has never been able to satisfy completely the growing need for such accommodation, especially for the seasonal and casual workers. Within their subset of the housing market the WHA would like to create a ladder of opportunity for workers who wish to settle in Whistler, one that would allow them to proceed from a rental to an ownership situation and move from apartment accommodation to more spacious and private accommodation if they are raising a family. Unfortunately, to date supplies of larger homes and ownership opportunities have not kept up with demand, so a significant number of people have had to move to outlying communities and face commutes of 30 minutes or more to work.

Questions

1 The introduction presents two definitions of 'community'. Examine those definitions from the perspective of resort management and assess their usefulness.

2 Some principles of effective collaboration have been presented within the chapter. Discuss these principles and assess which are most likely to be relevant to a resort management situation.

3 Nelson (1995) advocates three attributes of education/marketing. Assess the strengths and weaknesses of these attributes and critically apply this approach to the marketing of Simpson and Wall's (1999) Paradise or Santika resort.

4 Timeshare versus fractional ownership! As a resort developer where would you put your emphasis and why?

5 Venturoni et al. (2005) provide some graphic statistics linking second home development with social change within resort communities. Compare and contrast their evidence with what has been happening to the housing market in an urban centre near you.

6 Rothman (2002: 150) feels the retirement of baby boomers spells a transformation as great as any in American demographic history. Discuss what this transformation is likely to mean for an urban resort destination of your choice, and how you, as a resort developer, plan to ride this wave.

7 Hettinger (2005) maintains there are three externalities distorting local housing markets in popular tourist destinations. Discuss these three externalities and how you would respond to them with respect to staff housing in a resort setting of your choice.

References

Brown, F. (1998). *Tourism Reassessed: Blight or Blessing*. Oxford: Butterworth Heinemann.

Clifford, H. (2003). *Downhill Slide*. San Francisco: Sierra Club Books.

Disney Vacation Club (n.d.). *The Secret to Making Your Vacation Dreams Come True*. Promotional book obtained in Disney World, August 2005, no publisher.

Fisher, R., Ury, W., and Patton, B. (eds) (1991). *Getting to Yes: Negotiating Agreement without Giving In*, 2nd edn. New York: Penguin Group.

Go, F. (1992). Conference Report: The First International Assembly of Tourism Policy Experts. *Journal of Hospitality Leisure Marketing*, **1(1)**, 101–104.

Haywood, K.M. (1988). Responsible and responsive tourism planning in the community. *Tourism Management*, **9(2)**, 105–118.

Hettinger, W.S. (2005). *Living and Working in Paradise: Why Housing Is Too Expensive and What Communities Can Do About It*. Windham, Connecticut: Thames River Publishing.

Huffadine, M. (2000). *Resort Design: Planning, Architecture and Interiors*. New York: McGraw Hill.

Inskeep, E. (1991). *Tourism Planning: An Integrated and Sustainable Development Approach*. New York: Van Nostrand Reinhold.

Joppe, M. (1996). Sustainable community tourism development revisited. *Tourism Management*, **17(7)**, 475–479.

Lankford, S.V. and Howard, D.R. (1994). Developing a tourism impact attitude scale. *Annals of Tourism Research*, **21(1)**, 121–139.

Long, P.T., Perdue, R.R., and Venturoni, L. (2005). Home away from home: a research agenda for examining the resort community second home industry in Colorado. Paper presented at *Biannual Conference of the International Academy for the Study of Tourism*. Beijing, China.

Long, V. and Wall, G. (1995). Small-scale tourism development in Bali. In *Island Tourism: Management Principles and Practice* (M.V. Conlin and T. Baum, eds), pp. 237–257. Chichester: John Wiley and Sons.

Martin, B.S., McGuire, F., Allen, L., and Uysal, M. (1996). Growth, who cares? A study of resident perceptions of tourism development in Hilton Head. It's showtime for tourism: new products, markets and technologies. *Twenty-Seventh Annual Conference of the Travel and Tourism Research Association Proceedings*, Las Vegas, Nevada.

Murphy, P.E. (1985). *Tourism: A Community Approach*. London: Methuen.

Murphy, P.E. (1988). Community driven tourism. *Tourism Management*, **9(2)**, 105–118.

Murphy, P.E. and Murphy, A.E. (2004). *Strategic Planning for Tourism Communities: Bridging the Gaps*. Clevedon: Channel View Publications.

Nelson, R.R. (1995). The impact of tourism development on quality of life in host communities. In *New Dimensions in Marketing/Quality-of-Life Research* (M.J. Sirgy and A.C. Samli, eds). Westport, Connecticut: Quorum Books.

Ritchie, J.R.B. (1985). The nominal group technique – an approach to consensus policy formation in tourism. *Tourism Management*, **6(2)**, 82–94.

Roddick, A. (2000). *Business as Unusual*. London: Thorsons.

Rogers, M.F. (2001). The triple bottom line audit: a framework for community-based action. In *The Future of Australia's Country Towns* (M.F. Rogers and Y.M.J. Collins, eds), pp. 135–145. Bendigo, Victoria: Centre for Sustainable Regional Communities, La Trobe University.

Rothman, H. (2002). *Neon Metropolis: How Las Vegas Started the Twenty-First Century*. New York: Routledge.

Ryan, C. (2003). *Recreational Tourism: Demand and Impacts.* Clevedon: Channel View Publications.

Sanderson, T. (2005). *Fractional Resort Development – Defined. Tourism Monitor of Grant Thornton*, pp. 1–2. Victoria, BC: Grant Thornton (Canada).

Saveriades, A. (2000). Establishing the social tourism carrying capacity for the tourist resorts of the east coast of the Republic of Cyprus. *Tourism Management*, **21**, 147–156.

Simpson, P. and Wall, G. (1999). Consequences of resort development – a comparative study. *Tourism Management*, **20**, 283–296.

Susskind, L., McKearnan, S., and Thomas-Larmer, J. (1999). *The Consensus Building Handbook: A Comprehensive Guide to Reaching Agreement*. Thousand Oaks, California: Sage Publications.

The Economist (2006). Of gambling, grannies and good sense. *The Economist*, July 22, 41–42.

Urban Land Institute (1997). *Resort Development Handbook*. Washington DC: Urban Land Institute.

Venturoni, L., Long, P., and Perdue, R. (2005). The economic and social impacts of second homes in four mountain resorts counties of Colorado. Paper presented at the *American Association of Geographers Annual Meeting*. Denver, Colorado.

Wake, T. (2005). Interview with Tim Wake, General Manager of Whistler Housing Authority, Whistler, BC, September.

Whistler Housing Authority (WHA) (2002). *Building Our Resort Community – Overview 2002*. Whistler, BC: Whistler Housing Authority.

WTO (1996). *Timeshare – The New Force in Tourism.* Madrid: World Tourism Organization.

10

Human relations practices

Introduction

This chapter will examine some of the major human relations issues facing resorts. It has purposely been labelled 'relations' because in the tight business community of a resort people often live together as well as work together. Furthermore, the shift work and multi-skilling needed by core workers tends to break down the more formal industrial classifications and brings into prominence more personal qualities and attitudes and their effect on teamwork. Finally, new trends in hiring staff suggest that, under certain circumstances, businesses are outsourcing their traditional human resource responsibilities so they are developing relationships with those companies.

There will be considerable overlap between regular human resource practices and the human relations needs of resorts so the emphasis of this chapter will be on the specific human talent needs and issues of resorts. In terms of a resort's talents, staff and management require the appropriate motivation and training to provide the levels of quality service that were referred to as a resort differentiator in Chapter 1. With respect to the special issues of working in a resort, a major difference from regular employment situations is that many resort employees live and play at their place of work in isolated resorts; so it is often impossible for them to get that break or down time that most of us take for granted.

Resorts need to achieve high levels of service excellence in a competitive workplace, where there is a shrinking traditional labour pool and rising expectations on the part of many employees. We will see that resort management is attempting to raise the quality of service as part of its strategy to remain competitive with other forms of tourism and leisure in the world market. It is doing this by trying to develop more flexible and rewarding work opportunities within human relations and service management strategies.

Labour shortage

The traditional labour market for resorts has been the local labour pool of surrounding communities, with an emphasis on young and female workers for the front-line positions in developed economies. This works well for both management and employees in many labour market situations outside of the big cities, where the prior employment opportunities have been largely for males. However, as more national economies have experienced significant growth in their service sectors while manufacturing and primary industries have declined in relative and sometimes absolute importance, the competition for female employees has increased and the young have many more attractive options available to them. At the same time the number of young people (16–24 age range), that tourism and hospitality businesses have historically relied on for their entry level positions, has been decreasing. Meier (1991: 78–79) observes this age group in the US 'accounts for 42 per cent of the employees in travel-related firms and 60 per cent of the food service workforce. However this same group accounts for only 20 per cent of all employees nationwide and (was) expected to account for only 12.2 per cent by the year 2000, according to the (U.S.) Bureau of the Census'. What has been happening in the US has been happening elsewhere in the developed world, as the birthrate has shrunk since the post-World War II baby boom. A more recent study of employees in Cyprus resort destinations reports a similar dependency on young workers, where 37.7 per cent of the sample of Northern Cyprus hotels were 18–27 years of age, and a further 38.4 per cent were 28–37 years old (Karatepe et al., 2006).

This labour shortage has been a fact of life for the tourism industry for 20 years or more and various strategies have been adopted to solve the problem. The most prominent solution has been to hire migrant labour, both legal and illegal immigrants, to fill the gap, especially for the less popular positions back of house and general maintenance. This has been a natural and rationale solution in the eyes of economists, with the global transfer of unemployed people to countries where there are jobs waiting to be filled. However, for management it is not that simple. Such migrants usually need to learn the local language before they can start training and become fully proficient and then for some there are cultural differences to the western way of life that may require considerable adjustment on their part.

Another solution that has been mooted widely and tried by some companies is the employment of retirees. 'Older workers often bring experience, a strong work ethic, maturity, and reliability to a job. They also provide good role models for younger workers within the organization' claims Meier (1991: 81), who was in hotel management at the time. In contrast to the shrinking pool of young workers there is a growing number of retirees as the baby boomers enter retirement. Some of these retirees will either want to try something new or will need to extend their working lives if their pensions fail to provide adequate support. However, despite this logical solution it has not been the success to date that many had hoped. In part this has been due to management thinking more about the problems of hiring seniors than their benefits, and governments placing roadblocks in the way of earning extra income to supplement a pension rather than offering encouragement. It is also due to the stress involved with many resort positions, that many seniors did not appreciate until they looked closely at the situation or tried it for a while. Many front-line resort positions require people to be on their feet all day, are physically demanding due to lifting and carrying, can involve odd hours, and face-to-face customer service that can be challenging at times.

Another group that could assist with the labour shortage are the disabled. 'Studies have consistently shown that the work performance of disabled employees is as good or better than non-disabled employees. Disabled employees have also shown to have no significant effect on group health insurance or workers' compensation rates' according to Meier (1991: 82). There are often agencies that will pre-train disabled persons for basic positions and some governments provide subsidies or tax benefits to encourage the hiring of this labour segment. Again, many feel this opportunity has not reached its true potential and the main cause is our ignorance and prejudice, which means a re-education of the public and management.

Stress

'Doing more with less' has become a mantra of modern living for many, and this is certainly the experience of the modern workforce where business has raised productivity levels to remain competitive in the global market. Such management strategies inevitably create stress for everyone, from senior management to front-line positions the expectations regarding performance have been raised to provide the cost leadership and service differentiation expected within resorts. So it becomes vital to recognize and manage stress, especially in pressure situations like high season. In isolated resorts where the pressure builds up more than usual due to a lack of 'escape valves', occupational stress has been estimated to cause up to half of all absenteeism and up to 40 per cent of labour turnover (Sims, 2002: 672).

Stress has been defined as a 'demand made upon the adaptive capacities of the mind and the body' (Law et al., 1995: 277). It can be positive as well as negative, in that most of us need such demands to motivate ourselves to study or exercise. However, if we become overloaded our bodies and minds reach a point where they can no longer cope. Stress can be caused by a wide range of factors, both by physical factors such as the weather or the design of our work environment or by the attitudes of fellow employees and customers. In the final analysis 'it is not so much the event which causes stress but human reactions to the event' (Law et al., 1995: 277), which means it is possible to control this human response on a corporate (management) and individual (coping) level.

Law et al. (1995: 279) indicate stress research in the tourism industry has raised four particular characteristics that can create stress, but they point out there has been no empirical confirmation and as in the case of 'turnover', different stress levels can be explained in part by the different motives people have for working in a resort environment. The four general stresses Law et al. identify are:

■ *Anti-social work hours*, which in a resort environment includes not only shift work, but split shifts (breakfast, lunch and dinner shifts for wait/server staff), long shifts of 10–12 hours during the high season, and no shifts if the snow does not fall and the sun does not shine.

- *Insufficient pay* is a particular problem in those countries with no or insufficient minimum wage or award systems, but is generally restricted to front-line positions that often have tipping opportunities.
- *Poor management* occurs when management does not understand the true working conditions of its staff, and is seen more as an obstruction than an assistance in getting the job done properly.
- *Requirement to deal with the public on a continuous day-to-day basis*, is perhaps the least appreciated aspect of resort stress. Many of those drawn to tourism and resort employment are people-oriented extraverts who enjoy the same environment and activities, yet over-exposure to a demanding public and the need to be on top of the situation at all times can become exhausting.

When Law et al., surveyed front-line workers in the attractions sector of Australia, some of which would qualify as resorts, they found the overwhelming stressor was 'poor management'. It was mentioned by 65 per cent of the sample and such management was generally accused of creating stress through its lack of communication (28 per cent), lack of recognition (17 per cent) and lack of interest (7 per cent).

The same study reveals how front-line employees cope with their stressful situations. Coping is seen as 'ways to protect oneself against the adverse effects of any stress ... and at the same time take advantage of its positive outcomes' (Law et al., 1995: 278). This definition incorporates several important aspects, including:

- coping, like stress, is highly dependent on an individual's perception of the environment and situation;
- coping is an intentional and cognitive act of analysis;
- the costs and benefits of copying strategies involve criteria with which to evaluate stress.

In terms of their coping strategies the sample of front-line employees mainly talked with co-workers (45 per cent), followed by reporting to their supervisor (36 per cent), trying to enjoy themselves and make the best of the situation (33 per cent) or by taking the problem home to family and friends (27 per cent). This diverse array of coping strategies offers some direction for management intervention.

Based on these results and talking with resort management students over the years, resort management must pay more attention to the needs of its front-line employees if it wants to establish the quality service it so often promotes as part of a resort experience. It needs to shift from being a stressor to being a mentor (training and communicating) and counsellor. Management needs to ensure its strategic mission is converted into a caring culture for guests and staff, through better communication, increased responsibility and appreciation. Such action with regard to stress could reduce the major labour cost of turnover for all resorts.

Turnover

Turnover represents the regular movement of staff, ranging from frontline employees to managers, within the tourism and hospitality sectors and out of the industry into other forms of employment. It is most frequently defined as the number or percentage of employees separated from their employment during a particular period of time (usually over a year). The formula is:

$$\text{Employee turnover} = \frac{\text{Number of separations}}{\text{Number of employees}} \times 100\%$$

(Gee, 1996: 231)

The turnover rate varies a great deal within the tourism industry, ranging from zero for many small family run businesses to over a hundred per cent when a business has a steady turnover of staff throughout the year. Under the later conditions a business with 10 positions that hires and looses or fires 20 people throughout the year would record a turnover rate of $20/10 \times 100 = 200\%$. Resorts run the full gamut of these experiences, from small family run resort hotels or retail businesses to large corporations, but resorts with the highest turnovers are the more isolated and seasonal ones. Isolated resorts create their own stress situations of homesickness and lack of privacy; where seasonal resorts will shift from hundreds of staff during the high season to a skeleton crew of core employees during the low season or face a complete shutdown.

Turnover can be both beneficial and problematic to resort management. Beneficial in the sense that it can accommodate the seasonal demand fluctuations by hiring staff for specific periods and the need to terminate the employment of those who prove to be unsuited to the rigours and demands of resort work and living. It can prove to be problematic when a turnover culture develops (Deery, 1999); one that encourages capable and excellent staff to move to competitors or other areas of the tourism industry, or to loose them and their skills to other service industries after they have been nurtured and developed within the tourism industry. Rudall et al. (1996) report that only a third of those entering the industry with a tourism or hospitality degree are still in the industry after five years, for example. These will be skilled and motivated individuals who have committed several years of their life and considerable expense to obtain a degree; but they will also have been encouraged to think for themselves and to look for their best personal options, so they are unlikely to stay in positions where conditions do not suit them.

Turnover can be both avoidable or unavoidable (Pizam and Ellis, 1999: 10). *Avoidable turnover* occurs when a business fails to make enough effort to retain staff. This occurs when employees leave in search of better pay or working conditions, or when they are seeking career advancement. *Unavoidable turnover* has little to do with the work environment. Unavoidable turnover occurs when the employee leaves because of personal reasons, such as returning to school, or changing situations such as the end of the season. James (1996) illustrates this situation with resorts very clearly when describing the situation at Dunk Island resort in tropical North Queensland. Dunk Island had a staff turnover of 126 per cent at the time because of its 'uniqueness and remoteness, and the lifestyle that goes with working in remote areas. We tend to attract people – apart from senior management – who stay for short periods (to experience that lifestyle). Hospitality (under these conditions) is a transient business' (James, 1996: 62).

Regardless of whether turnover is good or bad for resort management, all have agreed it is expensive. In Australia, Van Der Wagen and Davies (1998) estimate the cost of recruiting and training new staff is at least A$1000 per head for entry level staff. Hogan (1992) citing US experience has suggested $1700–$2500 in direct costs and an additional $1200–$1600 in indirect costs for front-line employees. The high expense is due to the direct costs of advertising and recruitment, management and clerical time, overtime for others covering the shortage, training and support items like new uniforms; plus an assessment of the indirect costs involved, such as lack of productivity, low morale, loss of reputation and goodwill. Given such an expensive and disruptive process it is desirable to find ways to reduce this labour turnover.

The most effective way to reduce turnover is to satisfy the needs and priorities of employees as well as those of the customers. 'It isn't easy, inexpensive, or achieved without effort' according to Hogan (1992: 45), but if a resort wishes to deliver quality service amidst a happy and enthusiastic environment it will need to ensure it has a happy and effective staff. Various studies cited by Deery (1999) have found job satisfaction and organizational commitment to reducing employee turnover have been significant contributors to a reduction in the intention to leave, which in most human resource studies is the surrogate variable used to represent turnover. Specific commitments and practices that can be made in this regard throughout the regular human resource functions include the following.

Recruitment

- Good staff need to possess the twin skills of technical knowledge and people skills.
- Recruitment must ensure applicants are aware of and can handle local living conditions, especially in remote settings.
- Recruit from reliable sources, such as proven agencies or associated institutions of higher learning for permanent or temporary workers.
- Recruit ahead of when staff are required, to meet labour planning objectives and to leave sufficient time for training.
- Salary – although wages are important they are not the only consideration for many resort employees. Other benefits such as lifestyle, housing and medical benefits and bonuses are also important considerations, whose importance will vary from person to person.

Induction and orientation

- Each resort is different in detail and will need to induct the new employee into their particular culture and approach.
- Induction can take place at the point of recruitment and/or place of work. If some induction is provided under a preliminary or probation basis this often reduces misunderstandings and later turnover.
- Staff housing, wherever applicable, is often crowded and noisy due to shift work and a party atmosphere among young staff. Some staff may wish to find alternative accommodation, so a list of nearby private housing is advisable. The hardest employees to accommodate are married couples and families who need increased privacy and space in locations where house prices tend to be very high.

Motivation and reward

- Training needs to be undertaken at all times and talented staff can be encouraged to develop multiple skills, which helps to turn them into core staff and start them up the career ladder.

- Resorts are designed for fun, so the provision of access to facilities and activities is a major attraction, especially for young staff. Discount passes to activities and facilities can be supplied as a fringe benefit or as part of a reward system.
- Provide furlough time so staff can escape the resort environment and the need to be constantly on show, to reconnect with family and friends for a while.

Termination

- End of season bonuses are common inducements to encourage staff to stay for the whole season or contractual period.
- Exit interviews are a good way to determine how things went and whether staff are interested in returning.
- Some staff may be retained and added to the core year-round staff pool. In seasonal resorts these are likely to be the multi-skilled staff who can undertake several and very different roles over the low or off-season, including plant and grounds maintenance.
- Some staff may be offered the opportunity to work with another resort during the off-season, so they and their particular skills are kept within the resort sector. In this regard Mt Buller (Australia) has developed a dual employment package with Vail (US), that enables certain ski instructors to follow the snow seasons and ply their trade skills on a global basis.

Practices like those outlined above have been used to minimize avoidable turnover while accepting the unavoidable turnover circumstances. Even in the case of unavoidable turnover strategies can be developed to ameliorate some concerns, like an off-season, by developing intra-sector arrangements or encouraging good resort workers to return for future experiences. In addition to incorporating these tactical practices into a resort's human relations practices it is also possible to enhance staff relations and effectiveness via a variety of management techniques.

Flexibility

'Flexibility' is defined most often as being responsive to change and being pliable, with an ability to switch between products or product emphasis (Dastmalchian and Blyton, 2001). Flexibility within organizations is generally viewed as a positive quality for the enhancement of business in an increasingly competitive and changing world. Implicit in this relationship is the role of human relations in creating the necessary flexibility to enable business to adjust to changing conditions, some expected and others not. In the case of seasonal resorts that flexibility becomes an important part of labour relations for both management and employees.

There are four potential sources of workplace flexibility according to Dastmalchian and Blyton (1998) and Ng and Dastmalchian (1998). *Numerical flexibility* refers to the organization's ability to respond to fluctuations in demand by adjusting staff levels. It is the most common flexibility strategy in the resort sector, but it is not the only management option. There is also *functional flexibility* where adjustments are made to workforce skills, so workers can undertake a wider range of tasks. Within resorts this type of flexibility is behind the move to multi-skilling, which is most prevalent in seasonal resorts. Another is *distancing* where employment contracts with on-site personnel are replaced by outsourcing through commercial contracts. This type of flexibility is less common in resorts at present because of the importance of quality service developed through internal practices, as we will see in the case of Ritz-Carlton. Finally, there is *financial flexibility* which is the movement to more individualized payment systems from the more uniform ones established through union negotiations. Individual workplace agreements, as they are now called in Australia, provide more flexibility concerning shift work and contract conditions, and individual reward incentives. While the author only has limited anecdotal evidence of this form of flexibility being used in the resort sector, it generally seems to be applied to staff with key skills who are major attractions in themselves, such as a well-known chef or tennis coach.

James provides an example of numerical and functional flexibility occurring at Dunk Island Resort. He notes that the resort has flattened its management structure to improve communication and the need for number flexibility has increased, as demand not only fluctuates with the seasons, but also within weekly periods when changing weather and holiday periods alter demand. But the resort also encourages 'any staff member who has been with us longer than three months to apply to cross-train in any facet of the business' (James, 1996: 62). Along with this increased skill set and flexibility often comes an increasing confidence in the staff to handle a variety of 'moments-of-truth' situations with customers, so there is more confidence in them to make individual decisions on behalf of resort management.

A growing aspect of flexibility is the move to outsourcing and the important changes this can bring to a business's labour relations. Drucker

(2002: 70) has noted that an increasing number of businesses no longer have traditional employees under their direct control, because as more of them outsource employee relations 'they no longer manage major aspects of their relationships with the people who are their formal employees'. He feels this change has occurred because the growing burden of rules and regulations has taken senior management's eye off their principal responsibility, which is 'to focus on the business rather than on employment-related rules, regulations, and paperwork' (Drucker, 2002: 77). While Drucker does not mention resorts or tourism directly he does relate this trend to service industries that require a wide range of skills and have stressful work conditions. In fact more resorts are turning to agencies to help them find not just seasonal employees but senior people with professional and management skills, so we may see more distancing flexibility in the future.

Empowerment/enfranchisement

Empowerment encourages front-line workers, who are the major interface with guests to exercise initiative and imagination to prevent problems, to solve actual difficulties or to provide some form of service recovery if there has been a slip in the level of service. In an environment where hundreds of guests want to do the same things at the same time, where their plans may be forcibly changed by the weather or unexpected demands within their party, or those plans depend on the smooth coordination of several suppliers – the possibilities for friction and disappointment are endless. It needs someone on hand to assess the situation and determine the best solution for each particular incident with respect to the resort's image and branding. In the words of Jan Carlzon, who invented the very apt term 'moments of truth' and was a champion of empowerment:

> When problems arise, each employee has the authority to analyse the situation, determine the appropriate action, and see to it that the action is carried out, either alone or with the help of others.
>
> (Carlzon, 1987: 61)

Empowerment respects the ability of a trained professional to make the appropriate decision relating to a front-line contact with the guest, which permits the immediate resolution of most problems on the spot and with little fuss.

Empowerment in the tourism industry in general and in the resort sector in particular has become standard practice. Edward G. Sullivan, when he was regional Vice President of Hyatt Hotels and Resorts, has been quoted as saying:

> Managers in the hotel business must train employees and empower them
> to handle most guest incidents on the spot and with good judgement –
> promptly, professionally, and courteously. This will improve guest ser-
> vice and satisfaction, *create a better working environment for the employ-
> ees*, and free up more time for managers to focus on the tasks of being
> a manager.

(Brymer, 1991: 58)

The relationship of empowerment to the working environment has been
highlighted in the above quote by this author because too often the
human response of staff in these situations is overshadowed by empowerment's link to customer satisfaction and maintaining the brand image.
What empowerment offers to employees is a further way to become part
of the team, by enabling them to show their initiative and judgement in
the provision of quality service. It gives them status and personal satisfaction to be able to function as a caring and capable human being as well
as a mechanic performing their trained function(s).

The contribution of empowerment to staff morale and effectiveness,
however, should not be interpreted as a universal truth to be applied
everywhere. Empowerment compared to the rigidity of corporate policy
works best under certain conditions. For example, Disney finds the
tightly scripted presentations of its ride operators' works best because of
the high business volume and short contact time with the customer. In
contrast, Club Med staff are encouraged to interact with their guests in a
variety of settings, and over the week or so of a typical stay they will
require more flexibility in how to engage with guests. This is basically the
difference between a production line approach and a personal relations
approach. Bowen and Lawler (1992) have demonstrated that an empowerment approach is preferable when personal relations dominate over
production line considerations in any staff–guest interaction. They have
developed a table to illustrate when one approach should be favoured
over the other in terms of a management approach (Table 10.1).

From this table Bowen and Lawler make three recommendations:

1. The higher the rating of each contingency the better the fit with an
   empowerment approach.
2. The higher the total score from all five contingencies the better the fit
   with an empowerment approach overall.
3. The higher the total score, the more the benefits of increasing empowerment will outweigh the costs.

Table 10.1   The contingencies of empowerment

Contingency	Product line approach		Empowerment
Basic business strategy	Low cost, high volume	1 2 3 4 5	Differentiation, customized, personalized
Tie to customer	Transaction, short-time period	1 2 3 4 5	Relationship, long-time period
Technology	Routine, simple	1 2 3 4 5	Non-routine, complex
Business environment	Predictable, few surprises	1 2 3 4 5	Unpredictable, many surprises
Type of people	Theory X managers, employees with low growth needs, low social needs and weak interpersonal skills	1 2 3 4 5	Theory Y managers, employees with high growth needs, high social needs and strong interpersonal skills.

Source: Bowen and Lawler, 1992: 37.

They conclude by re-iterating that empowerment and production line approaches demand different types of managers and employees. They consider for empowerment to work well requires managers 'who believe their employees can act independently to benefit both the organisation and its customers' (Bowen and Lawler, 1992: 38). But it also needs employees who want that sort of responsibility and challenge. Not all employees can handle such responsibility and some back of house positions will rarely require it, so such a policy has to be implemented on a selective and appropriate basis throughout a resort.

Strongly related to empowerment is the concept of *enfranchising* service workers, where a combination of empowerment and pay for performance encourages employees to use their discretionary powers (Schlesinger and Heskett, 1991). Although the primary area to utilize enfranchisement has been the retail sector, Schlesinger and Heskett refer to one hospitality company that has used enfranchisement successfully, and that is the Fairfield Inn division of the Marriott Corporation.

The Fairfield Inn approach to the employment and management practices for housekeepers is provided as an example. Empowerment occurs through the assignment of 14 rooms to clean every day, without any conditions or policy regarding how much time should be spent on each room. If the rooms are cleaned to the required standard in less than eight hours the housekeeper (known as guest room attendants or GRAs), receives a full day's wage. If there are still rooms to be cleaned the GRAs can bid on those additional rooms, and are paid in half-hour increments. Such overtime is paid in cash at the end of each shift, 'reflecting the typical short-term needs for compensation that often motivate GRAs to clean additional rooms on a given day' (Schlesinger and Heskett, 1991: 90). In addition each inn establishes two discretionary budgets of $150 each for a 28-day period. The first is spent at the discretion of management on employee awards and morale-building events. The second is a 'guest relations' budget that is managed by employees. These budgets are 'managed with great care and spent with considerable creativity and by the third year of the programme Fairfield Inn's relative economic and human relations performance was ahead of the industry's norm', as shown in Table 10.2.

When compared to other economy lodging chains Fairfield Inn's compensation levels were around that group's norm but its occupancy rates were higher, customer satisfaction rates were higher and its turnover level was lower. This has helped Fairfield Inn eliminate the need for housekeeper supervisors in some locations, which not only reduced the cost of operation but 'represents a reallocation of a unit managers' time to more positive activities of selecting and motivating staff' (Schlesinger and Heskett, 1991: 91).

Quality service and total quality management

Throughout this chapter the emphasis has been on how to develop human relations so resorts can offer the service quality that should be one of their key differentiators. We have examined various specific issues, such as stress and turnover, which can impact on the quality of service and discussed some of the management techniques that have been used to enhance this feature, such as flexibility and empowerment. But it all needs to be pulled together in some way, to support the overall vision and purpose of a resort. One of the best ways to do this is through the application of total quality management (TQM) principles, as had been done so successfully by the Ritz-Carlton Company.

'The foundation for building and sustaining customer service and satisfaction is to establish an effective measurement and improvement system'

Table 10.2 Early results of Fairfield Inn's effort to enfranchise employees

Index of compensation	Fairfield Inn	Other economy lodging chains
Rates, hourly employees		
Wage	1.00	1.00
Incentives	1.10	1.00
Employee turnover (annual)		
1990	100–120%	167%
1989	120–140%	167%
Occupancy rates percentage of		
rooms filled on average		
1989–1990	70–75%	60%
Average number of trips per year		
among economy business travellers'	50–70	30–40
Management salary index (unit level)	1.05	1.00
Non-management labour costs as		
a percentage of revenue (unit level)	18–20%	16–19%
Indices of customer satisfaction		
Overall cleanliness of hotel	80–90	55–85
Overall value for money	70–80	55–65
Overall maintenance and upkeep of hotel	80–90	45–80
Hotel service overall	80–90	50–70
Speed and efficiency of check-in and check-out	70–80	40–70
Friendliness of hotel personnel	70–80	50–60

Source: Schlesinger and Heskett (1991: 92).

(Barsky, 1996: 27) and that is a key basis of TQM. TQM has been critically analysed by Flood (1993) and he has identified 10 principles of this management approach, 2 of which involve measurement and improvement (#8 and #9), but all of which involve human relations development, especially within a service industry like tourism. Flood's 10 principles are:

1. There must be agreed requirements, for internal and external customers.
2. Customers' requirements must be met first time, every time.
3. Quality improvement will reduce waste and total costs.
4. There must be a focus on the prevention of problems, rather than an acceptance to cope with a fire-fighting manner.

5. Quality improvement can only result from planned management action.
6. Every job must add value.
7. Everybody must be involved, from all levels and across all functions.
8. There must be an emphasis on measurement to help to assess and to meet requirements and objectives.
9. A culture of continuous improvement must be established (continuous includes the desirability of dramatic leaps forward as well as steady improvement).
10. An emphasis should be placed on promoting creativity.

(Flood, 1993: 48)

In terms of resorts, the first principle of a TQM approach is to *agree on the requirements* of both the guests (*external customers*) and staff (*internal customers*). To deliver the promised vacation experience requires that both of these groups be on the same page and acting in harmony to produce the successful vacation experience of a lifetime.

Other principles that may require some elaboration in a resort setting include the following. The focus on the *prevention of problems* emphasizes pre-planning and pro-active management. This goes beyond regular training to include risk management preparation as will be discussed in Chapter 11. Ensuring *everybody is involved* is necessary in such diverse and fragmented businesses as resorts, even when we are considering a single resort hotel facility. The different departments all have a role to play and value to add, but this will only work effectively if their goals and efforts are coordinated. *Measurement* of performance, in the role of the control function of management, is vital for resorts if they are to determine how well their efforts are meeting customers' expectations and to detect any areas of weakness. The need for *continuous improvement* is a fact of life in the global economy and resort marketplace, so there must be ongoing analysis of the measurements and a cross-department appraisal of how the product and service could be improved. This leads back to the first principle of ensuring the needs of both guests and staff can be met to provide the best possible service.

When addressing the application of TQM to the tourism industry Witt and Muhlemann (1994) emphasize that customer focus is the central element in a service industry, but that cultural change and a commitment to employees are essential support mechanisms to that central goal. They note the important differentiators between a tourism/resort experience

---

Table 10.3 Service characteristics for tourism/resort workers

---

1. Services produce intangible output
2. Services produce variable, non-standard output
3. A service is perishable; that is it cannot be carried in inventory, but is consumed in production
4. There is high customer contact throughout the service process
5. The customer participates in the process of providing a service
6. Skills are sold directly to the customer
7. Services cannot be mass produced
8. High personal judgment is employed by individuals performing the service
9. Service firms are labour intensive
10. Decentralized facilities are located near the customers
11. Measures of effectiveness are subjective
12. Quality control is primarily limited to process control
13. Pricing options are more elaborate

Source: Murdick, R.G., Render, B. and Russell, R.S. (1990). *Service Operations Management.* Boston: Allyn and Bacon, p. 26.

---

and a manufacturing system, for which TQM was initially developed (Table 10.3).

This means training must be as related to customer relations as it is to technical skills, because the perfect delivery of service will involve the guests' active participation. This can happen either directly in the recommended choice of a meal or personal equipment for an activity, or indirectly in observing how guests use a room and its various facilities. For example, are they heavy towel or shampoo users or have they exhausted the mini bar and video selection? In either case good service adjusts to these conditions and provides more or less of a specific item. To permit or encourage such flexible service requires a cultural change for many managers, to provide staff with the opportunity to adjust to changing circumstances, including that occasional 'customer from hell', through empowerment and supervisory responsibility.

Witt and Muhlemann (1994: 422–423) suggest three guidelines for the successful implementation of TQM in services; these are as follows with additional details from the author:

1. Elements of the product/service package.
   - Organizations should have a clear *strategy* for the key features of their service/product.

- *Design* of the service/product should be approached in a structured and collaborative manner with staff,
- Service/product should be broken down into *specific processes/components* to create the best value in terms of experience and return.
- Key *skills and competencies* for each task should be identified and enhanced through training and cross-skill development where applicable.
- *Contingency plans* should be developed for key problem areas (such as check-in and check-out at busy times) and occasional events such as accidents or festive celebrations.
- Delivery systems should be *robust* and able to handle a variety of demand levels.
- Processes should be *standardized* wherever possible to ensure *consistency* of delivery, but not to the extent of restricting flexibility when necessary to maximize the value of a guest's experience.

2. Human aspects of the delivery system
   - *Clear communication* of vision and objectives needs to be extended to the staff.
   - All staff should be *fully trained* in the necessary technical skills and competencies relevant to their role(s) and in interpersonal relations.
   - *Multi-skilling, problem-solving skills and job enrichment* should all be included in recruitment and training exercises.
   - Individuals should be prepared for taking over *ownership* of a situation.
   - Staff should be *empowered* to make decisions when necessary to ensure guest satisfaction.
   - *Total commitment* to quality objectives of the company should be a *motivation* force for staff.
   - *Customer's roles* within the delivery system should be specified explicitly and communicated clearly.
   - *Provision of facilities for staff* should be sufficient to allow them to complete their tasks at the levels expected.

3. Measurement issues in service quality
   - Both tangible and intangible aspects should be *quantified.*
   - Intangibles can be measured by using *focus group situations* to establish expectations and set standards.
   - Clear *standards* of acceptable service need to be set and communicated to both customer and provider.
   - *Benchmarking* should be used to compare performance levels with the competition.
   - Staff should be involved with the *feedback* on service performance.

- Feedback should be viewed as an *opportunity*, but not as a *threat*.
- *All* negative feedback should be followed up as soon as possible and appropriate joint action taken by staff and management.
- *Teamwork* can be used to evaluate and resolve general problems identified through feedback.
- *All difficulties* which have arisen should be *recorded and analysed* with the appropriate corrective action established and recorded. If necessary, based on this experience established practices *should* be modified or changed.
- Systems should be in place to *monitor customer expectations and levels of satisfaction*. Do not be restricted to invasive processes like questionnaires or interviews, but also use old-fashioned human skills of looking, listening and thinking about your product through the eyes of your guest.

Throughout these three guidelines one can see the central importance of having all employees, from front line to senior management, prepared and committed to provide the best service possible and working like a team to bring about the promised resort vacation experience.

Summary

This chapter has reviewed some of the labour conditions facing resorts and challenging management to deliver on the promised quality experiences. Traditional sources of labour have started to dry up in advanced economies, so recruitment and training processes become more vital and need to be adjusted accordingly. Even when staff have been hired there is the constant spectre of turnover which can be a very expensive process. Not everything about turnover is negative and some forms of turnover are unavoidable, but the evidence suggests that the cost of turnover can be reduced with strategies that make resort employment more fulfilling and relevant to individual interests.

This chapter emphasizes the importance of relations further when discussing the relationship between employees and the delivery of quality service. In this instance staff need to work with the resort companies and the guests in order to deliver the high-quality vacation experiences that have been promised via the marketing campaigns. Factors that will assist in this include the development of various types of workplace flexibility, the opportunities for empowerment and the integration of human relations into the strategic management of resorts through concepts like TQM.

Many of these human relations features have been incorporated into successful tourism and resort products, and some of the specific problems and responses will be explored in this chapter's two case studies. Sims' studies of isolated resorts in Australia demonstrates the added social pressures isolation places on workers, and his research suggests treating these workers as separate work groups who are seeking different objectives from their resort work. The Ritz-Carlton Company exemplifies what can be achieved by integrating human relations into the TQM strategies of a hospitality service company. By emphasizing the importance of selection, training and empowerment it has raised the professional levels of its staff to new heights, resulting in lowered turnover and increased earnings, a win–win situation for staff and management.

Case studies
Employee turnover in isolated resorts, Australia

Wiley Sims, a colleague at La Trobe University, has conducted several studies of turnover in isolated resorts within Australia, because high labour turnover levels can have serious effects on the efficient operation of hospitality enterprises within isolated resorts. He defines isolated resorts as 'resorts that are dependent on their own internal labour supply; they have no or a very limited access to an external casual labour pool' (Sims, 2002: 670). Sims considers the cost of labour turnover in such resorts comes in two forms. *Direct costs* include separation costs of the departing employee (exit interviews and severance pay), recruitment costs (advertising and search fees) and the costs associated with finding their replacement, the selection costs (interview and reference checking), hiring costs (induction and initial training, relocation expenses, uniforms) and lost productivity costs associated with the learning curve of the new employee. *Indirect costs* include decreased levels of general employee motivation as staff change regularly, and the sort of problems that precede any decision to quit such as tardiness and absenteeism.

Sims' studies started with a comparison of the situation at the *Ayers Rock Resort Company* (ARRC), which then operated seven resort properties in and around the township of Yulara that service the tourist interest in Ayers Rock (Uluru) and nearby Mt Olga (Kata Tjuta), and Thredbo Village which is located in the Kosciosko National Park and is the largest ski resort in Australia. Although Thredbo is a small community within a large national park it is not as cut-off as Yulara because it is within a three hour drive of Sydney, which is its major skier market.

The ARRC is challenged by its physical isolation, being over 2000 km from the nearest large urban centre and its lack of social activities and satisfactory accommodation. Despite careful selection and the promotion of a six-month renewable contract, backed up with financial incentives from the company and Australian Tax Office, 'less than 50 per cent of new employees complete a six-month contract of employment' (Sims, 2000: 594–595). Sims' survey of employees at ARRC revealed a personal turnover average of 0.89 years for staff and a 'very unstable youthful workforce' where the average age was 23 years. Thredbo's workforce was older, with an average age of 34.6 years and a lower turnover rate of 2.0 years. Although neither location has a local labour market and must bring in its employees, especially for the high seasons, Sims felt that more could be done to reduce labour turnover if resorts examined and promoted their lifestyle factors.

To test out this idea Sims moved his focus to three isolated winter resorts in the Victorian Alps – Mt Hotham, Falls Creek and Mt Buller, and examined whether these resorts were building a culture that could be seen as a positive from the employees' perspective and if it would help to overcome the isolation effects of their locations. Specifically he examined whether lifestyle factors such as skiing, environment and climate, escape from the city, the development of friendships and less formal working conditions could be developed into employee satisfiers and thereby reduce turnover rates in these isolated resorts. Of these variables only working conditions showed any significant statistical relationship with intent to stay. Far more significant was the age of the employee. 'The younger the employee the more likely the employee is to voluntarily terminate his/her employment. General managers and supervisory staff were found to be the most stable cohort' (Sims, 2002: 681). This suggests that older and core staff are more committed to the employment and lifestyle opportunities of resort life, while the younger staff treat it more as a transient step in their general growing up and travel plans. The strategic implications being that management should treat their young and older staff as separate labour markets with different priorities, and should therefore emphasize different factors in their individual workplace agreements.

The Ritz-Carlton Company, USA

There is no better way to demonstrate the importance of human relations and the TQM process than to review the experience of the Ritz-Carlton Company. It was the first hotel group to win the Malcolm Baldrige National (US) Quality Award in 1992 and has now won it a second time (1999). 'While winning the award is nice, to paraphrase

Shakespeare, the process is the thing' according to Partlow (1993: 16), so that is what will be examined here.

The Ritz-Carlton Hotel Company is a management company offering a traditional luxury hotel experience that has European roots. It has embraced the Malcolm Baldrige commitment to TQM as a way to get to the top and stay at the top of the luxury hotel and resort sector. It has used the categories and certification criteria of the Baldrige Award scheme as its road map for quality improvement, not just to compete for the award and prestige it brings but also to improve its business and to keep ahead of the competition. Now it is no longer just a hotel or resort business, it is in the development business by adding 'the residences at the Ritz-Carlton' (private residential units) as well as 'The Ritz-Carlton Club' (fractional ownership residences). But given the human relations emphasis of this chapter we will focus on those aspects of its success with TQM.

The Ritz-Carlton Hotel Company operated 36 hotels (25 city hotels and 11 resorts) worldwide in 1999 when it won its second award, a figure that has increased to 58 operations worldwide with its own enlargement and partnership with Bulgari Hotels. It has over 27 000 employees and 85 per cent of its staff are front-line employees. This diverse company is able to deliver customer satisfaction to guests and staff alike, as indicated by the following reported highlights:

> In an independent survey, 99 per cent of guests said they were satisfied with their overall experience; more than 80 per cent were 'extremely satisfied'.
>
> (Mene, 1999: 2)

> Since this improvement effort has begun we reduced our employee turnover from 80 percentage points to the middle 20s, and that's in an industry that runs at around 100 per cent.
>
> (Schulze quoted by Green, 2000: 2)

How it has achieved such milestones is examined below.

Leadership

TQM required leadership commitment from senior executives, general managers and middle management to succeed because it involves a transformation to the normal way of doing business. 'A focus on customer satisfaction must be built into the management processes of the organization and supported through an integrated system of information analysis, total employee participation, training, and the continuous effort to improve service and product quality' (Partlow, 1993: 24). This takes time and resources and Ritz-Carlton President and Chief Operating Officer Horst H. Schulze, says the process for the 1992 award began back in 1983 (Schulze, n.d.: 3) and 'its easier to get to the top than to stay there' admits Diane Oreck, Vice President of the Ritz-Carlton's Leadership Centre (trainingmag.com, 2006: 2).

A sign of human relations leadership within The Ritz-Carlton Hotel Company is its creation of its *Leadership Centre*, which is the company's corporate university and umbrella learning organization. It is made up of three schools: the *School of Performance Excellence* houses all of the training and development programmes for hourly employees; the *School of Leadership and Business Excellence* provides soft-skills training to develop identified leaders; the *School of Service Excellence* was created to address the increasing benchmark questions the company has received after winning its second Baldrige Award. This latter school brings in a 'yearly revenue of $1.5 million to the company – earnings that are invested back into internal training and development programs', while the other schools operate on a fee for service to internal and external customers (trainingmag.com, 2006: 1). So human relations leadership is looked upon as an investment and revenue generator at Ritz-Carlton, and to understand what it does to earn this respect and money we shall examine some of the issues that have been raised in this chapter.

Selection

The Ritz-Carlton Hotel Company's mission is 'to be the premier worldwide provider of luxury travel and hospitality products and services' and that process starts with selecting the appropriate management and front-line staff. Their commitment to planning and to realizing the full potential of their staff begins with a selection process that uses predictive psychological and behavioural instruments to determine each candidate's capability of meeting the requirements of 120 job positions. 'This technology: known as 'character trait recruiting' reduces service variability; acts as an aid to productivity and has enabled us to reduce turnover by nearly 50 per cent in the past three years' (Schulze, n.d.: 8).

It should be noted that as part of the teamwork or circles approach within TQM the selection of staff is not solely a human resources or management's responsibility. 'Human resources and operations personnel work together to select, orient, train, and certify employees' (Partlow, 1993: 22).

Training

This is the aspect of the Ritz-Carlton approach which has received most attention, and deservedly so, due to its recognition that any hotel or resort needs quality staff to bring the best out of quality facilities and products. After the first Baldrige Award Schulze (n.d.: 8) reports how the training manager and senior hotel executives worked as an orientation team over a two-day period to instill the company's Gold Standards service values in all new employees. These Gold Standards incorporate three pocket-sized memory prompters and the more detailed Ritz-Carlton Basics.

Within the Gold Standards 'three steps of service' define the activities and decisions of the customer interface. The 'Credo' acts as a guide, reaffirming that personalized customer satisfaction is the company's goal and that staff are an essential part of that process. The 'Motto' that staff are ladies and gentlemen serving ladies and gentlemen is a succinct and clever summary of the guest–server relationship. 'It is a culture, effectively created by senior leaders and experienced by (both) customers and employees' (Schulze, n.d.: 4). The Ritz-Carlton Basics describe their guest problem-solving process and the expected standards for personal grooming and safety procedures. After the orientation comes extensive on-the-job training, followed by job certification that requires constant upgrading.

The actual training for each position has evolved into a continuous improvement process where every employee receives an average of 284 hours of training each year (over 35 days a year), consisting of face-to-face training along with CD-Rom and Web-based training that leads to certification and regular updating.

'This process has allowed the housekeeping department to replace annual training certification with just-in-time training while increasing their customer satisfaction scores in guest-room cleanliness,' Oreck (Vice President of Ritz-Carlton's Leadership Centre) says. One Ritz-Carlton property increased its satisfaction with guest-room cleanliness from 82 to 92 per cent within six months.

(trainingmag.com, 2006: 2)

The commitment to and continuous nature of the training enables Ritz-Carlton to keep up with changing technical specifications and customer tastes, as illustrated by Schulze's remarks:

Things are changing dramatically. I can tell you that only three years ago, no customer asked for high-speed Internet access. Today, every customer asks for it. Guests today have knowledge of amenities totally different from guests of five years ago. There is a higher level of sophistication, higher expectations, because our customers travel. So there is an evolution – a constant revolution of new expectations.

(Green, 2000: 3)

To ensure the training is targeted appropriately and the material is relevant an important part of the TQM process is a focus on information and analysis.

Information and analysis

Ritz-Carlton places great emphasis on knowing what their guests desire, even to the point of anticipating those desires. To achieve this the company must measure and analyse their guests, which is a most challenging task if they are meant to be relaxing or are otherwise engaged, but the effort put into this is one of the key features distinguishing this company from its competitors.

It starts with 'understanding customers in detail'. Key processes in the customer–staff relationships are 'dissected to identify points at which errors may occur' in the company's bid to eliminate all errors. For example, Ritz-Carlton has determined that 'there are 970 potential instances for a problem to arise during interactions with overnight guests and 1071 such instances during interactions with meeting event planners' (Mene, 1999: 3). This degree of information and analysis makes it possible to determine where problems are most likely to occur and to prepare staff to handle them, be it a mundane issue regarding ice for drinks in the room or the unusual, such as managing the appearance of a wild animal mascot at a convention.

In addition to events and interactions the company seeks to cultivate customer loyalty through customer customization. This process 'relies on extensive data gathering' regarding the guest using 'the capabilities of advanced information technology'. The information is gathered during 'various types of customer contacts' or 'post-event reviews conducted with meeting planners'. So the million or so files held in the Ritz-Carlton data base can ensure James Bond's martini is shaken and not stirred, and that Corporation X places more importance on the chef's famous desserts than the team-building exercises available at the resort.

Empowerment

An important element in ensuring the steady quality improvement that has led to the Baldrige Awards is the empowering of staff, 'giving them the authority to identify and solve customer problems on the spot and to improve work processes' (Partlow, 1993: 23). For Ritz-Carlton 'effective involvement and empowerment grew in part from effective quality training' (Schulze, n.d.: 9).

At Ritz-Carlton each employee is trained to:

1. move heaven and earth to satisfy a customer;
2. contact appropriate employees to help resolve a problem swiftly (lateral service concept);
3. spend up to $2000 in order to satisfy a guest;
4. decide the acceptability of products and services;
5. decide the business terms of a sale (sales and marketing);
6. become involved in setting the plans of their work area;
7. speak with anyone regarding a problem.

(Schulze, n.d.: 9)

With such training and responsibility goes accountability, so in each instance when the empowerment function is used there needs to be a report and subsequent analysis of the actions taken. With thorough training and the detailed analysis referred to above these situations do not occur too frequently and are generally resolved without major time or cost impacts. In most cases it simply requires a caring person who is prepared to listen to a guest's request or problem and then proceed to have it granted or expedited as effectively and efficiently as possible – the traits of good management.

Staff perspective

While the Baldrige Award represents the official recognition of the Ritz-Carlton Hotel Company's overall TQM success; Paul Hemp, a senior editor at the *Harvard Business Review*, spent a week as a room-service waiter at a Ritz-Carlton Hotel to view the process from a staff member's perspective. As he says:

Managers love to talk about delighting their customers. But how does it feel to be one of the people who actually have to deliver the goods?

(Hemp, 2002: 50)

His assessment after his exposure to the Gold Standards, practicing under the tutelage of experienced co-workers, and going solo at the end of the week is that Ritz-Carlton's success in customer service involves an emotional partnership, which requires several ingredients.

Based on his exposure to the Ritz-Carlton system from the inside Hemp considers there are several lessons for all service businesses. Specifically he recommends:

■ 'Great customer service should be based on dynamic principles rather than a rigid formula'. That is some situational flexibility is called for when staff implement company policies.
■ 'It is employees' emotional commitment – which is achieved in part through symbols and rituals that enhance employees' sense of identity with the company – that contributes most to superior performance'.
■ '(Personal) commitment serves as a driver of excellent customer service only when employees are empowered to take initiative'.
■ '(It) isn't enough to truly anticipate customer needs. Another component is empathy – being able to imagine guests' emotional responses to their experience'.

(Hemp, 2002: 62)

Based on his experiences Hemp feels if any company can blend the Ritz-Carlton practices with like-minded staff, it will create a positive service environment that will be hard to beat.

Financial performance

Obviously the cost involved in preparing staff and management for such high levels of service quality is significant, and many will be wondering if all this effort in creating capable and motivated staff is worthwhile. Well, let us think about the words of a successful small tourism business operator and examine the financial statements of the Ritz-Carlton Hotel Company to assess this point.

Tom O'Toole, the owner and operator of successful bakery and tourism attraction in Beechworth, Victoria, Australia, has often been asked why he spends so much money training his staff, when they can up and leave for another job or worse still start up in competition with him. To which his usual reply is 'What if I don't train them and they stay?' (O'Toole with Tarling, 2000: 199). In business, as in life, one cannot stop people moving on and there is no harm in parting as friends and enhancing your reputation and network of colleagues, even among competitors. That is certainly preferable to holding back the potential and spirit of staff, which is bound to reduce the effectiveness of your business and increase the expense that turnover brings.

In the case of Ritz-Carlton it would appear the company is convinced the time and expense invested in their staff, as part of their TQM strategy, has been well worth the effort. Not only has the company won two Malcolm

Baldrige National Quality Awards, with all the positive media attention and prestige that brings, but it reports that such human relations policies have been good for the bottom line. Schulze has mentioned the dramatic decline in turnover rates, which are now well below industry averages and Mene (1999: 3) reports that 'earnings before income taxes nearly doubled (from 1995 to 1998), and revenue per available room continues to grow, exceeding the industry average by more than 3000 per cent'.

Questions

1 With a shrinking traditional labour pool of young people discuss what adjustment should resorts be considering in their recruitment processes and how they can make employment more attractive to alternative labour sources.

2 'Stress can be both good and bad'. Examine this statement in light of your exam *or* tourism work experiences, analysing how you handled it and what changes you need to make for the future.

3 Assuming that you are a tourism/hospitality graduate with life-long career aspirations in this industry, discuss what your future first employer should do to keep you for five years plus *and* what you should do to deserve that commitment.

4 Analyse the pros and cons of financial flexibility processes for resort management, and assess whether such individual agreements should supersede traditional union agreements.

5 Flood (1993: 142) in his critique of TQM considers that it 'emprisons' employees into a rigid system of behaviour that limits their true potential. He advocates 'disemprisoning (that will) enable genuine open debate for learning and understanding which leads to more meaningful work and to the realization of maximum efficiency from designs, which all adds up to maximum freedom'. Based on your experience as a tourism employee and your expectations as a future manager/owner within tourism explain how these two concepts might co-exist within a resort business.

6 Taking the Ritz-Carlton experience, discuss why and how you would transfer some of their methods to the operation of a non-accommodation component in an integrated resort complex.

References

Barsky, J.D. (1996). Building a program for world-class service. *The Cornell Hotel and Restaurant Administration Quarterly*, **37(1)**, 17–27.

Bowen, D.E. and Lawler, E.E. (1992). The empowerment of service workers: what, why, how and when. *Sloan Management Review*, Vol. 33, Spring, 31–38.

Brymer, R.A. (1991). Employee empowerment: a guest driven leadership strategy. *The Cornell Hotel and Restaurant Administration Quarterly*, **32(1)**, 58–68.

Carlzon, J. (1987). *Moments of Truth*. New York: Harper and Row.

Dastmalchian, A. and Blyton, P. (1998). Introduction to organizational flexibility in a cross-national perspective. *International Journal of Human Resource Management*, **9(3)**, 437–444.

Dastmalchian, A. and Blyton, P. (2001). Workplace flexibility and the changing nature of work: an introduction. *Canadian Journal of Administrative Sciences*, **18(1)**, 1–4.

Deery, M. (1999). *Turnover Culture, Internal Labour Markets and Employee Turnover: An Integrated Model*. Unpublished Ph.D. Thesis, La Trobe University, Melbourne, Australia.

Drucker, P.F. (2002). They're not employees, they're people. *Harvard Business Review*, **80**, 70–77.

Flood, R.L. (1993). *Beyond TQM*. Chichester: John Wiley and Sons.

Gee, C.Y. (1996). *Resort Development and Management*, 2nd edn. East Lansing, Michigan: Educational Institute of American Hotel and Motel Association.

Green, R. (2000). Baldrige Award Winner Profile. www.qualitydigest.com/aug00/html/baldrige.html.

Hemp, P. (2002). My week as a room-service waiter at the Ritz. *Harvard Business Review*, **80**, 50–62.

Hogan, J.J. (1992). Turnover and what to do about it. *The Cornell Hotel and Restaurant Administration Quarterly*, **33(1)**, 40–45.

James, D. (1996). Keeping staff happy on a tropical island. *Business Review Weekly*, **19**, 62.

Karatepe, O.M., Uludag, O., Menevis, I., Hadzimehmedagic, L. and Baddon, L. (2006). The effects of selected individual characteristics on frontline employee performance and job satisfaction. *Tourism Management*, **27(4)**, 547–560.

Law, J., Pearce, P.L. and Woods, B.A. (1995). Stress and coping in tourist attraction employees. *Tourism Management*, **16(4)**, 277–284.

Meier, J.D. (1991). Solutions to the hospitality industry's labour shortage. *Florida International University Hospitality Review*, **9(2)**, 78–85.

Mene, P. (1999). Malcolm Baldrige National Quality Award – 1999 Award Recipient, Service Category – The Ritz-Carlton Hotel Company. www.nist.gov/public-affairs/bald99/ritz.html. Accessed on 2 August 2006.

Murdick, R.G., Render, B. and Russell, R.S. (1990). *Service Operations Management*, Boston: Allyn and Bacon.

Ng, I. and Dastmalchian, A. (1998). Organizational flexibility in Canada: a study of control and safeguard rules. *International Journal of Human Resource Management*, **9(3)**, 445–456.

O'Toole, T. with Tarling, L. (2000). *Breadwinner: A Fresh Approach to Rising to the Top*. Melbourne: Information Australia.

Partlow, C.G. (1993). How Ritz-Carlton applies TQM. *The Cornell Hotel and Restaurant Administration Quarterly*, **34(4)**, 16–24.

Pizam, A. and Ellis, T. (1999). Absenteeism and turnover in the hospitality industry. In *Human Resource Management: HRM in Tourism and Hospitality, International Perspectives on Small to Medium-sized Enterprises* (D. Lee-Ross, ed.), pp. 109–131. London: Cassell.

Rudall, L., Deery, M. and Stewart, M. (1996). Hospitality graduates: course expectations and career destinations. In *Tourism and Hospitality Research: Australian and International Perspectives* (G. Prosser, ed.). CAUTHE Proceedings, Coffs Harbour, NSW, 171–181.

Schlesinger, L.A. and Heskett, J.L. (1991). Enfranchisement of service workers. *California Management Review*, **33(4)**, 83–100.

Schulze, H.H. (n.d.). *Application Summary for Malcolm Baldrige National Quality Award – 1992 Winner*. In-house brochure distributed by The Ritz-Carlton Hotel Company.

Sims, W.J. (2000). A tale of two resorts: a comparison of employee turnover and employee profiles in remote Australian resort communities. In *Tourism 2000: Asia Pacific's Role in the New Millennium*, Vol. II. *Proceedings of 5th Annual Asia Pacific Tourism Association Conference*, Hong Kong, pp. 589–596.

Sims, W.J. (2002). Towards an understanding of labour turnover in isolated resorts. In *Tourism Development in the Asia Pacific Region: Worldwide Views and Multidimensional Perspectives* (L. Changchong, K. Chon, H.Q. Zhang and X. Yanjun, eds). *Proceedings of 8th Annual Asia Pacific Tourism Association Conference*, Dailan, China, pp. 670–683.

trainingmag.com (2006). Ritz-Carlton Hotel Co. www.trainingmag.com/training/search/article_display.jsp?vnucontentid=1000. Accessed on 2 August 2006.

Van Der Wagen, L. and Davies, C. (1998). *Supervision and Leadership in Tourism and Hospitality*. Melbourne: Hospitality Press.

Witt, C.A. and Muhlemann, A.P. (1994). The implementation of total quality management in tourism: some guidelines. *Tourism Management*, **15(6)**, 416–424.

Part
D

Future directions

11

Risk management

Introduction

Risk management has been placed at the end of this book in affirmation of its crucial and central role in resort management, and as a prime example of pulling together the external and internal elements of Parts B and C. While some may think risk management is a recent phenomenon, a result of global warming and terrorism, it has been associated with resort management for a long time and in a variety of ways. In normal business, financial risk is a regular occurrence that should be recognized and managed like other factors of demand and supply. However, with the taking-in of guests comes an extra responsibility, known as 'duty of care', where management is obliged to protect their guests from harm to the best of their ability.

On the demand side guests are often looking for excitement and the spectacular, which can put them at risk. Those who seek excitement in adventure tourism, when they challenge themselves or look for an adrenalin rush, purposely place themselves at risk and it is up to resorts to ensure the real risk is minimalized by managing the situation. Even those who have not come to a resort to exert or excite themselves regularly demand spectacular views and sunsets that often require building on risky sites and in non-conformist style. The sounds of the sea and uninterrupted tropical sunsets attract resorts to the water's edge in areas where hurricanes and cyclones occur with regularity. In the mountains, similar demands for spectacular views place buildings at crests or on steep slopes where local climatic conditions are at their extreme and avalanches can occur.

On the supply side risk is present at the very start, requiring a correct interpretation of market research and feasibility studies over the 30–50-year life span of many resort investments. Risk is present in the location of many resorts on the 'edge of civilization', well removed from regular infrastructure and services that are the basis of quality service experiences. It is present in the operation of resorts where guests come to participate in challenging activities, regular sports or simply to unwind, a process that inevitably leads some of them to leave natural caution and common sense behind at home.

It is not surprising that 'risk management is not just good for business, but is absolutely necessary in order for tourism and related organizations to remain competitive, to be sustainable, and to be responsible for their collective future' (Cunliffe, 2006: 35). Resort management risk not only involves both demand and supply considerations, it can range in scale from minor yet important internal issues like a lack of staff in crucial situations and places to overwhelming natural disasters or human external interventions like terrorism or financial crises. Whatever form it takes the element of risk is ever present for resort management and some type of management structure needs to be in place to minimize its impact on the business.

General risk

If no event or business decision within resort management is risk free, a risk management framework needs to take on a statistical probability structure. Tarlow (2006) has suggested a useful framework would be one that considers the probability of an event and its likely consequences. Figure 11.1 provides some examples, using Tarlow's suggested framework, but it should be noted that the consequences will vary according to each incident's severity and relevance to the resort product offerings.

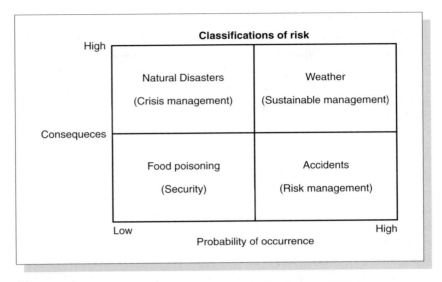

Figure 11.1   Classifications of risk source. (After Tarlow, 2006.)

Food poisoning is a serious occurrence for a resort because it means one duty of care has failed, ruining the visit of some guests and possibly closing a restaurant; but in the overall scheme of things, it has a low probability of occurrence and low consequences in a well-run establishment. The consequences are generally limited to some temporary bad publicity, financial compensation, a revision of safety procedures and possibly new equipment. This level of risk is discussed under the heading of 'Security' within this chapter.

Accidents are presented in the form of personal injury, where the probability of occurrence can be high when a resort is associated with adventure tourism or dangerous locations. Duty of care is still a major consideration, but if a guest chooses to undertake a risky activity they are expected to assume some of that risk. Under these circumstances resorts are expected to minimize the level of risk by preparing the site properly, instructing the guest where appropriate, and providing warning signs or professional help where warranted. This level of risk has been assigned a low consequences ranking in that it usually applies to individuals or small groups and through the implementation of 'Risk Management' these consequences can be minimized, but not eliminated.

Natural disasters have been a fact of life for the resort industry since its inception, with one of the earliest recorded disasters being the destruction of Pompeii by the Mount Vesuvius volcano in AD79. Natural disasters have high consequences because they cause severe damage and can destroy a resort or close it down for a long period. Fortunately, their probability of occurrence is generally low. This form of risk is more difficult to anticipate so 'Crisis Management' is presented more as contingency planning, preparing for the worst in order to minimize its impact, especially on the loss of life.

The *weather* had been classified as a high probability and consequence risk, because so many resorts are dependent on this feature yet it is something beyond their control. Bad weather or even the threat of it can reduce visits and sales, but in this era of global warming the signs of severe weather stress are starting to have an impact. The increasing number of Force 5 hurricanes is raising the insurance rates of all tropical resorts and not just those affected directly. The long-term drought in Australia's Alpine areas is creating poor snow seasons and raising questions about the ski industry's viability in these areas. Such events do not have the sudden impact of a site-specific natural disaster, but they can have a major say on the long-term viability of a resort business. In this regard such risks are incorporated into the overall framework of 'Sustainable Management', where the evolving weather patterns are integrated into the long-term resource planning for a resort.

Security

At the basic level a resort's 'duty of care' requires it to ensure the safety of its guests within reasonable limits. Possible threats to a guest's safety can arise from internal and external sources. Internally, the design of facilities should include safety considerations along with their functional role, whether that involves a ski lift or a hotel balcony. Staff should be trained to undertake their tasks safely, to keep an eye on guests and the general situation, and to note any external threats. These threats can include vandalism, theft or terrorism. The level of security will be determined by the perceived degree of threat in the local area, but some attention to this matter is necessary everywhere, for insurance and legal purposes alone.

Security of a resort involves three basic steps:

1. *Analyze and identify vulnerable areas/processes.*
   Resorts offer extensive and varied terrain with open and friendly access to welcome guests. They need to reduce the vulnerability of

property and guests by identifying the weakest and most exposed elements of the property, and the riskiest regular activities of the guests.

2. *Establish security priorities.*

As Figure 11.1 indicates not all risks warrant equal attention because their probabilities of occurrence and levels of impact on the operation will vary. In terms of basic security a differentiation should be made between public areas and private accommodation which ensures the privacy and security of guest accommodation can be maintained. In the restaurants and food outlets the storing, cooking and presentation of food must be undertaken with respect to health and safety regulations. In the most popular recreational areas like swimming pools and play areas, there must be qualified supervision. In guest rooms there should be a smoke alarm and sprinkler system to protect guests and the resort investment.

3. *Organization of a security system.*

The combination of guest enjoyment and security often requires a delicate touch in a resort environment, so as not to spoil the vacation experience. This means security should be present, but as invisible as possible. In a casino resort the presence of occasional guards can be re-assuring, but most of the security surveillance is conducted by closed circuit television (cctv). In other resorts there may be patrols for the grounds, especially at night, alarms in sensitive areas and instructions to staff and guests about possible dangers. In-room security is aided by instructions via notices or local hotel channel on the television, and an in-room safe.

When resorts are exclusive in terms of being up-market, providing extensive facilities and attracting wealthy guests they need to be particularly concerned with security because they can become a magnet for criminal activity and litigious activity. For example, the Jalousie Plantation Resort and Spa in the island of St Lucia would offer a tempting target according to the description offered by Pattullo (1996: 3):

> The US$60 million, 320 acre resort has 115 cottages and suites (with plunge pools), four restaurants, a ballroom, the Lord's Great Room furnished with Tennant's antiques, tennis courts, a helicopter pad, a hydroponic farm for growing non-traditional crops and *tight, high-tech security*. For US$350–475 per day in the 1994 high season, guests enjoyed all meals, unlimited drinks, water sports, saunas and beauty treatment and cable television in an 'ambiance of tranquility and serenity'.

(this author's emphases)

Security planning

A security system is only as good as its staff and cannot operate effectively in isolation from general staff and guests. Resorts can either hire their own security staff or outsource the responsibility to a professional company. Regardless of the approach used it must be integrated into the daily operations in such a way as to be effective yet undetected. 'Management should view the cost of developing a security training program as an investment. A resort in which all employees are attuned to the safety and security concerns can create a safer environment for guests and employees and a more profitable operation in the long run' (Gee, 1996: 415).

There are several aspects to security planning:

- *Security staff.*
  In major resorts it is now common to hire a professional security company to provide coverage for key areas and assets. In addition to being skilled in their task the individuals selected for resorts need to be presentable and able to interact with guests. Just like Disney theme park street sweepers are trained to know about their theme park and emergency procedures, resort security will find themselves called upon for directions and advice by the guests.
- *Staff training.*
  Even if a resort has a professional security arm it needs to include general staff in its security planning. They should be knowledgeable about basic procedures and able to advise guests. They should learn to keep their ears and eyes open for trouble.
- *Records and reports.*
  Recording what happens is vital because it can help identify danger spots and become invaluable evidence for insurance and litigation purposes. There are several types of reporting mechanisms; Daily Activity Report, General Incident Report, Loss Report, Accident Report, Monthly Statistical Report.

Security and the law

Failure to fulfil the 'duty of care' responsibility may result in a security related liability law suit. In a suit alleging negligence, the plaintiff (the accuser) must show the defendant (the resort) failed to provide 'reasonable care' regarding 'foreseeable' acts or situations. Judges often apportion blame for an accident. That is a certain percentage of the blame is seen as the responsibility of the operator and the remainder the responsibility of the guest.

Damages associated with negligence can be of two types:

1. *Compensatory damages:* to compensate for loss of income, for pain and suffering.
2. *Punitive damages*: to inflict punishment for outrageous conduct and to act as a lesson for others (setting precedence).

Examples of the legal consequences from insufficient attention paid to 'duty of care' abound, but in many cases involving private companies the cases are settled out-of-court with minimum publicity. To illustrate what can happen with regard to apportioned blame and the challenges in safeguarding tourists, the following two published accounts of Australian cases are presented.

The first involves a young man, who like many before him went to swim at a local waterhole in the Murray River. He dived from a log in the waterhole and struck the riverbed, suffered permanent spinal injuries and sued the Berrigan Shire Council and Forestry Commission of NSW for A$8 million in damages. 'Both defendants denied liability, but agreed that damages should be assessed at A$8.2 million' (Gregory and Hewitt, 2005: 6). In the original judgement the presiding judge reduced the assessment by 32 per cent to take account of the plaintiff's share of responsibility, through contributory negligence. For the remaining A$5.6 million he ordered the council to pay 80 per cent and the commission 20 per cent. As often happens in such cases involving large sums this 2004 judgement was appealed. In 2005 a new judge upheld the decision but placed all the blame and financial responsibility on the council. In his summary the new judge said:

> Council employees were aware of people diving from the log, and the changes to the riverbed that floods could cause. He said the council has means and opportunity to put up warning signs, and in the longer term, to remove the log.

> Justice Nettle said the council owed (the plaintiff) a specific duty (of care) to take reasonable steps to guard against the risk of harm resulting from the use of the log for diving.

> But he said the commission had a very different charter and purpose (responsible for managing the forest alongside the river), and arguably no actual knowledge of the use of the log (as a diving platform).
>
> (Gregory and Hewitt, 2005: 6)

The second case involves a man who on a warm day in 1997 went to Sydney's Bondi Beach for a swim and like a responsible Australian waded into the sea 'between the red-and-yellow "safe swimming" flags, (where) he dived under a foaming wave and collided with a sand bar' (Feizkhah, 2002: 46). By 2005, the plaintiff who is now a quadriplegic as a result of this incident, claimed:

> Waverley Council's life-guards should have put the flags in a different spot or installed warning signs. Perhaps 'a fellow diving and a cross through it or some words saying "sand banks"'. Last week a jury agreed, ordering the council to pay (the plaintiff) A$3.75 million.
>
> (Feizkhah, 2002: 46)

This judgement not only cost a local council a great deal of money, it sent shock waves through the industry because it meant standard procedures had failed to demonstrate sufficient 'duty of care' in the eyes of the law.

The wider implication of this case and others like it has been an increase in claims for negligence and a rise in public liability insurance. Feizkhah (2002: 46) reports:

> Between 1998 and 2000, the number of public liability claims Australia-wide rose by 60% to 88 000: total payouts rose by 52% to A$724 million. Most claims are settled out of court for less than A$20 000. But, 'there is a jackpot mentality, where people with minor injuries see reports of big payouts and see if they can get something too'.

One of the most affected tourism activities in this regard has been adventure tourism, an activity closely associated with resorts whose owners, such as international chains and public companies, are often viewed as possessing deep pockets. Claims in these activities and areas have been increasing over a long period and have been associated with rising public liability insurance costs to cover not just recorded claims; but to help cover the broader costs of global insurance increases.

Adventure tourism

Given its importance as a major attraction for many resorts and as a prime source of risk and insurance claims, adventure tourism deserves special attention. Depending on the level of risk and size of insurance claims, it can vary from a general security issue to a risk management issue. As can be seen in Table 11.1 representing the insurance claims for a whole state, the number and amounts are relatively minor, although they can be crippling for small businesses with limited resources. When accidents and claims involve major incidents, with extensive pain and suffering, loss of

Table 11.1   Rising adventure tourism insurance claims

Total claims in VTOA members insurance scheme 1997–2001

Classification	Cost of claims	Number of claims
Horse riding	$511 860	26
Climbing – outdoor	$167 526	3
Climbing – indoor	$316 526	10
Corporate training	$204 400	2
Whitewater activities	$140 361	3
Tours	$78 734	5
Other water sports	$52 741	4
Camel Rides	$1557	3
Walking Tours	$4761	1
Other	$104 539	7
Total	$1 580 266	64

Source: Victoria tourism operators association, Tourism News, **15(6)**, 2001: 2.

income and possibly life there is a need for more extensive risk management and control as will be discussed in the next section.

Adventure tourism is a very general term and hence a very inclusive subset of tourism, including a large array of activities. The term implies excitement and a change from normal daily life by pursuing an activity in a different environment.

Adventure tourism can take many forms because three dimensions have been linked to its structure (Page et al., 2005). These dimensions involve the following characteristics, with an indication in the brackets of who is the major player:

- *Active–passive dimension* (Guest).
  The amount of physical effort a person is prepared to put into the activity is a major feature of adventure tourism. In terms of an active situation the guest is an active participant who, with or without the help of a guide or instructor, is looking for excitement and an adrenalin rush. In a passive situation the guest is a spectator or observer, one who wishes to learn more about the world around them rather than about themselves and their personal limits.
- *Hard–soft dimension* (Business).
  These are the categories applied by the industry and relate more to the degree of preparation and pampering the guest requires for the activity.

A 'soft' activity is one where the guest is able to view the scenery or wildlife from a safe vantage point with low risk of injury. A 'hard' activity is more risky because the guest participates directly in the activity in order to obtain that adrenalin rush and requires more individual attention, before (preparation) and during (guidance) the activity.

■ *High risk–low risk dimension* (Business–Guest).

This is where guest perception and business management create the preferred and real tourism experience. Beedie (2003: 206) notes correctly that a paradox has been created, 'whereby the more detailed, planned and logistically smooth an adventure tourist itinerary becomes, the more removed the experience is from the notion of adventure'. This helps to explain why 'injury rates do not necessarily conform to the notion of perceived risk', with some soft activities having substantial injury and death rates while some hard activities have far fewer than commonly expected.

In bringing the guest's desires and expectations together with the resort's prepared and staged offerings, adventure tourism has been seen as a natural business opportunity by some (Cloutier, 2003) and a commodifiction of the human spirit by others (Beedie, 2003). Regardless of which interpretation is correct, for resorts it provides a varied and profitable business mix (Figure 11.2).

Many of the references quoted in this section have extensive lists of activities cited as adventure tourism, but most shy away from classifying them because whatever groups are selected cannot be mutually exclusive

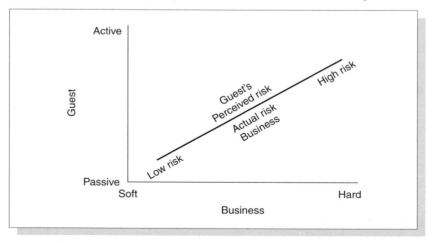

Figure 11.2 The three dimensions of adventure tourism risk.

given the three dimensional characteristics and the varying conditions under which they operate. For example, skiings' rating would be influenced by its location, whether it be in mountain areas with steep slopes and tricky runs or on the gentler beginner slopes attached to some resorts and urban centres. It would also depend on whether we are considering downhill or cross-country skiing, and of course on the skill and experience of the individual skier.

When resorts present hard adventure tourism products they face the challenge of providing an exciting adrenalin provoking experience in the safest way possible. In many tropical resorts scuba diving is one of the key attractions, and although not physically demanding does require a reasonable level of health and fitness. Wilks and Davis (2000: 596) observe, however, that a review of 100 consecutive scuba diving deaths found 'that in 25% of the fatalities there was a pre-existing medical contraindication to scuba diving' and those people should not have risked a dive. In this respect most dive companies rely heavily on personal honesty when guests fill in preliminary medical questionnaires, and at times this trust is abused through bravado and peer pressure.

At other times the bravado and peer pressure can be laid at the door of the adventure tourism company. This was one accusation and explanation offered in relation to the canyoning tragedy in Switzerland that claimed 21 lives in 1999 (Head, 1999: 3). According to Morgan and Fluker (2000: 2):

> Clearly the risks associated with this incident were beyond the capabilities of participants. Importantly, newspaper reports of the Interlaken tragedy speculated that early warning signs of danger had been ignored by the activity's guides. Expert opinions of experienced river guides were also reported. These reports expressed serious concerns that the Interlaken river guides employed by the adventure company may have been under pressure to put profits before safety, this being compounded by their lack of knowledge of local conditions.

The judge apparently agreed, stating the 'safety measures taken by the now defunct Adventure World were totally inadequate – with no proper safety training for the employees' (BBC News, 2001). Something that should have been undertaken before hand, as part of a risk management process.

Risk management

Risk Management is a way in which to prepare for the security risk and crisis issues outlined above. It is becoming a significant aspect of resort management given the adventurous nature of many of their activities, their exciting locations, the growing litigious nature of customers, and the growing threat of terrorism. Risk management should incorporate the following, which involves considerable overlap with the previous security planning. The difference being that risk management is more comprehensive, including environmental concerns and financial considerations as well as human safety.

Issue

The unique characteristic of adventure tourism, and those resorts offering that type of product, is that 'participants are deliberately seeking and/or accepting the chance of sustaining physical injury' (Morgan and Fluker, 2000: 4). This means that for adventure clients *perceived risk* becomes an important part of the adventure experience, while for the commercial operator the actual and managed level of risk is the *real risk* as shown in Figure 11.2. When guests pay money for the specialized knowledge, skills and equipment of the commercial provider, 'they reduce their need for risk awareness and responsibility. This transfer of risk responsibility to an activity operator, arising from the tourist's financial consideration (contract), raises a number of legal and ethical issues' (Morgan and Fluker, 2000: 3). The legal issues revolve around duty of care and individual responsibility, the ethical issues include the paradox that 'accidents can add to the allure of the adventure experience through providing a valid testimony of the risk' (Morgan and Fluker, 2000: 9).

Process

Risk management is a rational approach to deal with real risk. It is about managing risk rather than eliminating it because as we have seen some degree of perceived risk is inherent in adventure tourism and many resort locations. But 'it is important to grasp the concept that the level of risk management applied is relative to the tolerance of a specific business and its guests for risk, which can vary substantially from one operator to another' (Cloutier, 2000: 96).

Gee (1996: 437–440) has identified a general process, that can assist resorts in their management of risk for both adventure tourism and general operations which consists of four steps.

1. *Risk identification.*
   Risk is associated with all aspects of business, and like the adventure tourist that is part of the thrill for many entrepreneurs and business people.

Adventure tourism operations must be identified in terms of their real risk, and even when they are outsourced to separate organizations with their own liability insurance, their professionalism and record will still impact on a resort's reputation and business.

Asset risks involve the major investment in property and facilities that need to be protected. Identifying areas of particular danger and hazard is an important first step, such as the buildup of under growth and leaf-litter in woodland areas; the presence of currents or steeply shelving beaches along the beach-front; the physical dangers associated with wastewater treatment plants and with electrical substations; and the ever present danger of fire when people are relaxed and having fun.

Income risks are a major concern for resorts, which have a high dependence on external conditions often beyond their immediate control. Anderson (2006: 1290) in the introduction to her article on crisis management in the Australian tourism industry lays out a catalogue of disasters that have befallen that country's tourism over the past 20 years:

- 1989 – pilot's strike
- 1991 – Gulf War
- 1997 – Asian economic crisis
- 2000 – dot com crash
- 2001 – collapse of HIH Insurance Company (which was the major public liability insurer in Australia and with its demise there were major increases in insurance premiums for everyone).
    - World Trade Centre Attacks
    - demise of Ansett Airlines (which had a 35 per cent market share of the domestic airline business at the time).
- 2002 – Bali bombings which killed 202 people
- 2003 – Iraq War
    - outbreak of Severe Acute Respiratory Syndrome (SARS)

As if this is not enough some countries could add the outbreak of foot and mouth disease, avian flu epidemics, further terrorists attacks and unreliable weather. Although in Australia and most countries tourism has recovered from such experiences, the industry has learned valuable lessons along the way. One has been to recognize the potential loss of business that can occur through interruption or damage, and to prepare for it through contingency planning and market diversification.

Legal liability risks are increasing as society becomes more litigious. Resorts as businesses are responsible to their guests, employees and shareholders, all of whom are better educated regarding their rights and are more prepared and able to exercise those rights in court if need be. Now liability insurance is a major cost factor that all businesses must consider, including resorts.

Loss of key personnel risks are often under-appreciated until such a situation occurs and the resort discovers how much a certain individual contributed to the business' overall attraction. A key person like a chef, an entertainer or instructor whose skills and special qualities are hard to replace can leave a big hole in a resort's reputation. These people should be identified and retained wherever possible, and if they are lost to illness or poaching then succession plans should be in place.

2. *Risk measurement and evaluation.*

To control the frequency and magnitude of losses due to risk it is essential to develop recording procedures and to create a repository of past records. Detailed record keeping is a key to identifying where and when risks are occurring, and the staff who were or should be involved. If personal injury is involved it is particularly important to obtain independent witnesses to the incident, in case there are later legal or insurance claims. Such data should be recorded in a central registry on a daily and weekly basis to be deposited in an appropriate computer database. This will provide important information regarding the safety record, or otherwise, of individual operations and the total resort. Such data will prove useful when negotiating liability insurance or to demonstrate the resort's actual duty of care record.

3. *Risk reduction.*

Business, like life, is never risk free so in designing and operating a resort one important emphasis is safety – for guests and staff. Many of the common dangers like food, health and safety and fire are regulated and controlled by local by-laws or ordinances. However, such statutes often involve the 'minimum acceptable' precautions, so a resort may choose to follow the Walt Disney World lead and select higher standards. This will mean higher initial building costs, however it should reduce both the associated risks and annual insurance premiums.

'One of the most rewarding loss-control projects is training personnel to think in terms of accident and loss avoidance' according to Gee (1996: 439). This becomes particularly important in the operations phase and needs to be emphasized as part of the resort's duty of care. When accidents occur they become significant 'moments of truth' for the guests and if they are handled in an empathetic and professional manner many later difficulties can be avoided.

4. *Risk finance determination.*

Most businesses, including resorts can absorb small and infrequent losses brought on by seasonal fluctuations or occasional accidents, but will need to transfer the risk of large business interruptions or liability claims to outside suppliers of such coverage, such as insurance companies or brokers. Small losses and claims will still be a matter for management's discretion even when they have insurance coverage, due to the deduction or excess clause associated with their insurance premium. Most personal injury and damage claims can be accommodated within these parameters and involve negotiation with the affected parties rather than court cases, but if it becomes a major contentious court case insurance providers will become involved.

Resort owners can also transfer risk to other parties via non-insurance responsibility. In terms of major recreation equipment, like ski lifts or spas, the supplier can be encouraged to guarantee the safety of its equipment if it is properly installed and operated. This often involves the supplier installing the equipment and certifying the operators. In terms of more hazardous adventure tourism activities the resort can sub-contract these activities to specialist operators who carry their own and independent insurance policies.

Cloutier (2000: 104–105) provides some insights into actual risk management, as seen through the eyes of Will Leverette, who offers simple guidelines based on the real experience of lawsuits and consultations with adventure tourism companies. According to Leverette there are six basic rules to follow:

1. Develop a means to *prove* that guests were adequately warned and informed.
2. Any *guarantee* of safety made in a business' literature or marketing materials is an open invitation to be *sued*.
3. All field *staff* must have current training in basic *first aid*.
4. The *business* should develop a written *emergency/evacuation plan* for all areas and activities to be used.
5. One *good witness statement* will shut down a frivolous lawsuit faster, more cheaply and less painfully than will anything else.
6. The business must use a *properly drafted liability-release form*. (this author's emphases)

Such personal experiences are a guide as to how today's risk management is evolving into a legal discourse over duty of care, but when there is a major disruption to business through some form of disaster the emphasis changes from prevention to the rescue and recovery of crisis management.

Crisis management

'Crisis management is an extension of risk management' according to the Pacific Asia Travel Association (PATA, 2003: 3). Risk management can be viewed as management initiatives designed to minimize loss through poor decision-making; but it can also be viewed as an important proactive step in reducing the dangers of catastrophic business collapse due to crisis or disaster. The PATA booklet presents a 'four R' step process to crisis management:

1. *Reduction* – detecting early warning signs;
2. *Readiness* – preparing plans and running exercises;
3. *Response* – executing operational and communication plans in a crisis situation;
4. *Recovery* – returning the organization to normal after a crisis;

where risk management practices would dominate the first two steps. Risk management procedures that help to identify safety and security weaknesses in an operation will not only help to minimize danger and loss, they will expose the weak points in case a crisis occurs.

Crisis in a literate sense represents a moment of acute danger or difficulty, which in terms of the tourism industry has been defined as:

> an unwanted, unusual situation for an organization, which, due to the seriousness of the event, demands an immediate entrepreneurial response.
>
> (Glaesser, 2003: 8)

This approach places the emphasis of crisis management on the response and recovery phases of a crisis and brings it into line with disaster planning which has its own four-stage process of: assessment–warning–impact–recovery (Foster, 1980). It is natural disasters which often trigger crisis within the tourism industry be they earthquakes (Kyoto – 1995), volcanic eruptions (Mount St Helens – 1980), forest fires (Yellowstone National Park – 1988), tsunami (Phuket – 2004) or hurricanes (New Orleans – 2005). One should not forget that human beings can and do create their own crises for tourism and the resort industry. Wars, terrorism and political decisions can bring about dramatic declines in visitation due to the prospect of danger or the removal of access. King and Berno

(2002) provide a good example of this in their analysis of the impact of Fiji's two coups in 1987 and 2000 on the local tourist trade, which is heavily resort oriented. They note that:

> like many other tropical island nations, Fiji has long established procedures in place to deal with emergencies such as cyclones. This meant that the overall preparedness in 1987 was relatively good with provision to contact hotels across the country with advice on how to react
> (King and Berno, 2002: 49)

Such an experience demonstrates strong synergistic links can exist between natural disaster and human crisis management.

From past crisis experiences Ritchie (2004) sets out a strategic framework for the planning and management of crises by public or private organizations. His model outlines three main stages in managing such incidents – prevention and planning, implementation, evaluation and feedback. Ritchie's three strategic management stages, along with Faulkner's earlier crisis stages and their ingredients, has been combined with more resort oriented issues and actions in Table 11.2. If the process is divided into the three phases of pre-, actual and post-crisis it is possible to determine a clear pattern of events and responsibilities for resorts.

Pre-crisis stage

Pre-crisis for most resorts will be some form of preparation for a future possible disaster. Whether that be an 'inevitable' physical disaster like an earthquake in certain regions or a possible negative political change, such major 'unthinkable' events need to be considered and prepared for.

The recommended and common approach at this phase is to develop contingency plans – plans for actions that will mitigate the disaster's effects. This involves recognizing the potential scale and frequency of the expected disaster, and planning accordingly. In terms of the guests, all staff must be trained in emergency procedures and have a role to fulfil. In most cases there will be an obvious overlap with regular security measures such as fire drills, but in terms of major disaster preparation additional factors will need to be considered and plans prepared.

For human created crises the degree of notice may be shorter than for natural disasters but there will usually be a warning period of political unrest. In this case the experts will be political commentators and the global news services, and it will be up to owners and managers to keep abreast with their regional situations. More governments are becoming

Table 11.2 Strategic management for tourism crises

Disaster/Crisis stages	Principal ingredients for management strategies	Strategic actions
1. *Pre-event Stage* When time and opportunity to prevent or mitigate the effects of potential disasters/crises	*Risk assessment* ■ Assess probability and impact of crisis ■ Develop contingency plans	1. *Pre-crisis: crisis/disaster prevention and planning* ■ Problem recognition through environmental scanning and issue analysis ■ Strategic forecasting and risk analysis ■ Contingency planning for best options
2. *Prodromal* When a disaster or crisis is imminent		
3. *Emergency* Disaster/crisis occurs requiring action to protect people and property.	*Contingency plans* ■ Identify likely impacts and groups at risk ■ Assess community and visitor capabilities to cope. ■ Develop individual business preparations for disaster specific crises	2. *Actual crisis: strategic implementation* ■ Managers and staff ready to implement contingency plans, including evacuation. ■ Control over communications use of a public relations plan and credible spokesperson. ■ Collaboration with community
4. *Intermediate* Short-term needs of people have been addressed and focus turns to restoring services.		
5. *Long-term recovery* Rebuilding community and business, including post-mortem analysis and healing	*Crisis operations* ■ Media relations ■ Central and regional government collaboration ■ International agency assistance	3. *Post-crisis: resolution, evaluation and feedback* ■ Restore business and community as quickly as possible to a livable and revenue generating state. ■ Learn from the experience ■ Turn crisis into an opportunity for improvement of business and community
6. *Resolution* Routine restored in a new and hopefully improved state.	*Future goals* ■ Vision for a better business and community	

Source: After Faulkner (2001: 144) and Ritchie (2004: 674).

involved in this scanning process on behalf of their travelling citizens, and are offering travel advisories. For many resort destinations these advisories have both positive and negative features. On the positive side they provide up-to-date and comparable risk assessments for tourists; on the negative side they are susceptible to political influence and may not be as objective as one would hope; plus they paint the risk picture with broad strokes, so that relatively safe enclaves become included in the national summary. Glaesser (2003: 131–132) provides an example of how one crisis, the Bali bombing of 12 October 2002, produced various levels of advisory notice in Europe, ranging from a low level general security advice to warnings against travel under any circumstances.

Actual crisis stage

During the actual crisis there is going to be chaos and confusion and it is the prepared and cool-headed who will prevail. Hence the key management task at this stage is to have staff able to implement the contingency plan and to be empowered to show initiative when conditions do not exactly follow the predicted pattern of events. A major disaster or crisis is likely to affect more than one resort or destination, so collaboration with other tourism organizations and government agencies will be essential. Hopefully in the imminent stage all or most guests would have been evacuated with the help of public agencies and industry partners to safer areas, but generally a skeleton staff of key personnel will be required to stay on site as long as possible to ensure the safety of assets.

One of the biggest challenges during this period will be media relations, for in today's global village a disaster or crisis attracts the attention of the world and a media frenzy erupts. Glaesser (2003: 223) in his discussion of communications policy with respect to a crisis states 'the principle (sic) task is to convey information with the aim of influencing and guiding consumer behaviour, opinions and expectations'. To achieve this he advocates the affected organization creates a quick understanding of the situation and a transparency in its preparation and response, to build the credibility of the business. He recommends (Glaesser, 2003: 230–231) a communication process that follows the sequence of:

1. Portray the dismay and responsibility of the organization.
2. Describe decisions and measures introduced to cope with the crisis.
3. Indicate, based on the current experience, what further measures will be introduced to avoid future repetitions.

In the case of major disasters and crises resort destinations and businesses will need to collaborate with central and regional governments, for it is they alone who can mobilize the resources needed to handle major catastrophes. The evacuation of guests to other areas will require bus and truck transportation and possibly air evacuation. The chaos and confusion of a crisis provides the opportunity for crime and lawlessness, so governments will need to bolster regular police forces with federal police and possibly troops. In the case of the New Orleans hurricane of 2005 such a government response was widely criticized for its slowness and inadequacy.

Since much of the world's resort business occurs in the developing world when a major disaster or crisis occurs the host communities often need international assistance. It is at such times that the international community has revealed its better nature, ignoring old differences to come to the aid of fellow humans suffering from the ravages of nature or the actions of a few. Unfortunately, the generosity of individuals, charities and nations is not generally put to the best use. Partly this is because many receiving nations have neither their own contingency plans for such disasters nor the organization and infrastructure to handle a major in-pouring of generosity; and partly because some of the recovering nations have been susceptible to pilfering and corruption, which results in funds and materials not reaching the designated destinations and sufferers. Given the occurrence of irregularities and disappointments with various international aid programs, it is not surprising that their recovery period is often much longer and more difficult than many expect.

Post-crisis stage

The post-crisis phase occurs when the actual crisis has abated and is out of the international news headlines, and represents the business and community efforts to return to pre-crisis conditions. As many students of disaster/crisis management indicate this is not only the time to get back to business as quickly as possible, it is an opportunity to redevelop and learn from the mistakes of the past.

An immediate concern is to take advantage of the media attention that will have placed the resort destination in the world headlines, by demonstrating that the crisis has passed and life is returning to normal. It is quite likely that the global public has been presented an inaccurate and exaggerated picture of local devastation, which needs to be remedied as quickly as possible. For example, when hurricane Iwa struck the Hawaiian island of Kauai in November 1982 some international news media were reporting that part of the island had sunk and thousands of people had died, which was far from the truth, although the hurricane caused a lot of physical damage (Murphy and Bayley, 1989: 38). Such stories need to be refuted, and information about the undamaged areas and recovery put in their place wherever possible.

When it comes to repairing the damage an opportunity is presented to upgrade a resort's infrastructure and facilities. There will always be improvements (real or imagined) that the consumer society has developed since the original building of a resort destination which can and should be integrated into the new resort. There will be lessons learned from the disaster or crisis that can be incorporated into the design of the new resort which will make it more disaster-proof in the future. One example of how a disaster can be turned into a positive for tourism occurred with the Mount St Helens eruption.

Prior to the eruption Mount St Helens was a relatively quite tourist attraction, appealing mostly to outdoor recreationists and offering mainly basic facilities. The publicity of the 1980 eruption, including dramatic television coverage, increased interest in the volcano to the extent that 'a national monument was created by setting off 110 000 acres from the existing national forest to commemorate the eruption . . . a new visitor center was opened in December 1986, with illustrations and other graphics that depict the events and the subsequent natural regeneration of the devastated areas' (Murphy and Bayley, 1989: 42). This new visitor centre has good access to the local interstate freeway and now many more visitors are drawn to the area, incorporating a wider range of tourist types and market segments than before.

Sustainability crisis management

As has been mentioned, life is a risk and as we modify the earth's environment we are creating new and uncharted conditions that will bring increased risk. Signs that business conditions are changing come in various guises. Nature seems to be going through a period of instability, with evidence of climate change beginning to take on more significance as scientific evidence points more to a global shift in weather patterns rather than normal climatic cycles.

Climate change is a serious and urgent issue. While climate change and climate modeling are subject to inherent uncertainties, it is clear that human activities have a powerful role in influencing the climate and the risks and scale of impacts in the future. All science implies a strong likelihood that, if emissions continue unabated, the world will experience a radical transformation of its climate.

(Stern, 2006: 17)

Even the conservative periodical *The Economist* has come to the conclusion that 'the chances of serious consequences are high enough to make it worth spending the 'not exorbitant' sums needed to try to mitigate climate change' (*The Economist*, 2006b: 5).

Resort tourism is particularly vulnerable to climatic change given that many resorts are located in high risk areas like mountains and tropical beaches, and it uses high levels of energy drawing in its guests and on-site water to keep them happy. War has been joined by global terrorism as a major disruption and deterrent to travel, with tourists seen as 'soft targets' bringing maximum exposure to the terrorist cause. An ever-crowded world with over-stretched medical systems appears to be waiting for the next pandemic, with the recent outbreaks of SARS (2003) and avian flu (2006) revealing a certain lack of control and openness in dealing with global health crises.

Under these circumstances one of the most direct business signs of change has been the dramatic increase in insurance premiums that everyone seems to have faced in this new millennium. Increased liability insurance has put some single owner peripheral tourism operations out of business, regular security insurance as well as liability insurance has risen dramatically for resorts, and resort destinations in vulnerable locations are facing either dramatic increases in premiums or the loss of direct insurance. After a disastrous 2005, with insured losses of $55 billion in the US, of which $38 billion was caused by hurricane Katrina, American insurers 'are cutting back their exposure in coastal areas . . . home owners who can get insurance coverage face sharply higher rates. Some premiums have risen by as much as 200% . . . Many residents cannot get private coverage at all. As a result, state – backed insurance plans, meant to provide coverage as a last resort, are being inundated' (*The Economist*, 2006a: 74).

This is only the tip of the iceberg according to figures provided by Winn and Kirchgeorg (2005: 245) who quote Table 11.3 from the *Topics GEO 2003* report, which shows 'the number of natural catastrophes rose nearly five fold (and) economic losses nearly 16 fold over the last five decades'.

Winn and Kirchgeorg use such information to suggest business in general needs to rethink its strategic approach to the environment and

Table 11.3 Development of natural catastrophes and economic losses (in US$ billion, 2003 values)

Decade	1950–1959	1960–1969	1970–1979	1980–1989	1990–1999	Last 10 Years
Number of events	20	27	47	63	91	60
Economic losses	42.7	76.7	140.6	217.3	670.4	514.5
Insured losses	–	6.2	13.1	27.4	126.0	83.6

Source: Münchner Rück 2003: 15.

sustainable development. They view past and present management interest in environmental management and sustainable development as an 'inside–out' approach, 'one in which the primary perspective is to look from the firm out at the external environment' (Winn and Kirchgeorg, 2005: 240) that includes ecological and social considerations. But given the dramatic external forces in nature, politics and health which are leading to new levels of uncertainty in the ecological and societal realms, they see the need for 'a radical departure from the inside–out perspective of environmental management and its more systems theory-informed cousin from sustainability management' to one where sustainability management should be 'expanded and complemented, and may even need to be substituted by conceptual frameworks fairly new to organization theories, such as "resilience management" or "discontinuity management"' (Winn and Kirchgeorg, 2005: 250).

This is because if we are facing significant shifts in environmental and political conditions, the balancing nature of sustainable development will no longer apply in an unstable world. Rather, business will need to take on board the possibility or probability of structural shifts and the prospect of facing several global emergencies during their lifetime. 'Since ecological global systems cannot be affected significantly by actors in the short-term (the inside-out approach), broader adaptive behaviors that secure the survivability of the economy and society become increasingly relevant. Crisis management, risk management, and emergency responses need to be supplemented with long term management for survival' (Winn and Kirchgeorg, 2005: 252).

To put such thoughts into practice will require guidelines that incorporate all the knowledge that has been accumulated to date on risk and crisis management to be supplemented by a broader and more collaborative approach to business survival and sustainability. Given the noted exposure of tourism to the environmental, political and medical forces that seem to be in flux, it is not surprising to find some are already thinking along these lines. Santana (2003: 304) considers that

> if decision-makers acknowledge that in these complex and unpredictable times in which we live and operate, anything is possible, including a major crisis that may prove devastating to their organizations, management will be in the 'right frame of mind' to accept the contention that forms the basic foundation of crisis management; proper advanced planning.

As Santana points out, with the increasing impact of external forces on tourism operations, crisis should be looked upon as an evolving process in itself, one that develops its own logic and consequences, rather than be treated as an isolated event. 'It is the degree to which management heeds the warning signals and prepares the organization (that) will determine how well it responds to the impending crisis' (Santana, 2003: 310). Likewise, Hall et al. (2003: 2) note that tourism and destinations are 'deeply affected by the perceptions of security and the management of safety, security and risk'. They think the concept of security has broadened significantly since the end of the Cold War, with a dominant single political enemy being replaced by terrorism, wars of independence, indigenous rights, and religious differences. 'Security ideas now tend to stress more global and people-centered perspectives with greater emphasis on the multilateral frameworks of security management' (Hall et al., 2003: 12).

One of the few at this point to provide practical guidelines for sustainable crisis management in tourism is de Sausmarez (2004). de Sausmarez maintains that many future crises will require careful detection and collaborative efforts to minimize their impact, and she has outlined a six step approach to tackle such major external threats.

1. *Evaluation of the importance of the tourism sector.*
   We, as students of tourism, know tourism and resorts are important socio-economic functions for many people, communities and nations, but we cannot assume others give tourism the same degree of importance in the bigger picture and more comprehensive view of events, including crises. Hence, the first step in the establishment of a national or regional crisis management policy is to determine and demonstrate the relative importance of the tourism and resort sectors.

   Until this has been done, it is impossible to prepare any sound strategy for the response to a crisis. This was well illustrated by Sharpley and Craven (2001) who show that even though tourism contributes substantially more to the British economy than agriculture does, the British government's response to the foot and mouth crisis in 2001 was to slaughter rather than vaccinated animals and to close the countryside to visitors, moves which favoured the agricultural sector rather than the tourism sector and cost the taxpayer substantially more than was necessary.

(de Sausmarez, 2004: 4)

It is only when tourism in general and the resort component in particular are shown to be significant local and regional socio-economic activities that governments and planners will consider them seriously and integrate their needs into macro-crisis management planning.

2. *Identification of sources of greatest risk.*
   If resorts and tourism are to integrate crisis management with their sustainable development philosophy they will need to identify the anticipated areas of greatest risk. In the literature and this chapter the emphasis has been on natural disasters, which are essentially supply side characteristics as they change or eliminate the attractiveness of a destination. However, just as important are demand side characteristics such as international political relations affecting visa requirements, economic conditions affecting the ability to travel, world health and safety, and competition from other destinations and leisure activities. Although none of these supply and demand risks will fall under the direct control of resort management, knowledge of their existence and development will be essential for future strategic planning, and should be used to lobby government.

3. *Identification and monitoring of indicators.*
   While it is important to scan the environment continuously it is important to be able to measure trends in a relevant and timely manner. The evidence of global warming is building momentum, but it is often sending out confusing and at times conflicting information, little of which has any bearing on a single location or site. Managers and owners of resort properties need to know what this impending crisis means for them specifically.

   de Sausmarez (2004: 7) maintains tour operators and travel agents, along with government agencies, are in a 'strong strategic position to monitor and assess changes in the tourism status quo as they have access to data on both supply and demand'. She notes that the World Tourism Organisation's (1999) recommendation after the Asian financial crisis of

1997 was that destinations should develop three categories of indicators, to warn of impending crises.

  i. *Short-term indicators* of up to three months, that include advance bookings from key markets, or an increase in the usual length of time needed to settle accounts.
  ii. *Medium-term indicators*, with a lead time of 3–12 months such as that needed for tour operator allocations and take-up to be recorded.
  iii. *Long-term indicators*, with a lead time of a year or more that include planned capacity developments, international currency valuations and trends in GDP, interest rates and inflation in key markets.

  To which Sustainability Crisis Management would add a fourth category:

  iv. *Future indicators*, with a lead time of 10–50 years which covers the life of most mortgages and leases and provides sufficient time to determine whether the current climatic experiences are long-term phenomena or cyclical aberrations. These indicators would sub-jectively convert the environmental, political, business and health trends into local and more useful indices. They would be subject-ive because it would depend on local knowledge to disaggregate the global information meaningfully, and that process would be influenced by the outlook of the assessor – be they an optimist or pessimist.

4. *Resolving issues of implementation.*

  The type of global crises that tourism may be facing will be sufficiently large scale and evolving that they will require collaboration to imple-ment an effective management strategy. This means that responsibil-ities and coordination plans need to be drawn up at an early stage and should cover three essential areas: a speedy response, appropriate measures in terms of the local needs of impacted areas and communi-cation and coordination between different levels of jurisdiction and different sectors.

5. *The development of a crisis plan.*

  The development of a national crisis management plan is itself an example of macro-level proactive crisis management (de Sausmarez, 2004: 9), and a considerable achievement in itself. Such plans need to be flexible as we can expect a series of different crises in the future, with varying local and regional impacts within national jurisdictions. An important part of any large scale crisis management plan will be media relations, relying on the various forms of media to distribute the relevant information as quickly and effectively as possible and being transparent about the severity of the crisis and remedies being undertaken.

In some countries there may already be plans in place to cope with anticipated natural crisis such as cyclones (Fiji) or earthquakes (Pacific North West of America) that can be extended to include other forms of possible crisis. Such plans would need regular re-assessment by government departments and the private sector, but can build an invaluable data bank and procedural map. In an Asian context de Sausmarez (2004: 11) feels communication and inter-agency cooperation needs to overcome the perceptual association between a crisis and 'loss of face', as is claimed to have occurred with the SARS outbreak in East Asia in 2003. In terms of global warming and its associated crisis no single country or person is to blame, we all need to take joint responsibility.

6. *The potential for regional cooperation.*

Although de Sausmarez focusses on the creation of national crisis management she recognizes that global issues like climate change require an even larger operational scale. No single country can be isolated from its neighbors, as 'was clearly illustrated by the decline in tourism to Southeast Asia following the Bali bombings in October 2002' (de Sausmarez, 2004: 12). She points out that the combined effort of the Association of Southeast Asian Nations (ASEAN) was able to effectively contain the SARS epidemic through regional preventative action in 2003, and that success has been repeated with the later outbreak of avian flu in East Asia.

The six steps outlined by de Sausmarez do not follow a natural linear sequence, but should be viewed more as a continuous dynamic process which has been divided up to permit closer examination and appreciation of its component parts. The whole process depends on continual learning and adjustment, so as to be responsive and flexible in the face of future crises. For resorts which have survived as a separate form of tourism since the early days it becomes imperative to embrace risk and crisis management as a central part of their business strategy.

Summary

This chapter has discussed the growing importance of risk management to resorts as our business and natural environments have changed. Although financial risk has been a constant within business it is only in recent times, with the rise of a litigious society and a less stable natural environment, that it has become a more general and important issue for management. Its increased prominence in business and society now means resorts should make it a key feature of their strategic management, and possibly their central concern.

Risk management does make a logical central theme for resort management in that it provides a focussed context for its past, present and future directions. The past experiences and business literature (Part A) provide a guide as to what management may expect today, and the general level of risk associated with most options. Present management must consider both external factors (Part B) and internal strategies (Part C) to create the most viable and sustainable options for today's resorts. The future can be extrapolated from the present if global business conditions change slowly and in a familiar manner, as predicted in the forecast for a growing senior's market for resorts. But what if we are experiencing major changes to the physical well-being of our planet and in human behaviour to one another? The risk factors that we have calculated from the past and present may no longer work so well or even apply, and we will need to enlarge our risk management process to incorporate more fluid business and environmental situations (Part D).

The purpose of this chapter and book is to encourage the reader to think about the wonderful legacy that has been provided by resorts; how we should strive to ensure resorts continue to delight our senses and educate us about our planet and its various cultures; and how we can achieve this through appropriate business management, even in this era of global change. A risk management focus would not only assist with the general sustainability objectives of a resort business, it can help position resorts at the forefront of monitoring and adjusting to the predicted changes in our natural and human environments.

The chapter and book closes with an examination of one recent global crisis, which had a direct impact on resorts throughout a large area of the world, and one resort which learned a great deal from one hurricane season. The Indian Ocean Tsunami of 2004 illustrates how we can still be caught unawares by a natural disaster, how such disasters can become international in scale, and thanks to rising sea levels may have even more significance in the future. Walt Disney World Resort received its first hurricane direct hit in more than 40 years in mid-August 2004, only to have it followed by three others in the space of six weeks. In the process it learned some invaluable lessons.

Case studies

Indian Ocean Tsunami

The Indian Ocean Tsunami, also known in some quarters as the Boxing Day Tsunami, occurred on 26 December 26 2004. This tsunami was generated by an earthquake under the Indian Ocean near the west coast of the Indonesian island of Sumatra, and is estimated to have released the energy of 23 000 Hiroshima-type atomic bombs. By the end of that day 'more than 150 000 people were dead or missing and millions more were homeless in 11 countries, making it perhaps the most destructive tsunami in history' (National Geographic News, 2005: 1). These figures were subsequently revised upward, so that now the Indian Ocean tsunami is estimated to have 'left 216 000 people dead or missing' (Guardian Unlimited, 2006: 1). If this terrible natural disaster is examined using the threefold strategic action template of Table 11.2 certain key crisis management lessons emerge.

At the *pre-crisis stage* little formal preparation had been undertaken at either government or resort levels of responsibility. This is understandable because there had been little history of major tsunamis in the Indian Ocean, the last being associated with Krakatoa's eruption in 1868, but unforgivable for tsunamis are still a risk in oceans with volcanic and tectonic activity. What was missing was both an early warning system of seismic buoys and a way to convey that information to potentially threatened areas, so they could instigate evacuation plans. While the 'Pacific Tsunami Warning Centre in Hawaii had sent an alert to 26 countries, including Thailand and Indonesia, (it) struggled to reach the right people. Television and radio alerts were not issued in Thailand until 9 a.m. local time – nearly an hour after the waves had hit' (Global Security, 2006: 3). In this case there had been no regional forecasting or risk analysis and there was no internationally coordinated contingency plan to deal with such a situation. The result was that even if a coastal resort had its own evacuation plan there was nothing to trigger it until the arrival of the first wave, and by then it was too late.

The *actual crisis stage* was viewed by millions of us around the globe, as we were able to view tourists' video camera images of this spectacular and unusual Sunday morning feature on our television screens. The world press immediately brought us these graphic images to go along with the rising death and damage statistics, so that once again the selective reporting of a natural disaster convinced many that the whole region had been devastated. This was particularly the case with Phuket Island, where the images of destruction at Patong Beach on the west coast were transformed to represent the whole island in the minds of many, even though Phuket is a large island with many separate resort enclaves scattered around its varied shoreline and many of them were untouched by the tragedy. This confirms the need for control over communications, to ensure reporting remains factual and in proportion, rather than sensational and exploitive.

The *post-crisis stage* represents an opportunity to learn from the crisis and to rebuild. This is certainly the case with the Indian Ocean Tsunami. The biggest weakness was the lack of information and warning, which prevented the implementation of effective contingency planning. This is now being addressed with the building of the Indian Ocean Tsunami Warning System in 2006. This system has been coordinated by the United Nations' Educational, Scientific and Cultural Organization (UNESCO) and consists of 25 new seismographic stations, supplemented by three deep-ocean sensors to provide the required early warning. But this is just the start, for the information needs to get to the areas around the Indian Ocean that are likely to be affected and the people in those areas who need to know what actions to take. Therefore, UNESCO is continuing to work on international coordination and with governments to provide grassroots preparedness (*Terra Daily*, 2006). UNESCO is providing expertise to assist with the redevelopment of mangrove, sea grass and coral reef rehabilitation; it is strengthening disaster preparation for cultural and heritage sites and integrating this into its reconstruction processes; and it is teaching tsunami awareness in schools, training decision-makers and broadcasters and staging local practice drills.

The recovery is well underway around much of the Indian Ocean. In Phuket where the damage was highly localized, Patong Beach showed no outward sign of the tsunami by October 2005, when the author paid a visit. The local tourism industry and English newspaper reported that while business had been slow in the months immediately following the tsunami, things had started to pick up around June and 'we expect it will be 80 per cent to 90 per cent from New Year (2006) to the end of March (high season)' (Phuket Gazette, 2005: 3C). Another example of crisis recovery is provided in the Maldives. Like all low-lying islands the Maldives are particularly susceptible to this form of disaster; thousands of local inhabitants lost their homes and 82 were killed in the tragedy. However, only two tourists lost their lives and although most resorts were damaged their 'higher construction standards (meant they) withstood the waves much better than local housing did' (Travel Wire News, 2005: 2). Consequently, it did not take most resorts long to rebuild and re-open, but in the process local businesses and government wanted to be better prepared for the future.

Five months after the tsunami swept across these islands in the Indian Ocean, the tourism sector and government agencies are cooperating to ensure that low-lying resorts and the nation's airport are better equipped to handle any type of emergency.

(Travel Wire News, 2005: 2)

Among the changes proposed are improving communications through the installation of satellite telephones on each island and a centralized emergency information command. New resort regulations will require evacuation plans and emergency supplies. A higher seawall around the airport and safeguards for electrical power supplies are also being considered.

These and other accounts of the Indian Ocean tsunami indicate the challenges facing the resort sector with today's concerns over global warming and the negative impact of news coverage for such disasters. Major tsunamis are fortunately rare events, but this case has demonstrated the need for some international warning system, so that regional and local contingency plans can be put into operation to minimize the impact. This will clearly require coordination at government levels and the will to maintain vigilance and training over long time periods between natural disaster events – something that will test human nature to the full. One also has to ask, if future tsunamis are associated with the rising sea levels of global warming will such improvements be enough? This is the type of question that some academics and researchers are asking us to consider, and should certainly be examined in terms of the sustainability and risk management of many resorts and their relevance in an era of possible climatic shifts.

Hurricane season for Walt Disney World

This case is based on an article by Barbara Higgins (2005) who was Director of Operations Integration for Walt Disney World Resort when four hurricanes impacted the resort's operations in 2004, providing an invaluable learning opportunity for them and other resort operations.

Plans

Walt Disney World's hurricane plans, as part of its general emergency planning, had definite priorities and procedures. Priorities included (Higgins, 2005: 41):

- keep guests safe;
- keep employees safe;
- have a thoughtful plan for tie-down, ride-out and recovery; and

■ provide the ability to get our parks open and operating as soon as possible after the storm.

The procedures were designed to account for varying hurricane strengths, and whether the hurricane involved a direct hit or a near miss in terms of its path across central Florida. To prepare for this Walt Disney World has instituted a five-phase approach to its hurricane preparedness, with each phase being selected in consultation with the National Hurricane Centre and local authorities.

■ *Phase 5 – Monitoring*
  Reviewing hurricane plans and verifying contact numbers for employees.
■ *Phase 4 – General readiness*
  Further review of plans and beginning of preparation for possible shutdown of long-lead-time operations.
■ *Phase 3 – Clean-up and tie-down*
  Predetermined emergency supplies are delivered, the site is cleared of loose materials and where relevant lightweight equipment and buildings are anchored to the ground, and managers evaluate moving to next phase.
■ *Phase 2 – Closing guest and employee areas*
  Guests and essential staff take shelter in hurricane-proofed buildings or begin evacuation.
■ *Phase 1 – Shut down all activities*
  All activities closed down, with only essential ride-out crews remaining in designated shelters.

Despite these plans and the thoroughness of preparation the sequence of four very different hurricanes revealed some additional factors and priorities.

Lessons

One major lesson from that summer's hurricane experience is that no two hurricanes are alike, so a resort can only prepare for hurricanes in general and not the specific one(s) that come its way. 'The first lesson we learned was that our rigorous plans were only guidelines that needed to be flexible enough to adjust to changes dictated by our circumstances' (Higgins, 2005: 42). The most important elements in the general emergency plans turned out to be:

■ maintaining guest and employee communication, letting them know about the impending storm and providing the relevant information regarding each phase's action plan;

- operating the food service, with the provision of hot meals being the biggest priority;
- offering in-resort entertainment to guests who were room-bound for many hours;
- preparing guests for confinement in their rooms over long periods, which is not what they came to the resort to do;
- arranging for the ability to use news media to give (information on park closures and re-openings) and to get (weather details and various local government announcements regarding schools, police and emergency services).

One 'important lesson to be learned in the face of a crisis is to show compassion for your employees and the toll the situation has had upon them, their families and their loved ones' (Higgins, 2005: 45). It is important to release unessential staff from their duties as soon as possible so they can attend to the safety of their family and homes as the hurricane approaches. Likewise, in the aftermath it is likely some employees will require shelter and hot meals due to the hurricane damage. 'One lesson many Floridians learned in the wake of these storms was the high deductible (excess) associated with hurricane insurance claims . . . (As a consequence) we anticipate providing more than $8 million to as many as ninety-five hundred employees who desperately need the funds to recover from the damage to their homes' (Higgins, 2005: 45).

Thus, in the end we have a reaffirmation that the business of resort management is 'to think globally but act locally'. Although the driver is business and financial concerns, there needs to be an appreciation of the importance of the local environment and community to the long-term success of a resort. Furthermore, if resorts are to continue to survive by adjusting to changing social and technical circumstances, they will need to become more proactive with regard to the current climate and cultural changes that face us all.

Questions

1 'Risk management is not just good for business, but is absolutely necessary in order for tourism and related organizations to remain competitive, to be sustainable, and to be responsible for their collective future' (Cunliffe, 2006: 35). Analyse this assertion in light of the global warming warnings that are becoming more common and urgent.

2 Examine the ramifications of 'duty of care' for a department or business of your choice within a resort setting, and assess how a risk management strategy can assist in its delivery.

3 Adventure tourism is considered to consist of three dimensions that provide a varied and profitable business mix for resorts (Figure 11.2). Discuss how a resort could use a risk management strategy to optimize its returns along the perceived/actual risk dimension.

4 Your resort business has received advanced notice of increased liability insurance rates for the coming year, even though you have made no claims for the past two years. What actions would you take to (a) convince the insurance company that such an increase is unreasonable, and (b) what alternatives do you have to reduce your insurance costs.

5 Apply de Sausmarez's (2004) six step approach to major global crises to the 2004 Indian Ocean Tsunami experience. Assess if it offers a good fit in this case and whether it provides a helpful framework to analyse this tragedy.

References

Anderson, B.A. (2006). Crisis management in the Australian tourism industry: preparedness, personnel and postscript. *Tourism Management*, **27(6)**, 1290–1297.

BBC News (2001). Six guilty in Swiss canyoning trial. http.//news.bbc.co.uk/1/hi/world/europe1704669.stm. Accessed on 16 August 2004.

Beedie, P. (2003). Adventure tourism. In *Sport and Adventure Tourism* (S. Hudson, ed.), pp. 203–239. New York: Haworth Hospitality Press.

Cloutier, R. (2000). *Legal Liability and Risk Management in Adventure Tourism.* Kamloops, BC: Bhudak Consultants.

Cloutier, R. (2003). The business of adventure tourism. In *Sport and Adventure Tourism* (S. Hudson, ed.), pp. 241–272. New York: Haworth Hospitality Press.

Cunliffe, S.K. (2006). Risk management for tourism: origins and needs. *Tourism Review International*, **10(1/2)**, 27–38.

de Sausmarez, N. (2004). Crisis management for the tourism sector: issues in policy development. *Proceedings of Tourism: State of the Art II.* 27–30 June 2004. Glasgow: The Scottish Hotel School, University of Strathclyde.

Faulkner, B. (2001). Towards a framework for tourism disaster management. *Tourism Management*, **22(2)**, 135–147.

Feizkhah, E. (2002). She's not right, mate. *Time*, May 27, 46.

Foster, H.D. (1980). *Disaster Planning: The Preservation of Life and Property.* New York: Springer Verlag.

Gee, C.Y. (1996). *Resort Development and Management*, 2nd edn. East Lansing, Michigan: Educational Institute of the American Hotel and Motel Association.

Glaesser, D. (2003). *Crisis Management in the Tourism Industry*. Oxford: Butterworth-Heinemann.

Global Security (2006). Asian tsunami/tiger waves. http://www.globalsecurity. org/eye/andaman.htm. Accessed on 14 December 2006.

Gregory, P. and Hewitt, R. (2005). Dive quadriplegic keeps his millions, plans to buy a house. *The Age*, June 23: 6.

Guardian Unlimited (2006). Asian nations stage tsunami drill. http://www.guardian. co.uk/tsunami/story/0,,1776974,00.html. Accessed on 14 December 2006.

Hall, C.M., Timothy, D.J. and Duval, D.T. (2003). Security and tourism: towards a new understanding. In *Safety and Security in Tourism* (C.M. Hall, D.J. Timothy and D.T. Duval, eds), pp. 1–18. Binghamton, NY: Haworth Hospitality Press.

Head, M. (1999). Profit drive blamed for Swiss canyon tragedy. *World Socialist Web Site*. www.wsws.org. Accessed on 16 August 2004.

Higgins, B.A. (2005). The storms of summer: lessons learned in the aftermath of the hurricanes of '04. *Cornell Hotel and Restaurant Administration Quarterly*, **46(1)**, 40–46.

King, B. and Berno, T. (2002). Tourism and civil disturbances: an evaluation of recovery strategies in Fiji, 1987–2000. *Journal of Hospitality and Tourism Management*, **9(1)**, 46–60.

Morgan, D. and Fluker, M. (2000). *Accidents in the Adventure Tourism Industry: Causes Consequences and Crisis Management*. Working Paper 80/00. Faculty of Business and Economics, Monash University, Melbourne, Australia.

Münchener Rück (2003). *Topics Geo – Annual Review*, National Catastrophes, Munich.

Murphy, P.E. and Bayley, R. (1989). Tourism and disaster planning. *Geographical Review*, **79(1)**, 36–46.

National Geographic News (2005). The deadliest tsunami in history? January 7, 1.http://news.nationalgeographic.com/news/2004/12/1227_041226_tsunami.h tml. Accessed on 14 December 2006.

Page, S.J., Bentley, T. and Walker, L. (2005). Tourist safety in New Zealand and Scotland. *Annals of Tourism Research*, **32(1)**, 150–166.

PATA (2003). *Crisis: It Won't Happen to Us!* Bangkok, Thailand: Pacific Asia Travel Association.

Pattullo, P. (1996). *Last Resorts: The Cost of Tourism in the Caribbean*, London: Cassell.

Phuket Gazette (2005). Rush for seats to Phuket. *The Nation*, October 22, 3C.

Ritchie, B.W. (2004). Chaos, crises and disasters: a strategic approach to crisis management in the tourism industry. *Tourism Management*, **25(6)**, 669–683.

Santana, G. (2003). Crisis management and tourism: beyond the rhetoric. In *Safety and Security in Tourism* (C.M. Hall, D.J. Timothy and D.T. Duval, eds), pp. 299–321. Binghamton, NY: Haworth Hospitality Press.

Sharpley, R. and Craven, B. (2001). The 2001 foot and mouth crises – rural economy and tourism policy implications: a comment. *Current Issues in Tourism*, **4(6)**, 527–537.

Stern, N. (2006). Stern review on the economics of climate change. *London: H.M. Treasury*.www.hmtreasury.gov.uk/Independent_Reviews/stern_review_economics_climate. Accessed on 1 November 2006.

Tarlow, P.E. (2006). Disaster management: exploring ways to mitigate disasters before they occur. *Tourism Review International*, **10(1/2)**, 17–25.

Terra Daily (2006). Indian Ocean tsunami warning system up and running. http://www.terradaily.com/reports/Indian_Ocean_Tsunami_Warning_System_Up_And_Running. Accessed on 14 December 2006.

The Economist (2006a). The price of sunshine: hurricanes and insurance. *The Economist*, June 10, 74–75.

The Economist (2006b). The heat is on: a survey of climate change. *The Economist*, September 9, 1–18.

Travel Wire News (2005). Maldives takes steps to improve crisis response. http://www.travelwirenews.com/news/27May2005. Accessed on 30 May 2005.

Wilks, J. and Davis, R.J. (2000). Risk management for scuba diving operators on Australia's Great Barrier Reef. *Tourism Management*, **21(6)**, 591–599.

Winn, M.I. and Kirchgeorg, M. (2005). The siesta is over: a rude awakening from sustainability myopia. In *New Perspectives in Research in Corporate Sustainability* (S. Sharma and M.Starik, eds), Volume 3 – Corporate Environmental Strategy and Competition, pp. 232–258. Mass and London: Edward Elgar.

World Tourism Organisation (1999). *Impacts of the Financial Crisis on Asia's Tourism Sector*. Madrid: World Tourism Organisation. 5

Index